Municipal Shared Services and Consolidation

"*Municipal Shared Services and Consolidation* accomplishes the important task of translating insights from academic research into the realities of working government professionals. Municipal leaders of all stripes will get valuable guidance about when to pursue collaborations among governments and how to manage them." —**Matthew Potoski**, University of California, Santa Barbara

"This book provides an excellent review of the conceptual issues related to interlocal collaboration and shared service management. It contains critical insights for students, scholars, and practitioners who are interested in local service provision and governance." —**Alfred T. Ho**, University of Kansas

Municipal Shared Services and Consolidation provides a clear and comprehensive review of the theories and practices associated with the structuring and management of complex local government services. Intended for academics, students, and practitioners, this volume addresses concepts and processes of shaping collaborative public-service arrangements, keeping in mind the goals of effectiveness and efficiency.

The *Handbook* begins by reviewing various approaches to shared services and consolidation, highlighting conceptual foundations, practical barriers, and related cultural considerations. In-depth analysis of the processes of creating, implementing, and managing shared services and consolidation agreements is backed up by solid advice and practical solutions. This exceptional resource is complemented by numerous examples, cases, illustrations, and a thorough bibliography.

About the Editor:

Alexander C. Henderson is an assistant professor in the Department of Health Care and Public Administration at Long Island University, Post Campus. He holds a BA and MPA from Villanova University, and a PhD in public administration from Rutgers University-Newark. He previously served as a chief administrative officer, operational officer, director, and volunteer with several emergency services organizations in suburban Philadelphia.

MARC HOLZER, SERIES EDITOR

MUNICIPAL SHARED SERVICES
A Public Solutions Handbook
Alexander C. Henderson, Editor

E-GOVERNMENT AND WEBSITES
A Public Solutions Handbook
Aroon Manoharan, Editor

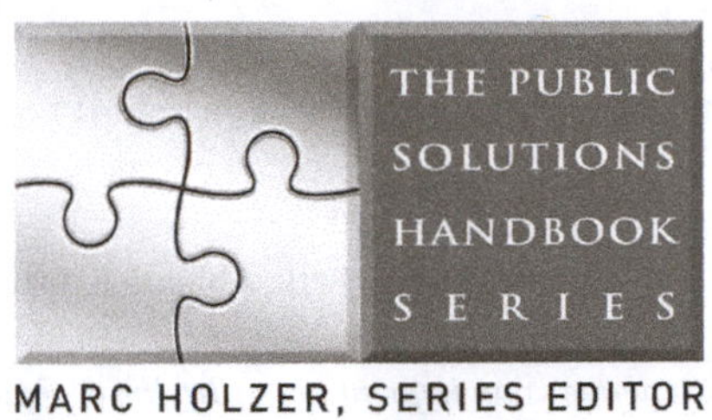

MARC HOLZER, SERIES EDITOR

Municipal Shared Services and Consolidation

A PUBLIC SOLUTIONS HANDBOOK

Alexander C. Henderson, Editor

NEW YORK AND LONDON

First published 2015

by Routledge
711 Third Avenue, New York, NY 10017

and by Routledge
2 Park Square, Milton Park, Abingdon, Oxon, OX14 4RN

Routledge is an imprint of the Taylor & Francis Group, an informa business

Library of Congress Cataloging in Publication Data
Municipal shared services and consolidation : a public solutions handbook /edited by Alexander C. Henderson.
pages cm. — (The public solutions handbook series)
Includes bibliographical references and index.
1. Municipal services—United States—Management 2. Municipal government—United States. 3. Shared services (Management)—United States. I. Henderson, Alexander C., 1980–HD4605.M86 2014
363.6068—dc23

ISBN: 978-0-7656-4561-6 (hbk)
ISBN: 978-0-7656-3723-9 (pbk)
ISBN: 978-1-315-72076-0 (ebk)

Contents

Series Editor's Introduction

The impetus for this series of public management handbooks is simply that public managers must have ready access to the best practices and lessons learned. That knowledge base is surprisingly extensive and rich, including insights from rigorous academic studies, internal government reports and publications, and foundation-supported research. Access to that knowledge, however, is limited by substantial barriers: expensive books and academic journals; "thick" academic language and hard-to-decipher jargon; the sheer volume of information available. Our objectives in initiating this series are to identify insights based in practice, build competencies from that knowledge base, deliver them at an affordable price point, and communicate that guidance in clear terms.

GROUNDED INSIGHTS

Each volume in the series will incorporate case-based research. Each will draw helpful insights and guidelines from academe, government, and foundation sources, focusing on an emerging opportunity or issue in the field. The initial volumes will, for example, address: Shared Services for Municipalities and Counties, Managing Generational Differences, Government Counter-Corruption Strategies, Public Sector Innovation, E-Government and Websites, and Performance Measurement and Improvement.

COMPETENCIES

We are initiating this series of Public Solutions Handbooks to help build necessary competencies, empowering dedicated, busy public servants—many of whom have no formal training in the management processes of the public offices and agencies they have been selected to lead—to respond to emerging issues, delivering services that policymakers have promised to the public, carrying out their missions efficiently and effectively, and working in partnership with their stakeholders. Enabling practitioners to access and apply evidence-based insights will begin to restore trust in their governments through high-performing public, nonprofit, and contracting organizations.

Just as importantly, students in graduate degree programs, many of whom are already working in public and nonprofit organizations, are seeking succinct, pragmatic, grounded guidance that will help them succeed far into the future as they rise to positions of greater responsibility and leadership. This includes students in Master of Public Administration

(MPA), Master of Public Policy (MPP), Master of Nonprofit Management (MNPM), and even some Master of Business Administration (MBA) and Law (LLD) programs.

AFFORDABILITY

Handbook prices are often unrealistically high. The marketplace is not serving the full range of public managers who need guidance as to best practices. When faced with the need for creative solutions to cut budgets, educating for ethics, tapping the problem solving expertise of managers and employees, or reporting progress clearly and transparently, a grasp of such practices is essential. Many handbooks are priced in the hundreds of dollars and are beyond the purchasing power of an individual or an agency. Journals are similarly priced out of the reach of practitioners. In contrast, each volume in the Public Solutions series will be modestly priced.

CLEAR WRITING

Although the practice of public administration and public management should be informed by published research, the books that are now marketed to practitioners and students in the field are often overly abstract and theoretical, failing to distill published research into clear and necessary applications. There is substantial, valuable literature in the academic journals, but necessarily to standards that do not easily "connect" with practitioner audiences. Even in instances where practitioners receive peer-reviewed journals as a benefit of association membership, they clearly prefer magazines or newsletters in a straightforward journalistic style. Too often they set the journals aside.

I am proud to announce the initial volume in the Public Solutions Handbook series: *Municipal Shared Services and Consolidation*, edited by Alexander C. Henderson. As a clear guide to an emerging menu of possible solutions to enduring and complex problems across neighboring municipalities, it emulates the goals and values of the series. As the first in a series of responses to enduring problems of stretching, optimizing, and conserving scarce municipal resources, this is an important new volume for public managers who are pursuing the promise of municipal shared services or even consolidations. This handbook will necessarily find a permanent niche on the desks of many public managers, empowering them to deliver public services as promised—efficiently, effectively, and within the budgets that citizens have entrusted to their municipalities.

Marc Holzer
Editor-in-Chief, Public Solutions Handbook Series
Dean and Board of Governors Distinguished Professor
of Public Affairs and Administration
Rutgers, The State University of New Jersey–Campus at Newark

Introduction

Alexander C. Henderson

Local governments are in a near-constant search for strategies to increase efficiency and effectiveness in the provision of public services. Given the reduced resources and increased demands facing many of these units of government, methods of sharing services or consolidating have emerged as important means to create cost savings while maintaining effectiveness and meeting organizational goals. Creating shared service arrangements or consolidating with other units can be tremendously complex activities, and are made increasingly challenging given the intrinsic links to underlying political, economic, and social systems. This volume helps to navigate these complexities and challenges by providing a clear and straightforward overview of the theoretical bases of cooperative activity, supported and refined with pertinent examples drawn from practice.

Students, practitioners, and scholars will undoubtedly find great utility in the content included here. Students of public administration and in-service practitioners, especially those with an interest in local government management, nonprofit administration, public budgeting and finance, and performance measurement and management, will find strong connections between their academic interests and the tangible, real-world examples. Scholars of public administration will find this text useful in supporting and framing academic research. The clarity and depth of the core concepts reviewed can serve as a key summative resource in developing literature reviews and outlining complex concepts related to the topics listed above.

Part I provides a theoretical and conceptual foundation for the discussion of shared services and consolidation, and also grounds the discussion in the realities of local government. In Chapter 1 Mildred Warner cogently lays out core concepts that have shaped views of how to structure local public services, specifically focusing on questions of economies of scale and efficiencies, political considerations revolving around jurisdiction and responsibilities, equity considerations, and governance of shared services and consolidation efforts. In Chapter 2 Christopher Hawkins and Jered Carr continue this conversation, providing an equally important and realistically grounded look at the barriers to consolidation and shared service delivery. Hawkins and Carr highlight previous work on transaction costs—central to cooperative activity—and discuss how the inherent risks found in these activities can be reduced through an understanding of service types, institutional design, and the social networks of administrators involved in these processes. In Chapter 3 Sydney Cresswell and Anthony Cresswell write about the nature of communities and culture in shared services and consolidation, a crucially important area of inquiry in discussions of how to shape local government. They also examine issues of community involvement and citizen engagement, focusing on processes that balance citizen input and weigh alternatives while tailoring these to specific local conditions.

Part II moves from discussion of conceptual and theoretical issues to the realm of practice. In Chapter 4 Michael Hattery outlines the processes of creating and shaping shared service agreements and consolidation of functional areas, providing specific considerations for initiating agreements, evaluating service delivery alternatives, capacity issues involved in changing public service provision, and the importance of flexibility in service provision and organizational change. Lauren Miltenberger continues the conversation in Chapter 5 by linking the discussion to the area of nonprofit management, focusing on those aspects of the nonprofit-municipal relationship that may be both pertinent and useful to those considering shared services and consolidation. Miltenberger begins with a discussion of the development of nonprofit–municipal relationships over the last several decades, reviews a number of best practices emerging from these relationships, and presents a typology that addresses possible barriers while offering suggestions for smoothing the establishment of collaborative relationships.

The discussion continues with Eric Zeemering's work in Chapter 6 on the necessity of attention to the management of shared service relationships. Zeemering examines evidence from interviews of both city managers and elected officials in the San Francisco Bay Area who engage in shared service activities, and brings to the fore a number of important considerations for managing complex shared local services. Specifically, he highlights the importance of fostering contract management skills among local government managers—including the process of initiating the contracting process and determining the necessity of altering contracts once in place—while concomitantly allowing for democratic oversight and popular input. One specific component of the broader set of activities associated with shared service management is that of performance measurement, the focus of Daniel Bromberg's work in Chapter 7. Bromberg discusses the role of performance measurement in interlocal agreements, and presents evidence of performance and monitoring challenges associated with shared property tax assessment in New Hampshire.

The conversation then shifts to an example of the failure of an attempt at functional consolidation. In Chapter 8 William Hatley, Richard Elling, and Jered Carr provide an engaging example of the failed consolidation efforts of five local fire departments in the suburbs of Detroit, Michigan. Hatley, Elling, and Carr outline the importance of a number of factors that created substantial barriers to these efforts, including difficulties developing understanding of expected costs and benefits of collaboration, the influence of state rules and unions on collaborative efforts, considerations of the loss of local control and communicating benefits to citizens and politicians, and lack of trust, the combination of which ultimately resulted in a complete breakdown of efforts.

In Chapter 9 Ricardo Morse and Charles Abernathy bring together the elements of this discussion of shared services and functional consolidation by presenting a typology of shared service agreements. Morse and Abernathy outline the complexity and variety of different types of shared service relationships, and create a two-dimensional framework centered on the extent of consolidation and shared governance. In Chapter 10 Suzanne Leland and Reid Wodicka outline the importance of creativity and innovation in thinking about ways to structure local government services, pulling ideas from current practice that could be expanded with the right attention to application.

Local governments provide important services in an evolving and complex environment, and are undoubtedly worthy of our focus and attention in an effort to both cultivate understanding and improve public service provision. The theories and linkages to practice found here substantively contribute to this crucial conversation.

Part I

Introduction and Theoretical Considerations

1

Municipal Size, Resources, and Efficiency

Theoretical Bases for Shared Services and Consolidation

Mildred E. Warner

The United States has a fragmented system of local governments, and many ills are blamed on this fragmentation. Inadequate watershed management, inequality and segregation in public education, poorly integrated regional transportation systems, suburban sprawl, and local government fiscal crisis are all blamed in part on our fragmented local government system. The problem is not unique to the United States. The challenge of suboptimal local government size has bedeviled government reformers for more than a century. The problem is common across continental Europe, Australia, and North America (Lago-Peñas and Martinez-Vazquez 2013). When local government units are too small or too fragmented in a region, this makes it difficult to provide quality services or to coordinate services across jurisdictions. While urban planners typically look to political consolidation as the solution (Rusk 1993; Orfield 2002), public choice theorists point to the possibility for voluntary shared service arrangements even inside a fragmented polycentric local government system (Bish and Ostrom 1973). Such voluntary shared service arrangements offer the possibility for a solution short of political consolidation, which is both unpopular and uncommon (Leland and Thurmaier 2004, 2010). But how can such shared service arrangements be promoted? What guidance does theory offer?

This chapter explores some theoretical bases for shared service arrangements. A theoretical framework must be grounded in an understanding of culture and history and recognize the path dependence of the problem of governmental fragmentation and the possibilities for its solution. We must give attention to political considerations that address service responsibilities, finance, and accountability in a multilevel federalist governmental system, equity considerations that look at externalities and spillovers across jurisdictions in an urbanizing world, and economic considerations of efficiency and economies of scale at both the governmental unit and the service level. Each of these issues is critical to a comprehensive theoretical framework (see Figure 1.1).

In this chapter, I give special attention to the concerns and insights raised by economic, political, and equity considerations. Theories that give emphasis to one or the other of these considerations offer contrasting views regarding the problem of governmental fragmentation and its solution.

Regarding political considerations, fiscal federalism and public choice theories gener-

Figure 1.1 **The Theoretical Framework**

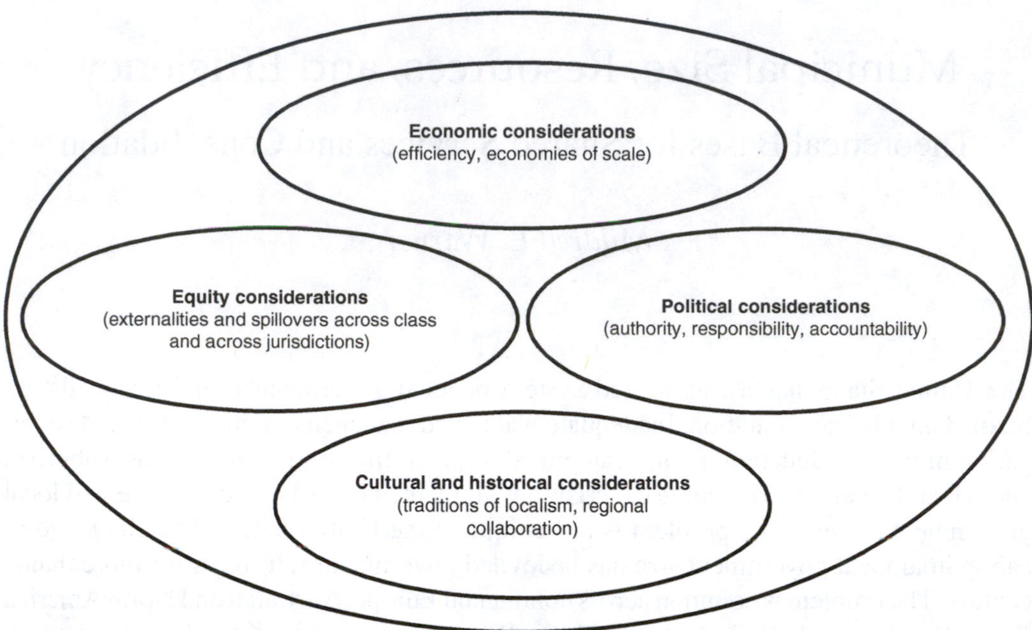

ally celebrate the efficiency and democracy potential of a fragmented local government system. While fragmentation may create coordination problems, it also offers the solution with economic incentives for collaborative action. For example, Nobel laureate Elinor Ostrom (2010) argued that fragmented government systems create a polycentric system of many independent local governments, which in turn promotes innovation, enhanced citizen voice and diversity due to localism, and a marketplace for public services that promotes efficiency and fiscal equivalence. If coordination and allocational efficiency problems arise, they can be addressed voluntarily through shared service arrangements.

Theories that emphasize economic efficiency, by contrast, often focus on economies of scale as a solution to the problem of suboptimal local government size. This can lead to a consolidationist view. However, achieving efficiencies in a fragmented government system depends on the nature of the service and changes in the technology of service production, and this offers a wider array of possible solutions (Holzer and Fry 2011). Both production and transaction costs must be considered in assessing alternative arrangements—unit consolidation, functional consolidation, or shared services. Governance arrangements are critically important in determining transaction costs of alternative shared service arrangements (Feiock 2009).

Finally, regional equity considerations give attention to the heterogeneity of need and resources across local governments and the need for coordination. Geographic differences by metro status create different challenges in rural and metropolitan regions (Warner 2006). Coordination and allocative efficiency questions are paramount. Differences in interests may undermine the potential for voluntary solutions. Regional equity theories explore the political bases for cooperation and often argue for consolidation approaches, although some recent research has focused on the possibility for voluntary action as well (Leland and Thurmaier 2004; Pastor, Benner, and Matsuoka 2009).

Each of these perspectives provides a diagnosis of the problem and a basis for its solution. While celebrating fragmentation and efficiency, fiscal federalism and public choice theory acknowledge the problem of suboptimal size but point to the positive potential of a voluntary approach to shared services. Economies of scale give attention to service characteristics but also acknowledge the transaction costs associated with different governance arrangements. Regional equity theory explores the political interests and challenges in a fragmented governance system and the means to overcome them. In each of these considerations we find the seeds of a theory for shared service delivery—the role of a market, the nature of service, the nature of governance arrangement, and the means to address differences in interests. Under the economic efficiency paradigm, concern about public goods, externalities, economies of scale, transaction costs, and market failures justify the use of consolidation or coordinated service provision (Boadway and Shah 2009).

However, society is not only interested in economic efficiency. Values such as equity, equality of opportunities, and security matter. And political concerns regarding the roles of the government, the importance of self-determination, and the appropriate level of centralization or decentralization all come into play (Mikesell 2007; Boadway and Shah 2009). More recent theoretical attention has focused on a framework for understanding collective action at the local government level and the role of norms, networks, and political interest groups (Feiock, 2009; Leland and Thurmaier 2004, 2010). But first, let us turn to a discussion of history.

HOW DID WE GET HERE?

The United States has a tradition of fragmented local government that began with the founding of the nation (Warner 2013). In many ways, local government structure reflects economic development trajectories. In the Northeast and Midwest, early settlement patterns were based on a small farm yeoman economy. Economic democracy led to a form of direct local democracy captured in the town meeting form of local government. Township boundaries were roughly determined by the distance a person could travel to do business and return in a day.

In the South and West, this township tier is not found. Plantation agriculture in the South and ranching in the West did not require (or desire) a township tier of government, in part because of the larger territorial expanses of these economic forms. In these regions, county governments (without townships) were established. With urbanization, cities formed within counties to address the more complex service coordination needs that urbanized settlements require. As new cities and suburbs formed, they created their own city governments, leading to what is today a dense, fragmented system of 38,910 multipurpose local governments (townships, villages, cities, and counties), according to the 2012 Census of Governments.

This historical layering of local government organization reflects the economic realities of an earlier time. The challenge for the twenty-first century is that the earlier layers are locked in a palimpsest that makes difficult the creation of a local government layer that better reflects the coordination needs of a modern-day economy and society. Urban geographers argue that we are now in the era of the "city region," and that this is the relevant economic unit for a global economy (Brenner 2004). Similarly, rural planners point to the need to coordinate activity across a resource base—such as a watershed—and the challenges that a fragmented underlying local government system creates for environmental management and coordination (Homsy and Warner 2013).

It is in this context that this book explores the possibility for shared services and consolidation. Given the rich palimpsest of history, how can we achieve a more geographically and economically rational form of local government today? This volume explores two possibilities: political unit consolidation or functional consolidation via shared services.

Political unit consolidation has not been an attractive option for U.S. local government. Scholars who study consolidation note the importance of crisis in generating interest in consolidation, and the role of trust, power, and policy entrepreneurs in providing the leadership for change (Leland and Thurmaier 2004, 2010; Carr and Feiock 2004). Political support for localism is very high in the United States because it supports local voice and democracy, and because it justifies differentiation in local services by race and class (Briffault 2000). While regional planners have called for consolidation as a solution to the problems of coordination on a regional scale, the number of consolidations that actually have occurred is minimal. Empowered counties, where cities merge with their surrounding county, have been recommended (Rusk 1993, 1999), but these, too, are rare.

Instead, scholars and practitioners have shifted attention toward voluntary forms of coordination—from councils of governments and metropolitan planning organizations at the regional scale, to intermunicipal cooperation for shared production and delivery at the service scale (Holzer and Fry 2011). Such voluntary intermunicipal cooperation is quite common. The International City/County Management Association tracks the level of intergovernmental contracting at the service level. The most recent 2007 data show that cooperation accounts for 16 percent of all local government service delivery, an increase of 30 percent from 2002 (Hefetz, Warner, and Vigoda-Gadot 2012).

Such intermunicipal contracting is sometimes understood as functional consolidation, because the cooperating governments join in producing and delivering a single service without consolidating the entire political unit. This preserves localism but allows for a level of consolidation at the service level.

This chapter explores the theoretical bases for understanding shared service delivery given the problem and context of our fragmented local government system. It covers theoretical bases focused on political structure (fiscal federalism and public choice), economic considerations regarding economies of scale and transaction costs, and equity considerations for externalities and spillovers. The critical importance of governance structure is then presented, and challenges relating to the factors that promote or limit governance of intermunicipal collaborative agreements are explored.

FISCAL FEDERALISM

Fiscal federalism does not see a problem with fragmented local government. Fragmentation creates a market, which provides the solution to concerns with productive efficiency. Coordination, to the extent not achieved through a competitive local government market, can be accommodated with a voluntary cooperative approach. This is the basis for polycentric collective action articulated by Ostrom and colleagues. Prospects for cooperation are wide.

The U.S. government is a federal system built up from the states. Local government structure and authority is determined by the states. This creates a lot of diversity in local government form, local government autonomy, finance, and service delivery (Frug and Barron 2008). Fiscal federalism is an institutional arrangement for governmental finance and administration in a multilevel system. It is based, in part, on public choice theory, which argues that such fragmentation promotes productive efficiency, fiscal discipline, diversity, and citizen voice (Oates 1998).

Writing in the middle of the great suburban post–World War II development wave, Charles Tiebout, in his famous 1956 article *A Pure Theory of Local Expenditures*, argued that the multitude of local governments created a market for public services. This market is the basis for the efficiency claims of the fiscal federalists. Competition on both the supply and demand sides creates the basis for efficient production of local services. On the supply side, local government managers see a market of competing local governments; managers compete with their neighbors to offer the most efficient mix of services and taxes in order to attract residents. Residents, Tiebout maintained, create a market on the demand side.

There was a great deal of geographic mobility during this post–World War II period. Tiebout argued that residents are mobile consumers who evaluate the relative efficiency in service delivery offered by different local governments and choose where to live based on their true preferences, thus sending a clear market signal to city managers. Subsequent research has challenged this naïve view of sorting, pointing out that factors other than economics (such as race and class) drive the decision making of both residents and local government managers (Lowery 2000; Troutt 2000; Marsh, Parnell, and Joyner 2010; Lichter et al. 2007).

The budget constraint is an important factor in promoting efficiency in the local government market. U.S. local governments are the most fiscally autonomous in the advanced industrialized world. Services, by and large, are funded by local revenues. This creates a strict budget constraint on both citizen demand and local manager supply. Fiscal equivalence ensures fiscal discipline in the system—residents get what they pay for and must pay for services received (Oates 1998). If more services are desired, a higher level of taxes or user fees must be incurred.

But the benefits of a fragmented system do not stop with market-based efficiency and budget constraints. Fiscal federalists argue that a further benefit of a fragmented system is the potential for innovation, diversity, and voice (Ostrom, Tiebout, and Warren 1961).

The United States is a diverse country. Local government services vary according to need and preference, and a fragmented system allows this diversity to flourish. Localism supports voice and diversity. And from such diversity springs innovation.

Most famous among the fiscal federalists is Elinor Ostrom, who argued that public goods problems are best resolved at the most local level through a system of voluntary collective organization (Ostrom 1990). Her research, primarily in rural settings concerned with natural resource management, pointed to the importance of trust, sanctioning power, and iterative interaction between local actors to ensure successful collective management without dissipating the resource (Ostrom 2010).

The parallel to Ostrom's argument at the local government level is voluntary intermunicipal cooperation. Popularized in the famous public policy writing of Robert Bish and Vincent Ostrom (1973), the theory offers a critical alternative to regional consolidation by showing that communities can voluntarily cooperate to address issues of cross-community coordination and that such cooperative service delivery could be more efficient than consolidated service delivery (Parks and Oakerson 1993). Thus, a fragmented, polycentric local government system is not a problem needing correction, but rather a system that is self-correcting both due to market pressures and to voluntarily coordination for collective action.

REGIONAL EQUITY

> *Regional equity theorists see a serious problem with a fragmented local government system and give central importance to the need for regional coordination. Heterogeneity of need and resources across the region makes allocative efficiency of paramount concern, but differences in interests undermine the potential for voluntary solutions. Regional equity theories typically argue consolidation approaches are superior.*

The late twentieth and early twenty-first centuries show the increasing importance of city regions as drivers of economic competitiveness in a global world, and the need for more system-wide coordination of resources—watersheds, food systems, energy waste, and so forth. Fragmented and overlapping political jurisdictions undermine the potential for coordinated management. This is both an environmental management and an equity concern. While voluntary coordination across jurisdictions is welcome (Pastor, Benner, and Matsuoka 2009), it is difficult to achieve without some higher level of governmental authority.

Reviews of the evidence on fragmented local government point to problems with information asymmetry, resource inequality, and lack of mobility—especially for the poor (Lowery 2000; Troutt 2000). Community choice is driven by more than preference for a specific tax and service combination. Resource and service inequality in a fragmented local government system leads to a "privatized" view of local services to members of a single jurisdiction and this undermines the potential for equity across the metropolitan region (Frug, 1999). The supply and demand for local services is not simply based on a competitive market sorting mechanism regarding the efficiency of local services and taxes, but on race and class differences, which distinguish communities across both the metropolitan and rural landscape (Troutt 2000; Lichter et al. 2007; Marsh, Parnell, and Joyner 2010). For both urban and rural areas, fragmentation and suboptimal government size lead to problems of poor governments whose lower service levels result in reduced opportunities for residents. This problem has been well documented in poorer rural communities (Warner 2001; Warner and Pratt 2005), inner cities (Wilson 1987), and recently in inner ring suburbs (Kneebone and Berube 2013).

Consolidation is typically promoted by planners as the preferred option (Rusk 1993; 1999; Orfield 1997, 2002). Consolidation allows for greater attention to technical efficiency (Prud'homme 1995) and managerial capacity to ensure a more effective local government administration (McKinlay 2011). Australia has probably gone the farthest in promoting a consolidationist agenda, but even there scholars do not find significant evidence of cost savings (Dollery and Johnson 2005). The argument instead is for a more effective local government organization that matches the geographic scale of economic activity in the twenty-first century city (Aulich et al. 2011).

Support for consolidation in the United States is limited and weak. The most common consolidation is single-purpose, functional consolidation focused in a specific service area such as transportation. Metropolitan planning organizations typically play a consolidation role, but the technical orientation of these efforts can undermine equity goals (Downs 1994). This has led regional planners to argue for a democratic, people-based regionalism (Frug 1999; Bollens 1997).

Recent scholarly research has focused on political interests and power strategies that can encourage and support voluntary regional coordination. Norms of trust and reciprocity are built up over time to support network ties, which promote collaboration among local public administrations (Agranoff and McGuire 2003). Scholarly attention also is being focused on politics, social movements, and shifting market preferences in order to achieve support for regional integration (Pastor, Benner, and Matsuoka 2009). Voluntary forms of interlocal cooperation, such as shared services, may become an important, practical alternative to regionalism (Carr and Feiock 2004; Thurmaier and Wood 2004).

The question remains, how likely is voluntary cooperation among heterogeneous local governments that differ widely in resources and need? Empirical research is equivocal on this point. Looking over a fifteen-year period with International City/County Management Association (ICMA) data, we find intermunicipal contracting is pro equity in some years and neutral in others, whereas for profit contacting is never pro equity (Hefetz, Warner, and Vigoda-Gadot 2012). Our measures—income and poverty—are rough proxies for the array of variables that differentiate communities across the region. In a comprehensive review of the literature, Lowery (2000) argues that residential and service choice is often based on racial or class discrimination and leads to preference alignment problems as residents and local governments choose services that create externality problems for neighbors.

Polycentrists and consolidationists find common theoretical ground in their search for mechanisms that promote more coordinated action in a fragmented local government system. While Elinor Ostrom (2010) focused primarily on individuals coming together at a community level and the role of trust, norms, sanctioning, and iterative experience, regionalists have focused on what causes communities to come together to solve regional problems. Feiock (2007, 2009) has articulated a theory of institutional collective action, which looks at political institutions, the structure of policy networks, and the nature of transaction costs in cooperative agreements. Foster and Barnes (2012) address the importance of actors, agendas, internal and external capacity, and implementation experience. Agranoff and McGuire (2003) look at the intensity and strategic nature of collaborative action, while Leland and Thurmaier (2004, 2010) address political strategies and power. Boadway and Shah (2009) combine economic and political arguments in an international comparative framework.

Each of these theories combines economic rationality with institutional organization theory and offers a fruitful way forward in a more comprehensive theoretical framework for shared services. Before turning to a more detailed discussion of governance, let us shift our focus from the local government as the organizational unit to the service as our unit of analysis and explore economic concerns about economies of scale and transaction costs.

ECONOMIES OF SCALE

> *Economies of scale theories focus on the nature of the service, and changes in the technology of service production. Both production and transaction costs are important drivers of service delivery choices, whether the choice is unit consolidation, functional consolidation, or shared service delivery. While production costs are determined by economies of scale, transaction costs are determined by governance arrangements.*

One of the main drivers of shared services is the notion that municipalities are missing out on economies of scale because they are too small. When economies of scale are present, the marginal costs of production drop as the number of units provided increases. (For a thorough discussion of economies of scale, see Bel and Warner 2013.) Holzer and Fry (2011) argue that for most local services, economies of scale are reached at a population level of about 20,000–25,000. When you look at the question from an individual service perspective, shared services may be most attractive for small rural municipalities. By joining together, they can lower costs. This is also true for suburbs, but larger urban communities already enjoy internal economies of scale—without cooperation. Indeed, ICMA data show intermunicipal cooperation rates are consistently higher in rural and suburban communities than in urban communities (Hefetz, Warner, and Vigoda-Gadot 2012). As size increases, marginal costs drop, but only up to a point. Economies of scale depend on both size of population and density (Ladd 1992).

Large urban areas often require a more complex production technology to address the challenges of congestion and higher density. Thus, scholars often find a U-shaped cost curve with the highest marginal costs at the rural end due to the costs of sparsity, and at the urban end due to the costs of congestion (Warner 2006; Warner and Pratt 2005). Some services have constant returns to scale or declining returns to scale. In these cases, economies of scale would not drive interest in shared services.

Production costs are only part of the equation, however. Economists recognize the search and design costs involved in structuring shared service agreements. There are also ongoing implementation, maintenance, and monitoring costs (Shrestha and Feiock 2011). These transaction costs exist in addition to production costs. Transaction costs are often difficult to fully evaluate in advance and can be quite high. Not only do they include budget accounting and technical design costs, they also include important political costs, both from local officials and from citizens. Resistance to shared services can be high. Turf battles, concern over loss of local control, and accountability and differences in service and resource levels among partners can make design difficult. Some research suggests these transaction costs may be lower in intermunicipal contracting than in contracting for profits due to shared values among public partners and a wider array of partners with which to cooperate in a fragmented government system (Girth et al. 2012; Hefetz and Warner 2012; Warner 2011). Others challenge this view, noting the weak sanctioning power among intermunicipal partners and how this raises the transaction costs of monitoring (Marvel and Marvel 2007).

Most economic analysis focuses within a single service area. Cost savings are typically assumed in both consolidation and cooperation, but the empirical evidence is equivocal and no cost savings are the more common result (see Holzer and Fry 2011, and Bel and Warner 2013 for a review of studies). One explanation for lack of cost savings lies in the failure to adequately assess and measure transaction costs. When we look at service coordination across an array of services, transaction costs rise further. Regionalists challenge the individual service focus of shared services by pointing out that the intersections between water, waste, transport, and environment are what require multifunctional coordination, something a shared services strategy cannot meet. While some metropolitan planning organizations and councils of government are trying to address the multifunctional coordination problem, they typically lack the democratic legitimacy, governmental authority, and broad funding base needed for regionalism (Lowe 2010; Frug 2002). Thus, the economic argument does not leave us with a clear choice between consolidation or cooperation.

THE CRITICAL IMPORTANCE OF GOVERNANCE STRUCTURE

Each of the three theoretical foundations outlined above has concluded with attention to governance structure. While fiscal federalism and public choice give primary attention to the positive aspects of intermunicipal competition, and economists give primary attention to economies of scale and transaction costs, the bigger challenge may be regional equity concerns. Markets allocate to the highest bidder, but public services require some level of universality and coordination based on social and environmental values, not just cost and return. Here, governance is essential, and it extends beyond the dimension of transaction costs related to the nature of governance within a service, and raises the trickier transaction costs related to cross-organizational collaboration in a multiservice framework (Shrestha and Feiock 2011).

The theoretical work of Richard Feiock (2007, 2009) on institutional collective action, Elinor Ostrom (1990, 2010) on common pool resources, and Kathryn Foster (1997) on regional governance all give attention to economic considerations but then move into theoretical arenas, which draw heavily on sociology and public administration. Norms of reciprocity, strong and weak ties, short- versus long-term horizons, trust, authority, and ability to sanction are all elements in these theories.

The importance of such governance factors are confirmed by practitioners who often report breakdown of shared service agreements due to conflicts in these areas. None of these theories offers much hope for coordination among many heterogeneous actors. Even Ostrom (2010) acknowledges that voluntary coordination is more likely to occur among similar partners, in small numbers, where norms are shared and the possibility of sanction is high. This raises concern that voluntary intermunicipal cooperation will not be sufficient to address the critical social equity and environmental challenges that face twenty-first-century local governments.

However, recent theoretical work offers some promise. Network ties among local governments create the conditions for future collaboration (Agranoff and McGuire 2003). Political factors related to power and interest group politics show the potential for more collaborative activity across the metropolitan region (Leland and Thurmaier 2004, 2010). Historical institutionalism helps explain both the reasons for breakdown in collaborative action and the potential for future success.

Some balance is needed between local autonomy and regional coordination. While Ostrom (2010) sees a limited role for higher-level coordination, I argue a multilevel governance structure is needed that provides an overarching guidance and sanctioning framework within which semi-autonomous local governments can pursue shared arrangements in a polycentric system (Homsy and Warner 2013).

CONCLUSION

Economic theories dominate our understanding of service delivery. While markets have proven to be powerful motivators on both the supply and demand side, they alone are not sufficient to explain the rise in intermunicipal cooperation that we have seen in recent years. Economics looks at the margin, but government also must address the long term. Markets reward winners, but government concerns itself with all residents. Competition promotes market efficiency, but government is concerned with social efficiency. Market choice is based on effective demand, but citizen voice is based on democracy and participation.

The rise in intermunicipal cooperation calls for a broader theory, one that emphasizes the bases of cooperation (Warner 2011). While cooperation arises from market characteristics, it also arises from shared values and norms. Indeed, it is norms that make such shared agreements sustainable. Theories of institutional collective action give attention to norms, politics, and values and how these play out in collaborative governance networks

(Feiock 2009; Agranoff and McGuire 2003). How to embed both economic incentives and normative values in cooperative governance structures is the challenge that the later chapters in this book explore.

Intermunicipal cooperation also raises concerns about how to balance fiscal discipline and local voice and autonomy with the need for cross-jurisdictional coordination and equity. If intermunicipal cooperation and shared services are to be a solution to the problem of local government fragmentation, scholars and practitioners need to identify the relative allocation of roles (fiscal and administrative) in a multilevel governance system.

This is both a problem for theory and for practice. If we are to solve the critical problems of environmental management and social equity we must devise a better governance system that promotes cooperation at the regional scale. Pastor and colleagues argued in their 2009 book that "this could be the start of something big." It had better be if the challenges of watershed management, regional transportation, and equitable service delivery are to be met. Much work remains to be done. The chapters in this book represent a first step in outlining some of the potential and challenges of such an approach.

KEY POINTS

- A theoretical framework must be grounded in an understanding of culture and history and recognize the path dependence of the problem of governmental fragmentation and the possibilities for its solution.
- Discussion of shared services and consolidation must include political considerations that address service responsibilities, finance, and accountability in a multilevel federalist governmental system.
- Likewise, equity considerations that look at externalities and spillovers across jurisdictions in an urbanizing world are important in our discussions of local government form.
- Governance structure of sharing arrangements is critical to reduce transaction costs, ensure accountability, and build norms of reciprocal trust required for ongoing cooperation.
- Finally, discussions of shared services and consolidation must include central discussions of economic considerations of efficiency and economies of scale at both the governmental unit and service level.

ACKNOWLEDGMENTS

This research was supported in part by U.S. Department of Agriculture National Institute for Food and Agriculture grant # 2011-68006-30793.

REFERENCES

Agranoff, Robert, and Michael McGuire. 2003. *Collaborative Public Management: New Strategies for Local Governments.* Washington, DC: Georgetown University Press.

Aulich, Chris, Melissa Gibbs, Alex Gooding, Peter McKinlay, Stephanie Pillora, and Graham Sansom. 2011. *Consolidation in Local Government: A Fresh Look.* Broadway, NSW: Australia Center of Excellence for Local Government.

Bel, Germà, and Mildred E. Warner. 2013. Inter-municipal cooperation and costs: Evidence from experience in Europe. Working Paper, University of Barcelona, Spain.

Bish, Robert L., and Vincent Ostrom. 1973. *Understanding Urban Government: Metropolitan Reform Reconsidered.* Washington, DC: American Enterprise Institute for Public Policy Research.

Boadway, Robin, and Anwar Shah. 2009. *Fiscal Federalism: Principles and Practice of Multiorder Governance.* New York: Cambridge University Press.

Bollens, Scott A. 1997. Concentrated poverty and metropolitan equity strategies. *Stanford Law and Policy Review* 8(2): 11–23.

Brenner, Neil. 2004. Urban governance and the production of new state spaces in western Europe, 1960–2000. *Review of International Political Economy* 11(3): 447–488.

Briffault, Richard. 2000. Localism and regionalism. *Buffalo Law Review* 48(1): 1–30.

Carr, Jered B., and Richard Feiock, eds. 2004. *City-County Consolidation and Its Alternatives: Reshaping the Local Government Landscape.* Armonk, NY: M.E. Sharpe.

Dollery, Brian, and Andrew Johnson. 2005. Enhancing efficiency in Australian local government: An evaluation of alternative models of municipal governance. *Urban Policy and Research* 23(13): 73–85.

Downs, Anthony. 1994. *New Visions for Metropolitan America.* Washington, DC: Brookings Institution.

Feiock, Richard C. 2007. Rational choice and regional governance. *Journal of Urban Affairs* 29(1): 47–63.

———. 2009. Metropolitan governance and institutional collective action. *Urban Affairs Review* 44(3): 356–377.

Foster, Kathryn A. 1997. *The Political Economy of Special-Purpose Government.* Washington, DC: Georgetown University Press.

Foster, Kathryn, and William Barnes. 2012. Reframing regional governance for research and practice. *Urban Affairs Review* 48(2): 272–283.

Frug, Gerald E. 1999. *City Making: Building Communities Without Building Walls.* Princeton, NJ: Princeton University Press.

———. 2002. Beyond regional government. *Harvard Law Review* 117(7): 1766–1836.

Frug, Gerald E., and David Barron. 2008. *City Bound: How States Stifle Urban Innovation.* Ithaca, NY: Cornell University Press.

Girth, Amanda, Amir Hefetz, Jocelyn Johnston, and Mildred E. Warner. 2012. Outsourcing public service delivery: Management responses in noncompetitive markets. *Public Administration Review* 72(6): 887–900.

Hefetz, Amir, and Mildred E. Warner. 2012. Contracting or public delivery? The importance of service, market and management characteristics. *Journal of Public Administration Research and Theory* 22(2): 289–317.

Hefetz, Amir, Mildred.E. Warner, and Eran Vigoda-Gadot. 2012. Privatization and inter-municipal contracting: US local government experience 1992–2007. *Environment and Planning C: Government and Policy* 30(4): 675–692.

Holzer, Marc, and John Fry. 2011. *Shared Services and Municipal Consolidation: A Critical Analysis.* Alexandria, VA: Public Technology Institute.

Homsy, George C., and Mildred E. Warner. 2013. Climate change and the co-production of knowledge and policy in rural USA communities. *Sociologia Ruralis* 53(3): 291–310.

Kneebone, Elizabeth, and Alan Berube. 2013. *Confronting Suburban Poverty in America.* Washington, DC: Brookings Institution.

Ladd, Helen F. 1992. Population growth, density and the costs of providing public services. *Urban Studies* 29(2): 273–295.

Lago-Peñas, Santiago, and Jorge Martinez-Vazquez, eds. 2013. *The Challenge of Local Government Size: Theoretical Perspectives, International Experience, and Policy Reform*. Cheltenham, UK: Edward Elgar.

Leland, Suzanne M., and Kurt M. Thurmaier. 2004. *Case Studies of City-County Consolidation: Reshaping the Local Government Landscape*. Armonk, NY: M.E. Sharpe.

———. 2010. *City-County Consolidation: Promises Made, Promises Kept?* Washington, DC: Georgetown University Press.

Lichter, Daniel.T., Domenico Parisi, Steven M. Grice, and Michael Taquino. 2007. Municipal underbounding: Annexation and racial exclusion in small southern towns. *Rural Sociology* 72(1): 47–68.

Lowe, C. 2010. Institutions and environmental justice in regional transportation planning. Paper presented to the American Collegiate Schools of Planning Conference, Minneapolis, MN.

Lowery, David. 2000. A transactions costs model of metropolitan governance: Allocation versus redistribution in urban America. *Journal of Public Administration Research and Theory* 10(1): 49–78.

Marsh, Ben, Alan Parnell, and Ann M. Joyner. 2010. Institutionalization of racial inequality in local political geographies: The use of GIS evidence. *Urban Geography* 31(5): 691–709.

Marvel, Mary K., and Howard P. Marvel. 2007. Outsourcing oversight: A comparison for in-house and contracted services. *Public Administration Review* 67(3): 521–530.

McKinlay, Peter 2011. Integration of urban services and good governance: The Auckland supercity project. Paper presented to Pacific Economic Cooperation Council (PECC) Seminar on Environmental Sustainability in Urban Centres, Perth, Western Australia, April 13.

Mikesell, John. 2007. *Fiscal Administration: Analysis and Applications for the Public Sector*. 7th ed. Belmont, CA: Thomson/Wadsworth.

Oates, Wallace E. 1998. *The Economics of Fiscal Federalism and Local Finance*. Northampton, MA: Edward Elgar.

Orfield, Myron. 1997. *Metropolitics*. Washington, DC: Brookings Institution Press.

———. 2002. *American Metropolitics: The New Suburban Reality*. Washington, DC: Brookings Institution Press.

Ostrom, Elinor. 1990. *Governing the Commons: The Evolution of Institutions for Collective Action*. New York: Cambridge University Press.

———. 2010. Analyzing collective action. *Agricultural Economics* 41(S1): 155–166.

Ostrom, Vincent, Charles M. Tiebout, and Robert Warren. 1961. The organization of government in metropolitan areas: A theoretical inquiry. *The American Political Science Review* 55(4): 831–842.

Parks, Roger B., and Ronald J. Oakerson. 1993. Comparative metropolitan organization: Service production and governance structures in St Louis (MO) and Allegheny County (PA). *Publius* 23(1): 19–40.

Pastor, Manuel, Chris Benner, and Martha Matsuoka. 2009. *This Could Be the Start of Something Big: How Social Movements for Regional Equity Are Reshaping Metropolitan America*. Ithaca, NY: Cornell University Press.

Prud'homme, Remy. 1995. The dangers of decentralization. *The World Bank Research Observer* 10(2): 201–220.

Rusk, David. 1993. *Cities Without Suburbs*. Washington, DC: Woodrow Wilson Center Press.

———. 1999. *Inside Game/Outside Game: Winning Strategies for Saving Urban America*. Washington, DC: Brookings Institution Press.

Shrestha, Manoj K., and Richard C. Feiock. 2011. Transaction cost, exchange embeddedness, and interlocal cooperation in local public goods. *Political Research Quarterly* 64(3): 573–587.

Thurmaier, Kurt, and Curtis Wood. 2004. Interlocal agreements as an alternative to consolidation. In *City-County Consolidation and Its Alternatives: Reshaping the Local Government Landscape,* ed. J.B. Carr and R. Feiock, 113–130. Armonk, NY: M.E. Sharpe.

Tiebout, Charles M. 1956. A pure theory of local expenditures, *Journal of Political Economy* 64(5): 416–424.

Troutt, David D. 2000. Ghettoes made easy: The metamarket/antimarket dichotomy and the legal challenges of inner-city economic development. *Harvard Civil Rights–Civil Liberties Law Review* 35(2): 427–507.

Warner, Mildred E. 2001. State policy under devolution: Redistribution and centralization. *National Tax Journal* 54(3): 541–556.

———. 2006. Market-based governance and the challenge for rural governments: U.S. trends. *Social Policy and Administration* 40(6): 612–631.

———. 2011. Competition or cooperation in urban service delivery? *Annals of Public and Cooperative Economics* 82(4): 421–435.

———. 2013. Does local government size matter? Privatization and hybrid systems of local service delivery. In *The Challenge of Local Government Size: Theoretical Perspectives, International Experience, and Policy Reform*, ed. S. Lago-Peñas and J. Martinez-Vazquez, 271–296. Northampton, MA: Edward Elgar.

Warner, Mildred E., and James E. Pratt. 2005. Spatial diversity in local government revenue effort under decentralization: A neural-network approach. *Environment and Planning C: Government and Policy* 23(5): 657–677.

Wilson, William J. 1987. *The Truly Disadvantaged: The Inner City, the Underclass, and Social Works.* Chicago: University of Chicago Press.

2

The Costs of Services Cooperation

A Review of the Literature

Christopher V. Hawkins and Jered B. Carr

The context of service delivery has changed substantially for cities over the last half-century. Demographic shifts to exurban areas and resultant central city decline have had profound effects on the service delivery responsibilities of local governments. The "Great Recession" has also led to greater oversight of the use of public funds. Some suggest the fiscal realities many local governments now confront represent a "new normal" in which accountability is a public agenda priority (Martin, Levey, and Cawley 2012). Thus, for many communities, delivering high-quality services within the financial constraints they face is a serious concern. Moreover, local government officials must overcome inefficiencies in service delivery due to issues of scale, resource inequalities from residential sorting in terms of income and race within the region, and negative environmental externalities created by the actions of neighboring jurisdictions (Feiock and Carr 2001; Perlman and Benton 2012).

In light of these and other issues, arguments in favor of more shared service delivery among local governments have been advancing in practitioner and academic communities for several decades (Lowery 2000; Rusk 1999; Andrew 2009a). This increased interest in establishing more shared service delivery arrangements has focused attention on managing the complex relationships among participants in cooperative efforts (LeRoux and Carr 2010; Andrew and Carr 2013). Managing risk is a major focus of research on the development and maintenance of shared service delivery. Of particular significance to the creation of shared service arrangements are the difficulties of defining the outcomes that indicate achievement of the objectives and the time and financial costs of monitoring and enforcing participant contributions per the agreement. Dealing with problems of monitoring and enforcing contracts can be particularly challenging when public officials lack information from which to make sound policy decisions (Feiock 2007).

The purpose of this chapter is to review the academic research literature on shared service delivery to identify major obstacles to establishing and managing shared service agreements. Shared service delivery among municipal governments in the United States is widespread. Despite the absence of regular national surveys on the topic, the broad use of arrangements that create some version of shared service production is clear from many single-state surveys on the topic (Deller, Hinds, and Hinman 2001; Wood 2004; LeRoux 2006; LeRoux and Carr 2007; Zeemering 2007; Andrew 2009a).

However, what is collectively known about the process of municipal cooperation, the mechanisms of shared service delivery, and the nature of interlocal cooperation in general is fragmented across several different research literatures. Moreover, the existing research base on shared service delivery is shaped by a variety of factors that are directly tied to these independent research efforts, such as the sample on which the study results are based, the questions asked of study participants, the methods of analysis, and the theoretical orientation that guides the particular study. In this sense, academic research continues to lag well behind what is happening in communities across the United States.

Nonetheless, because a relatively large body of literature now exists on shared service delivery, students of public administration have a firm base from which to improve their understanding of the challenges in establishing and managing service agreements. Regardless of whether one is a new student of public administration or a seasoned city manager, the challenge, of course, lies in identifying important obstacles in interlocal cooperation and learning how to overcome these obstacles to be successful in managing shared service delivery. Our primary objective is to identify what has been learned about the process of interlocal cooperation for a broad range of readers.

For this information to be useful for practitioners and students we emphasize in this chapter the theoretical basis from which conclusions are drawn regarding the opportunities and challenges in developing shared service agreements. This approach is critical, since the theoretical foundation from which the academic literature has been built is closely intertwined with the perceptions of local officials who are responsible for crafting and managing service agreements. In fact, many studies of shared service delivery that we review in this chapter are based on data collected directly from local officials and complemented with data collected from various federal and state government agencies.

Because much of the research on shared service delivery utilizes a transaction cost approach, we begin this chapter by providing an overview of this concept. We then emphasize how participants in a cooperative agreement manage risks from defection and other transaction costs in these arrangements. We also emphasize how the different institutional mechanisms used to support shared services affect the transaction costs of these exchanges. The costs of engaging in services cooperation is a different issue than the question of how differences in production characteristics affect the potential for gaining cost reductions through shared services. (This issue is discussed in the previous chapter by Mildred Warner.) The chapter ends with suggestions for future research on this topic.

CHALLENGES FOR PUBLIC MANAGERS: TRANSACTION COSTS IN SHARED SERVICE DELIVERY AGREEMENTS

A relatively large and continuously growing body of literature utilizes transaction cost economics to explain local production decisions in general and interlocal cooperation and shared service delivery more specifically. The concept of transaction costs has been commonly applied as a theoretical explanation for why a private enterprise organizes activities vertically or horizontally (the decision to contract out, for example). According to Williamson (1975, 1985), uncertainty, limited information, and the features of the investment are considered the critical components of a transaction, or the "friction" in market exchanges.

Williamson links these issues to a conceptual explanation for organizational arrangements of a firm. He defines transaction costs as the "comparative costs of planning, adapting, and monitoring task completion under alternative governing structures" (1981, 552–553). Extension of this concept to the fields of public administration and urban policy is used to explain public sector action and organizational arrangement in a variety of policy domains. This literature has been instrumental in highlighting obstacles due to the coordination, division, and commitment problems that often must be managed effectively if the effort at cooperation is to be successful.

The adoption of interlocal agreements is commonly examined as a decision among several different options, which include in-house production and a number of possible contracting arrangements (Brown and Potoski 2003a, 2003b; LeRoux and Carr 2007; Andrew 2009a; Carr, LeRoux, and Shrestha 2009). This approach borrows heavily from the contracting literature, and the analyses tend to specify economic, political, and other local contextual variables to explain the motivations of local public officials in selecting different production options.

When establishing a service agreement, each jurisdiction has different policy preferences that must be reconciled through bargaining. This can be very time consuming and create a disincentive for local public officials to enter into interlocal service agreements (Williamson 1981; Feiock 2007; Hatley 2010). Therefore, local officials must weigh the anticipated benefits of such a shared service delivery arrangement against the time and monetary costs of negotiating the terms of the agreement. Furthermore, local officials must also consider the financial costs and the time required to monitor and enforce the agreement once it is finalized. However, these activities depend upon the services involved in the agreement. Metrics quantifying what each partner receives through an agreement are more difficult to develop for some services. Successful services cooperation often depends in large part on the ability of administrators to effectively monitor and manage provider performance (Atkins 1997; Brown and Potoski 2003a; Feiock 2009; Hawkins 2009).

Studies using the transaction cost approach describe the process of establishing a shared service delivery agreement as a coordination problem (Feiock 2007; Hawkins 2009; Scholz and Feiock 2010). Coordination problems result from the complexity of organizing tasks among the partners of an interlocal agreement. Local governments are not uniform in demographic or fiscal characteristics, and coordinating agreements is more difficult when the needs of potential collaborators diverge. Oakerson (2004) emphasizes the similarity of the population within cities in enabling public officials to "speak with one voice" when making governing decisions on behalf of their residents.

Depending on the services that are to be jointly produced, this may require extensive communication to specify the tasks that are to be completed jointly or individually by the participants. For example, Bae (2009) found that larger differences in terms of socioeconomic characteristics of the population has a negative effect on the formation of agreements among local governments in Georgia's metropolitan areas. Similarly, respondents to Hawkins's (2009) survey noted that a lack of agreement among communities on development goals was a significant barrier for local governments seeking to establish an agreement.

Significant differences across communities in socioeconomic characteristics require local officials to develop agreements that support the service delivery goals of all cities, yet also address the needs of their own diverse populations (Feiock 2007; Kwon and Feiock 2010). The formation of interlocal agreements is not a trivial process. These agreements often require the approval of each city council, and depending on the nature of the transactions, they may involve several rounds of negotiation and bargaining to determine the terms and conditions of the agreements. Hatley's (2010) case analysis of an effort by five cities to replace their fire departments with a single multijurisdictional fire authority illustrates that these bargaining costs may be so high that the effort to share services is abandoned.

Other studies have examined the effects of homogeneity in terms of the similarities and differences among local government departments that establish interlocal agreements. For example, Andrew and Hawkins (2012) find that service agreements are more likely to be established among local government departments that have the same goals. They argue that more diverse policy preferences increase the time and effort required for local governments to ensure decisions are made consensually. Participants in an intergovernmental agreement with a similar specialized function (such as law enforcement) can take advantage of redundancy in resources and similar governance structures in executing joint activities, thus minimizing coordination problems.

Difficulties in dividing costs and benefits among the participants may further inhibit the establishment of a shared service agreement (Zeemering 2007; Hatley 2010). Division problems occur when local governments agree on the general goals for an interlocal agreement, but encounter difficulty in dividing and distributing the benefits among themselves (Steinacker 2004, 2010; Feiock 2007; Hawkins 2010). If the distribution of resources or benefits from an agreement is perceived to be unequal or benefit some participants at the expense of others, this may deter a local government's disclose of fiscal or administrative capacities during the negotiation process. Division issues shape the rules that are agreed upon for managing the agreement and determining the benefits that may accrue to participating cities (Shrestha 2010).

Although coordinating services and establishing interlocal collaborative agreements can produce substantial benefits, local governments also confront a credible commitment problem. Without a credible commitment, there is the likelihood that one or more of the negotiating parties will not fulfill its obligations under the agreement (Feiock 2009). Bargaining requires a careful outlining of the terms and conditions of the exchange in order to ensure credibility of commitment, to adapt to environmental uncertainties, and to resolve conflicts that may arise in the future. As Brown and Potoski (2005, 328) note, policy decisions are particularly risky when local governments are faced with "limited information, uncertainty about the future, and the prospect that people or organizations behave opportunistically." In essence, each participant must be confident that the others have consistent policy preferences, will maintain the underlying goals and objectives of the agreement, and have a commitment to fulfill their obligations (Hatley 2010; Hawkins 2010).

Defection problems emerge when the decision of one participant in the agreement results in a worse condition for the other participants. This is exacerbated when an agreement is poorly specified or lacks requirement for reporting (Brown and Potoski 2003a). Mechanisms can be designed to minimize this risk and increase trust and reciprocity, which have been demonstrated to minimize monitoring and enforcement problems. The literature examining how these mechanisms can affect the transaction costs of an agreement to share services are reviewed in a subsequent section.

REDUCING RISK IN SERVICE SHARING AGREEMENTS: IMPORTANT CONSIDERATIONS FOR PUBLIC MANAGERS

In general, researchers have focused on three different approaches to reducing the risks in providing shared services as described in the previous section. First, the key characteristics of services that create these costs have received a lot of attention. A second area of emphasis has been to consider how different institutional arrangements affect the risks of collaborative service provision. Finally, researchers have also devoted attention to understanding how the social networks of administrators and elected officials mitigate risk in sharing services.

This section briefly explains the research on these three topics and draws insights from this work to gain an understanding of the costs of creating shared service arrangements. Table 2.1 provides a synopsis of these points.

Understanding the Effects of Service Characteristics on Transaction Costs

Analysts have devoted significant effort to thinking about how certain characteristics of services affect the risks of purchasing or jointly providing services with other local governments. These works focus on attributes of the service that affect their visibility with the public and difficulty in ensuring that contractors perform effectively. The implication of this research is that some services are more difficult to deliver effectively through shared service arrangements than others.

Political Salience of Service to the Public

A few scholars have grappled with the effects of differences in the political salience of local public services with the public and, consequently, elected officials. The best known of these efforts is Williams's (1971) analysis of metropolitan politics. He divided public services into two groups: system maintenance services and lifestyle services. System maintenance functions generally relate to physical infrastructure and provide the structure that supports the creation of multiple residential location options in the region. Lifestyle services, in contrast, provide access to social amenities and generally enhance the quality of life for the residents of each city.

Table 2.1

Key Considerations for Establishing a Shared Service Delivery Agreement

Challenges in Shared Service Agreements	Important Dimensions	Considerations for Public Managers
Transaction costs	Organizing and coordinating tasks, dividing costs and benefits, and monitoring and managing performance among partners of an interlocal agreement	Variation in economic, political, and local contextual factors among potential partners of an interlocal agreement shape transaction risk of shared service delivery.
Managing risk	Characteristics of services	The political salience of system maintenance functions versus lifestyle services can impact the establishment of a shared service agreement. Developing adequate measures of service inputs and outcomes for enforcing agreements and properly gauging the performance or the delivery of a service by another local government are essential for success.
	Institutional arrangements	Depending on the transaction costs, the characteristics of different governing mechanisms (e.g., coordinated agreement, restrictive, or adaptive agreements) provide a way for local governments to resolve their service provision problem.
	Social networks	Interpersonal relations among administrators and elected officials minimize monitoring and enforcement problems through the accumulation of social capital, such as trust, norms, and common professional values.

System maintenance services are "necessary to make the system of specialized areas work" (Williams 1971, 90). Roads, water distribution and treatment, solid waste disposal, and watershed management are examples of system maintenance functions. Examples of lifestyle services include education, public safety, parks and recreation, public housing, and economic development, since commerce provides employment opportunities. These services reflect amenities that vary dramatically in quality from city to city. Williams argued that these services distinguish the lifestyles of wealthier suburban residents and represent the public amenities over which communities compete with one another to attract residents and businesses. He concluded, "if we are to have area specialization, it follows that lifestyle policies are likely to be decentralized" (91).

Williams argued that in the absence of any mandate from federal or state governments, "policies that are perceived as neutral with regard to controlling social access may be centralized, but those that are perceived as controlling social access will remain decentralized" (1971, 4). As this quote suggests, he was talking about the potential functional consolidation of these services at the level of the county or even metropolitan area. However, others have used his argument to examine the potential for more localized cooperation on public services "where important and diverse values are involved" (Rawlings 2003, 55).

These propositions have great intuitive appeal, but their empirical support is not clear. One study found that intergovernmental service delivery arrangements among governments in the Kansas City Region are just as common in system maintenance services as in the lifestyle services (Wood 2006). However, two other studies reported findings more consistent with Williams's theory. For example, Rawlings's (2003) examination of intergovernmental fiscal transfers between localities in metropolitan areas concluded that the transfers were higher for system maintenance services than the lifestyles services she studied. LeRoux and Carr (2010) examined the service delivery networks for eight services among the 44 local governments in Wayne County, Michigan. They found that the networks for the four system maintenance services were more centralized than the networks linking the governments in the case of the four lifestyle services.

Tackling Measurement and Enforcement Costs: An Essential Element for Successful Shared Service Delivery

Another aspect of service characteristics that affect the risks involved with shared service arrangements relate to measuring the performance of the participants in the agreement and enforcing their obligations under the agreement (Romzek and Johnston 2002, 2005; Brown and Potoski 2003a; 2005; Carr, LeRoux, and Shrestha 2009; Shrestha 2010; Hawkins and Andrew 2011).

Public services differ in regard to the costliness of developing adequate measures of inputs and outcomes for monitoring shared service delivery and in the effective enforcement of service agreements (Feiock 2007; Hawkins 2011). Deciding on the inputs of an agreement in a way in which participants can determine the effectiveness of shared service agreements in achieving their intended results requires appropriate monitoring (Taylor and Bassett 2007; Zeemering 2008). Jang (2006) described these challenges in her analysis of shared service agreements for parks and recreation. These services can be relatively difficult to negotiate because of the challenge of identifying tangible service outputs and the complexity of service products.

A series of research articles by Brown and Potoski (2003a, 2003b, 2005) and Brown, Potoski, and Van Slyke (2006) provide a detailed explanation and assessment of the consequences of measurement difficulty. Ease of measurement refers to the ability of the contracting organization, such as local government, to gauge the performance or the delivery of a service by another local government. Easily measured services "have identifiable performance metrics that accurately represent service quantity and quality" (Brown, Potoski and Van Slyke 2006, 330). In contrast, they suggest "a service is difficult to measures when neither the outcomes to be achieved nor the activities to be performed are easily identifiable" (330).

As an example, based on responses to their survey of city managers, mental health programs and facilities are the most difficult to measure and payroll is the easiest. For some services, the design of contracts is fairly straightforward, such as waste collection and disposal or road construction and maintenance. In these cases, clear engineering standards, costs of materials, labor, or capital required of participants in a shared service can be written into agreements. For other services, however, it is much more difficult to define clear measures of what is provided by the participants and the resultant outcomes of an agreement (Girard et al., 2009).

The implication of this performance measurement issue is that for some services the development of effective measures to determine contractor performance is costly. Studies have provided strong evidence that the ease with which service level and quality can be measured affects the likelihood of agreements being established. Kwon, Lee, and Feiock (2010), for example, investigate changes in city-level service delivery arrangements between 1997 and 2002. They found that problems of measuring services that are shared by communities caused additional costs in terms of monitoring and, as a result, services that are difficult to measure were more often provided internally. Similarly, Deller, Hinds and Hinman's (2001) study of Wisconsin municipalities found higher rates of interlocal cooperation when contracts were easily crafted and monitored.

Institutional Design Matters: Reducing Risk Through Mechanisms That Lead to Success

Scholars have also focused on understanding how the different institutional mechanisms used to support shared service delivery affect the risks to the participants. Contracting for services or the consolidation of functions is a two-part problem (Kwon and Feiock 2010). Participants must first decide to seek a contracting partner as buyer or seller, or join a group of local governments planning to consolidate their services. Second, they must engage in collective action to create the institutions that will support the shared service arrangement. In this second stage, participants must overcome the barriers to collective action and create the institutions to implement service cooperation.

Institutional structures delineate roles and responsibilities and define tasks to facilitate and coordinate joint activities across the independent jurisdictions. Institutional structures also establish monitoring and enforcement mechanisms that are needed for conducting effective collective action. There is a growing body of work that identifies the potential for opportunism in these arrangements and discusses how different institutional arrangements can mitigate these risks.

Feiock (2009), for example, presents a range of intuitional mechanisms that can be established among local governments and that operate to reduce coordination problems and the potential for defection. He refers to these as "managed" and "coordinated" mechanisms, which are cooperative agreements among cities designed or coordinated by third parties such as state or federal governments. In these mechanisms, a higher-level government provides funding and mandates the formation of collaborative relations among local governmental actors. Existing institutions or actors—such as the state, a council of government, or a policy entrepreneur—serve as broker and assume responsibility for helping to craft an agreement (Wood 2006).

A "contract network," on the other hand, links individual units through joint ventures, interlocal agreements, and service contracts. This institutional mechanism links local governments in formalized and legally binding agreements but also preserves the autonomy of local actors. Andrew (2009b) noted that interlocal agreements can create a formation of contractual ties across a region. Furthermore, because shared service agreements can overlap among multiple functional areas, norms of reciprocity among local government actors are important for the maintenance of agreements. This is important to reducing transaction risk, particularly opportunism, because defection is widely known among the partners in such an agreement. Sanctions for noncompliance can also affect the establishment of agreements in other functional areas (Andrew 2010).

The patterns of voluntary and self-organizing networks provide a mechanism for governments to resolve their service provision problem. For example, Wood's (2004, 2006, 2008) analysis of shared service arrangements in the Kansas City region showed that many of the local government officials in the region were interconnected through the same social and professional networks and associations. Wood (2006, 348) concludes that "intergovernmental arrangements are generally cooperative and result in a more perfect union by overcoming the disarticulation of the state and collective-action problems created by governmental fragmentation and externalities."

A third type of institutional mechanism, a policy network, emphasizes the social network in which a local government is embedded. A policy network consists of the direct and indirect ties among public, non-profit and private organizations within a region and provides the greatest degree of autonomy in decisions to enter and exit agreements. According to Feiock (2009), this mechanism is strongly tied to the embededness of local government in informal, self-organized exchange relationships. An important feature of a policy network is that local governments pay attention not just to a potential partner's individual characteristics, but that they also consider the relations of the potential partner with other cities in the region (Andrew and Carr 2013). Thus, repeated interactions among local government actors mitigate the transaction costs of forming a shared service agreement. Underpinning this institutional mechanism are the characteristics of the relationships between the actors, such as mutuality, bonding, and trust (Scholz, Berardo, and Kile 2008; Andrew 2009b; 2010; Shrestha 2010).

Coordinating agreements is critical even when they are informal or fall outside the parameters of formal agreements specified through state statutes or enabling legislation (Andrew 2009a). In this case, a cooperative arrangement may be an unwritten agreement that is a function of meetings of staff and committees composed of partners in a joint effort (Graddy and Chen 2006). Jurisdictions often use memoranda of agreement or understanding as a means of addressing short-term and specific policy issues rather than as long-term solutions to more regional concerns. Nonetheless, a precondition to a successful memorandum is the ability of the participating local governments to reach consensus on broad policy goals for their communities (Lynn 2005).

Although policy networks may provide a mechanism for local governments to establish and maintain informal agreements, cities also have the autonomy to exit agreements. This can limit the kinds of conflicts that more flexible and self-organizing institutional mechanisms, such as a policy network, are capable of resolving. Thus, less formal arrangements are still expected to have relatively high transaction costs due to the attention to bargaining, negotiation, consensus building, and conflict resolution required to initiate and maintain the cooperative effort.

Contracts that formalize service delivery and that clearly outline the responsibilities of partners also entail transaction costs related to monitoring the contract and evaluating the performance of the service provider. But as Wood (2004) contends, such interlocal arrangements require less frequent interaction by the participants and thus involve lower transaction costs. These prove to be more stable and, ultimately, more permanent arrangements.

The advantages of different institutional mechanisms for managing shared service agreements are also discussed by Andrew (2010) and Andrew and Hawkins (2012) as adaptive and restrictive agreements. Through adaptive agreements, local governments can craft a flexible arrangement that allows participants to provide joint services but contains language that is broad enough to leave room for renegotiation and adjustment. The nature of some shared services, such as emergency preparedness and response, where conditions and events can change quite rapidly, may prohibit local governments from specifying in advance the exact processes and outcomes of joint activities. Adaptive agreements provide flexibility in order to reallocate resources or tasks among participants in order to respond to changing circumstances. A downside to an adaptive arrangement, however, is the potential difficulty associated with verifying outputs related to ambiguous and complex transactions.

In comparison, Andrew and Hawkins (2012) describe a restrictive interlocal agreement as one that specifies outputs before certain investments are made by participating parties. A restrictive agreement is more binding than an adaptive agreement and often includes detailed procedural safeguards to reduce uncertainty. This is particularly important when local governments design rules governing a transfer of total responsibility for the provision of a service to another governmental unit and when transactions involve some exchange of payments, revenue sharing, or impact fees (United States Advisory Commission on Intergovernmental Relations 1985; Atkins 1997).

An advantage of a restrictive agreement is that clearly specified rules can reduce uncertainty and risk among parties created by the turnover of local decision makers. Extensive turnover may erode or obscure the original basis of the agreement, leading cities to avoid contracting with cities experiencing increased administrative turnover (Feiock, Clinger, Shrestha, and Dasse 2007).

Studies examining the effects of executive turnover on transaction risk in interlocal cooperation are even more compelling. For example, the results of Feiock and colleagues' (2007) study of executive turnover suggests that cities conduct less external contracting when there is an increase in turnover of city leadership positions irrespective of the type of policy or service. Because of the instability that administrative turnover creates, shared service agreements become a more expensive and risky choice compared to alternative service production options.

At the organizational level, a restrictive arrangement, for example between public safety agencies, can produce a relatively strong functionally organized bureaucracy to ensure stability and decisiveness of coordinating efforts (Kettl 2007). Additionally, a stable set of rules governing processes and administrative procedures can reduce future conflicts when coordinating policy across multiple jurisdictions. In addition, Andrew and Hawkins (2012) identify specific state statutes or legally and defensible local ordinances as providing an additional layer of certainty to ensure outcomes are consistent with agreed-upon performance measures.

Networks Matter: The Role of Social Networks in Shared Service Delivery

Social networks are considered by many researchers as playing an important role in reducing the risks associated with establishing shared service agreements, particularly in the analysis of how networks mitigate the risks of opportunistic behavior. A network approach to analyzing production decisions in service delivery focuses on exchange relations and interdependencies among cities (Shrestha 2010; Andrew 2009a). Research that employs this approach couples the nature of the transaction, resource endowments, and political institutions of the participating governments (see especially Feiock and Scholz 2010) with the structure of the networks and the role of professional affiliations among the contracting parties (LeRoux and Pandey 2011; LeRoux, Brandenburger, and Pandey 2010; LeRoux and Carr 2007; Hawkins 2010).

Hawkins and Andrew (2011, 18–19) note that "while the threats of legal sanctions to resolve collective action problems are always a feasible option, they are often costly to consider without involving valuable resources in the litigation process." As an alternative, social networks can provide a monitoring and enforcement mechanism, thus reducing transaction risks.

Research has explored the role of networks in the establishment and maintenance of shared service delivery from two perspectives. The first perspective focuses on the structure of networks. This line of research has emphasized the varying configurations of shared service agreements across a region. The second perspective focuses on professional affiliation networks. This perspective emphasizes the importance of shared values, trust, and reciprocity among city managers and other officials of city government. These two perspectives are discussed in this section.

Network Structures

While the web of relations in a network of agreements can be relatively simple, as in the case of a single jurisdiction in which many local governments have established a tie, the relations can also be highly complex where local governments form multiple relations with one another across a region (Shrestha 2010). Research has begun to examine how the configurations of shared service delivery networks reduce the transaction risk in cooperative endeavors. For example, networks of shared service agreements have been characterized as closed or clustered. Alternatively, some networks have been characterized as centralized, with a network concentrating around a particular city or regional actor (Scholz, Berardo, and Kile 2008; Andrew and Carr 2013).

The characteristics of the network relations can provide a monitoring mechanism by ensuring that stakeholders play by the "rules of the game" (Coleman 1988; Scott 2000; Lin 2001). Some scholars have argued that close-knit social ties are important for building trust, maintaining norms of reciprocity, and developing social support (Podolny and Baron 1997). For example, Andrew (2010) argues that the advantage of having a clustered network reduces the cost of enforcing an agreed set of working rules because any actions taken or not taken by a recipient are made public. Any threat of collective sanction among the participants in a shared service agreement will enhance the credibility of punishments or sanctions being imposed.

Others argue that a dense network structure creates social capital (Coleman 1988). According to this view, obligations, information channels, and social norms reduce risks of uncertainty. A dense network structure creates efficiency and trust of information due to the limited number of people involved in the communication (Podolny and Baron 1997). Moreover, it increases the confidence with which each can trust the other to cooperate (Burt 2000, 352).

A sparse network structure, in comparison, is more diffuse. In this type of network a city may have social ties to a relatively small number of other cities. These other cities may also have few ties throughout the region. This type of network structure may allow cities the opportunity to reap the benefits of innovations or visions that are not available within a highly clustered network (Burt 2005; Granovetter 1973). A sparse network structure may also reduce coordination problems across a region because information held by one jurisdiction can be transmitted throughout the network via social ties.

In some cases, shared service delivery reflects cooperative arrangements where there are multiple agreements among various city departments between two cities. A "multiplex service relationship" is where an individual jurisdiction engages with other units in multiple policy relationships simultaneously. For example, a city may have a police service contract with another city in the region, as well as shared service contracts for fire or emergency medical services with the same city. Multiple service contracts that link more than one service can reduce credible commitment problems and minimize the potential for defection. Similarly, Shrestha and Feiock (2009, 806) suggest "The risks involving contractual arrangements in one service area can be mitigated if these contracts are embedded in broader multiplex service relationships." Multiple service contracts may signify more trust. It also can influence future exchanges and the maintenance or expansion of existing shared service delivery arrangements.

Get Connected: The Importance of Interpersonal Relations

The research on social networks also highlights the role of interpersonal relations in building "social capital" among local governing officials (LeRoux, Brandenburger, and Pandey 2010). Trust and norms of reciprocity are argued to be key elements of social capital that is formed and maintained through local government networks (Hawkins 2010). As trust among local officials increases, entering into cooperative agreements becomes more attractive, because bargaining and negotiating the agreements requires less time and the subsequent monitoring and enforcement costs are also reduced. Moreover, since shared service agreements often overlap among multiple activities and governing units, they may also be supported by norms of reciprocity (Andrew 2009b). Networks thus aid in minimizing transaction costs that serve as obstacles to negotiating and maintaining agreements (Carr, LeRoux, and Shrestha 2009).

Hawkins and Andrew (2011), for example, describe the role of networks in their study of joint ventures in twelve metropolitan areas. They suggest that interactions among city officials and regional organization complement and reinforce formal contractual mechanisms and facilitate the establishment of informal joint ventures by engendering trust (see Feiock 2009). In the absence of specific and formalized contractual obligations, trust among local governments becomes essential because it reduces the monitoring costs and improves the chances of a successful cooperative endeavor. This is particularly important when there is a misalignment or changes in goals and common expectations over time, which a formal contractual agreement does not anticipate or the parties have difficulty resolving through legal mechanisms. Thus, informal agreements are strongly linked with the assets generated from a network of government and non-government organizations.

The benefit produced by social ties lies in quantitatively unobserved resources that scholars often refer to as social capital. These resources signal that "something of value has been produced for those actors who have [these resources] available and that the value depends on social organization" (Coleman 1988, 101). One way to identify the benefits of social resources is through concrete personal relations and networks of relations that generate trust, obligations and expectations, and information channels (Coleman 1988).

From this perspective the networks of administrators and elected officials can be crucial to reducing risks from collaboration. Linkages among public officials can be created when they are bound by common knowledge, share a common information source, or are united by shared professional norms, values, and practices. Thus, as pointed out by Carr, LeRoux, and Shrestha (2009, 406) "professional associations represent another type of network, or institutional linkages that may help to promote interjurisdictional cooperation. Local government administrators who share an affiliation as members of a professional association are more likely to arrive at consensus related to 'best practices' and to see the value of increased cooperation." Frederickson (1999) argues that disciplines and professions, for example membership in the International City/County Management Association (ICMA), or having a public administration degree, function as institutions, imparting a shared system of norms and values among members. Thus, transaction costs of interlocal service delivery arrangements are likely to be lower if government officials share the same professional networks.

This perspective also focuses on the multiple actors that make strategic decisions in order to improve their individual benefits. Carr, LeRoux, and Shrestha (2009), for example, studied this network among administrators in the establishment of one of three production choices (in-house production, intergovernmental arrangements, and nongovernmental production) for 109 city governments in Michigan in 2005. Their indicator of social relations (measured by the index of local officials' participation in professional networks) is statistically related to cooperation with other local governments. Their results provide supporting evidence of the role social embeddedness plays in promoting exchanges of information and building trust among partners, thus resulting in increased outsourcing with other local governments.

Other evidence is provided by LeRoux, Brandenburger, and Pandey (2010), who measure interlocal cooperation for 1,538 local governments with a population of 50,000 or more, examining the number of interlocal agreements. They find that interlocal service delivery increases when managers network in regional associations, which provide opportunities for ongoing interactions among local government officials. They also find that professional networks matter, in particular networks created by shared disciplinary training in the profession of public administration. This, they argue, may also enhance trust, as managers may seek out cooperation with partners that they know will be like-minded and share the same goals and values. Exchange relations over time help develop trust and credibility of commitment between the transacting cities.

As part of their disciplinary training, public managers are socialized with values of efficiency and effectiveness, and therefore may share common assumptions that facilitate interlocal cooperation (LeRoux and Pandey 2011; Frederickson 1999; Frederickson and Smith 2003; LeRoux, Brandenburger, and Pandey 2010). A council–manager form of government is often considered more efficiency-oriented than mayor–council government (Carr and Karuppusamy 2010). Moreover, the longer tenure of career public servants forces them to look farther into the future when considering standardizing services and alternatives to managing jurisdictional problems that come with the actions of neighboring cities (Frederickson 1999; Frederickson and Smith 2003; Wood 2006). The literature suggests that local governments managed by professional managers are more likely to adopt advanced technology or managerial innovation in order to achieve managerial efficiency than their counterparts without professional managers (Musso, Weare, and Hale 2001).

CONCLUSION

The interdependency among local governments is clearly evident in the use of shared service delivery arrangements. For many cities, shared service agreements are now a relatively common feature of public administration and urban management activities. Thus, understanding the process by which agreements are formed, governed, and maintained over time is important for improving the design of institutional mechanisms and increasing the success of interlocal cooperation.

In this chapter we primarily focused on the transaction costs that inhibit shared services delivery, and how local governments can craft institutional structures to mitigate these barriers. The literature we reviewed provides some insight into these challenges. As suggested at the outset of this chapter, local governments are far from uniform across a region, and coordinating tasks among diverse communities can be fraught with difficulty. Local officials must also negotiate and bargain over the benefits that are to be distributed among the participants of an agreement. The difficulties are enhanced depending on the ease with which transactions can be measured. The risks associated with shared services often stem from enforcing and monitoring agreements under less than ideal conditions.

Moreover, some services are more apt to be shared across communities, depending on whether they are considered lifestyle or system maintenance functions.

Although uncertainty related to opportunistic behavior increases the bargaining and negotiation costs of coming to an agreement on service delivery, they are not insurmountable. As the literature suggests, local governments can overcome transaction risk by crafting agreements that fit the context. Restrictive agreements or flexible and more adaptive agreements, for example, provide alternative arrangements for dealing with the risks associated with changing environmental conditions. Through some types of institutional mechanisms, such as a managed network, third parties play an important role in negotiating agreements and reducing environmental uncertainty that can undermine cooperation.

Alternatively, contract networks and policy networks rely more extensively on social capital as a precursor to cooperation. The configuration of shared service delivery networks across a region provides a mechanism to mitigate transaction risk, as do the networks of professional affiliations among local government officials.

This chapter, of course, is not an exhaustive review of the literature on shared service delivery. Yet, it does provide a discussion of public service production arrangements that complement the research on cost savings and management efficiencies from interlocal agreements discussed in the previous chapter.

More research is undoubtedly needed. Autonomous political jurisdictions are establishing more diverse shared service delivery arrangements and placing greater emphasis on managing the complexity of interlocal relationships. Future research efforts should focus on examining shared service agreements over time. This is challenging given the lack of a centralized database of specific information on interlocal cooperation.

Consequently, to examine the emergence or termination of shared service agreements and changes in mechanisms used for managing risk, scholars are likely to collect data on cooperation from the sample of cities on which their previous research is based. Although this may approach may have its limitations, it is a necessary first step to improve our understanding of shared service delivery, particularly of how cooperation is maintained and how shared service agreements evolve and are adjusted to accommodate changes in contextual factors.

KEY POINTS

- Local officials must weigh the anticipated benefits of a shared service delivery arrangement against the costs of negotiating the terms of the agreement, as well as the monitoring and enforcement costs once the agreement is finalized.
- The political salience of local public services, the costliness of measuring performance, monitoring participant contributions, and enforcing the agreement shape the transaction risks of service cooperation.
- Institutional structures can mitigate transaction risk by delineating roles and responsibilities, defining tasks to facilitate and coordinate joint activities across the independent jurisdictions, and establishing monitoring and enforcement mechanisms that are needed for conducting effective collective action.

- The structure and content of networks among cities and the interpersonal relations among local public officials can mitigate transaction risk by facilitating the establishment of shared service agreements and constraining the behaviors of local officials.

REFERENCES

Andrew, Simon A. 2009a. Recent developments in the study of interjurisdictional agreements: An overview and assessment. *State and Local Government Review* 41:143–142.

———. 2009b. Regional integration through contracting networks: An empirical analysis of institutional collective action framework. *Urban Affairs Review* 44: 378–402.

———. 2010. Adaptive versus restrictive contracts: Can they resolve different risk problems? In *Self-Organizing Federalism: Collaborative Mechanisms to Mitigate Institutional Collective Action Dilemmas*, ed. Richard Feiock and John Scholz, 91–113. New York: Cambridge University Press.

Andrew, Simon, and Jered B. Carr. 2013. Mitigating uncertainty and risk in planning for regional preparedness: The role of bonding and bridging relationships. *Urban Studies* 50(4): 709–724.

Andrew, Simon, and Christopher V. Hawkins. 2012. Regional cooperation and multilateral agreements in the provision of public safety. *American Review of Public Administration* 43(4): 460–475. Accessed May 1, 2013. doi:10.1177/0275074012447676.

Atkins, Patricia S. 1997. *Local Intergovernmental Agreements: Strategies for Cooperation.* Management Information Systems Report 29. Washington, DC: International City/County Management Association.

Bae, Jungah. 2009. Institutional choices for local service contracting and collaboration. *International Review of Public Administration* 14: 27–42.

Brown, Trevor L., and Matthew Potoski. 2003a. Transaction costs and institutional explanations for government service production decisions. *Journal of Public Administration Research and Theory* 13: 441–468.

———. 2003b. Managing contract performance: A transaction costs approach. *Journal of Policy Analysis and Management* 22: 275–297.

———. 2005. Transaction costs and contracting: The practitioner perspective. *Public Performance & Management Review* 28: 326–351.

Brown, Trevor L., Matthew Potoski, and David M. Van Slyke. 2006. Managing public service contracts: Aligning values, institutions, and markets. *Public Administration Review* 66: 323–331.

Burt, Ronald. 2000. The network structure of social capital. *Research in Organisational Behaviour* 22: 345–423.

———. 2005. *Brokerage and Closure: An Introduction to Social Capital.* New York: Oxford University Press.

Carr, Jered B., and Shanthi Karuppusamy. 2010. Reassessing the link between city structure and fiscal policy: Is the problem poor measures of governmental structure? *American Review of Public Administration* 40: 209–228.

Carr, Jered B., Kelly LeRoux, and Manoj Shrestha. 2009. Institutional ties, transaction costs, and external service production. *Urban Affairs Review* 44: 403–427.

Coleman, James S. 1988. Social capital in the creation of human capital. *American Journal of Sociology* 94: S95–S121.

Deller, Steven.C., David G. Hinds, and Donald L. Hinman. 2001. *Local Public Services in Wisconsin: Alternatives for Municipalities with a Focus on Privatization.* University of Wisconsin–Madison, Department of Agricultural and Applied Economics.

Feiock, Richard C. 2007. Rational choice and regional governance. *Journal of Urban Affairs* 29: 47–63.

———. 2009. Metropolitan governance and institutional collective action. *Urban Affairs Review* 44: 356–377.

Feiock, Richard C., and Jered B. Carr. 2001. Incentives, entrepreneurs, and boundary change: A collective action framework. *Urban Affairs Review* 36: 382–405.

Feiock, Richard C., James C. Clinger, Manoj Shrestha, and Carl Dasse. 2007. Contracting and sector choice across municipal services. *State and Local Government Review* 39: 72–83.

Feiock, Richard C., Moon-Gi Jeong, and Jaehoon Kim. 2003. Credible commitment and council–manager government: Implications for policy instrument choices. *Public Administration Review* 63: 616–623.

Feiock, Richard C., and John T. Scholz. 2010. Self-organizing governance of institutional collective action dilemmas: An overview. In *Self-Organizing Federalism: Collaborative Mechanisms to Mitigate Institutional Collective Action,* ed. Richard C. Feiock and John T. Scholz, 3–32. Cambridge, UK: Cambridge University Press.

Frederickson, George H. 1999. The repositioning of American public administration. *PS: Political Science & Politics* 32: 701–711.

Frederickson, George H., and Kevin B. Smith. 2003. *The Public Administration Theory Primer.* Boulder, CO: Westview Press.

Girard, Peter, Robert D. Mohr, Steven C. Deller, and John M. Halstead. 2009. Public-private partnerships and cooperative agreements in municipal service delivery. *International Journal of Public Administration* 32: 370–392.

Graddy, Elizabeth A., and Bin Chen. 2006. Influences on the size and scope of networks for social service delivery. *Journal of Public Administration Research and Theory* 16: 533–552.

Hatley, William. 2010. The art of collaboration: Interlocal collaboration in the provision of fire services in the Detroit area. PhD diss., Wayne State University.

Hawkins, Christopher V. 2009. Prospects for and barriers to local government joint ventures. *State and Local Government Review* 41: 108–119.

———. 2010. Competition and cooperation: Local government joint ventures for economic development. *Journal of Urban Affairs* 32: 253–275.

———. 2011. Local economic development joint ventures and metropolitan networks. *Public Administration Quarterly* 35: 60–93.

Hawkins, Christopher V., and Simon Andrew. 2011. Understanding horizontal and vertical relations in the context of economic development joint venture agreements. *Urban Affairs Review* 47: 385–412.

Jang, HeeSoun. 2006. Contracting out parks and recreation services: Correcting for selection bias using a Heckman selection model. *International Journal of Public Administration* 29: 799–818.

Kettl, Donald F. 2007. *System Under Stress: Homeland Security and American Politics.* 2d ed. Washington, DC: CQ Press.

Kwon, Sung-Wook, and Richard C. Feiock. 2010. Overcoming the barriers to cooperation: Intergovernmental service agreements. *Public Administration Review* 70: 876–884.

Kwon, Sung-Wook, In Won Lee, and Richard C. Feiock. 2010. Transaction cost politics and local service production. *International Review of Public Administration* 14: 37–52.

LeRoux, Kelly. 2006. The role of structure, function, and networks in explaining interlocal service delivery: A study of institutional cooperation in Michigan. PhD diss., Wayne State University.

LeRoux, Kelly, Paul W. Brandenburger, and Sanjay K. Pandey. 2010. Interlocal service cooperation in U.S. cities: A social network explanation. *Public Administration Review* 70: 268–278.

LeRoux, Kelly, and Jered B. Carr. 2007. Explaining local government cooperation on public works: Evidence from Michigan. *Public Works Management and Policy* 12: 344–358.

———. 2010. Prospects for centralizing services in an urban county: Evidence from self-organized networks of eight local public services. *Journal of Urban Affairs* 32(4): 449–470.

LeRoux, Kelly, and Sanjay Pandey. 2011. City managers, career incentives and municipal service decisions: The effects of managerial ambition on interlocal service delivery. *Public Administration Review* 71: 627–636.

Lin, Nan. 2001. *Social Capital: A Theory of Social Structure and Action*. New York: Cambridge University Press.

Lowery, David. 2000. A transaction costs model of metropolitan governance: Allocation versus redistribution in urban America. *Journal of Public Administration Research and Theory* 10: 49–78.

Lynn, Phil. 2005. *Mutual Aid: Multijurisdictional Partnerships for Meeting Regional Threats.* Report No. NCJ 210679. Washington, DC: U.S. Department of Justice, Office of Justice Program, Bureau of Justice Assistance.

Martin, Lawrence L., Richard Levey, and Jenna Cawley. 2012. The "new normal" for local government. *State and Local Government Review* 44:17S–28S.

Musso, J., C. Weare and M. Hale. 2001. Municipal reinvention: Municipal values and diffusion among municipalities. *Journal of Public Administration Research and Theory* 11: 327–352.

Oakerson, Robert, J. 2004. The study of metropolitan governance. In *Metropolitan Governance: Conflict, Competition, and Cooperation,* ed. Richard C. Feiock, 17–45. Washington, DC: Georgetown University Press.

Perlman, Bruce, and J. Edwin Benton. 2012. Going it alone: New survey data on economic recovery strategies in local government. *State and Local Government Review* 44: 5S–16S.

Podolny, Joel, and James Baron. 1997. Resources and relationships: Social networks and mobility in the workplace. *American Sociological Review* 62: 673–693.

Rawlings, Lynette. 2003. The determinants of cooperation among local governments in metropolitan areas. PhD diss., George Washington University.

Romzek, Barbara S., and Jocelyn M. Johnston. 2002. Effective contract implementation and management. *Journal of Public Administration Research and Theory* 12: 423–453.

———. 2005. State social services contracting: Exploring the determinants of effective contract accountability. *Public Administration Review* 65: 436–449.

Rusk, David. 1999. *Inside Game/Outside Game: Winning Strategies for Saving Urban America.* Washington, DC: Brookings Institution Press.

Scholz, John T., Ramiro Berardo, and Brad Kile. 2008. Do networks solve collective action problems: Credibility, search, and collaboration. *The Journal of Politics* 70: 1–14.

Scott, John. 2000. *Social Network Analysis*. 2d ed. London: Sage.

Shrestha, Manoj. 2010. Do risk profiles of services alter contractual patterns? A comparison across multiple metropolitan services. In *Self-Organizing Federalism: Collaborative Mechanisms to Mitigate Institutional Collective Action,* ed. Richard C. Feiock and John T. Scholz, 114–141. Cambridge, UK: Cambridge University Press.

Shrestha, Manoj, and Richard C. Feiock. 2009. Governing U.S. metropolitan areas: Self-organizing and multiplex service networks. *American Politics Research* 37: 801–823.

Steinacker, Annette. 2004. Game theoretic models of metropolitan cooperation. In *Metropolitan Governance: Conflict, Competition, and Cooperation,* ed. Richard C. Feiock, 46–66. Washington, DC: Georgetown University Press.

———. 2010. The institutional collective action perspective on self-organizing mechanisms: Market failures and transaction cost problems. In *Self-Organizing Federalism: Collaborative Mechanisms to Mitigate Institutional Collective Action*, ed. Richard C. Feiock and John T. Scholz, 51–72. Cambridge, UK: Cambridge University Press.

Taylor, Gary D., and Ellen Bassett. 2007. Exploring boundaries in governance: Intergovernmental boundary agreements. *State and Local Government Review* 39: 119–130.

United States Advisory Commission on Intergovernmental Relations. 1985. *Intergovernmental Service Arrangements for Delivering Local Public Services*. Washington, DC: ACIR.

Williams, Oliver P. 1971. *Metropolitan Political Analysis*. New York: Free Press.

Williamson, Oliver E. 1975. *Markets and Hierarchies, Analysis and Antitrust Implications*. New York: Free Press.

———. 1981. The economics of organization: The transaction cost approach. *American Journal of Sociology* 87: 548–577.

———. 1985. *The Economic Institutions of Capitalism*. New York: Free Press.

Wood, Curtis. 2004. Metropolitan governance in urban America: A study of the Kansas City region. PhD diss., University of Kansas.

———. 2006. Scope and patterns of metropolitan governance in urban America: Probing the complexities in the Kansas City region. *American Review of Public Administration* 36: 337–353.

———. 2008. The nature of metropolitan governance in urban America: A study of cooperation and conflict in the Kansas City region. *Administration & Society* 40: 483–501.

Zeemering, Eric. S. 2007. Who collaborates? Local decisions about intergovernmental relations. PhD diss., Indiana University.

———. 2008. Governing interlocal cooperation: City council interests and the implications for public management. *Public Administration Review* 68: 731–741.

3

Communities and Culture

Sydney Cresswell and Anthony Cresswell

Restructuring or consolidating services is a growing imperative for many local governments. In responding to that imperative, local officials encounter difficult and complex decisions, particularly about how to engage the public on these issues. In fact, virtually all local decisions related to restructuring or consolidating services involve the community in some manner. Restructuring is likely to affect services in a material way, impact employment in the community, or impinge on the quality of neighborhood life. Consequently, most proposed redesign strategies ultimately bring the community into the process. Engagement is critical because whether the involvement of a community is deliberate, occurring at the front end of the process, or surfaces as a reaction to changes, it seems to be a fairly important influence on what is achieved.

Why is this the case? Done well, community involvement in local government's decision making has the *potential* to add value to the way we go about solving problems. When local officials are puzzling through questions about the nature of a problem—how big it is, whom it affects, what results it produces—members of the community can answer those questions from their unique vantage points. Once officials see the problem more completely and are ready to consider what to do, citizens can narrow the task by identifying which options they can live with and which they cannot. When it is time to see what resources can be committed to a solution, community members may have assets and valuable information to offer. At the end of the process, local leaders have a wider swath of the community that understands the central issues and backs the decisions made.

Without community involvement in restructuring or consolidation decisions, crucial assumptions held by the public concerning service delivery may remain unknown to officials, who will find it more difficult to anticipate the likely consequences of various options for service changes. Without involvement of the community, officials could fail to perceive whether all or only part of a service is needed or desired, and valuable expertise existing in the community will likely remain untapped.

Candidly, even though community involvement can make a substantial contribution to restructuring decisions, front-end engagement does not occur with sufficient frequency. Though there are a host of reasons for this, the most obvious is that community engagement is neither simple nor especially natural, even among social beings. Individuals and groups that comprise a community have different outlooks, histories, and preferences that are only partially visible in expressions of culture. Those who share a cultural bond honor a shared history and set of values, and strive to preserve established preferences

Figure 3.1 **Cultural Bonds**

- Cultural bonds honor a shared history and set of values
- Cultural bonds preserve established preferences shared by the group
- Cultural bonds are reflected in outlook and basic assumptions about what is best

(see Figure 3.1). Underlying differences in outlook and values across different cultures, coupled with the natural tendency to vigilantly guard one's own interests, make community decision making likely to be fraught with conflict.

Problem solving among individuals with different cultural perspectives requires a "deliberative space" that is hard to create and maintain. In the end, coming to agreement about local problems and service decisions usually entails sacrifices, with the strong likelihood that some will run counter to cultural interests.

In light of the difficulties of community involvement, local officials face a complex decision of whether or not to engage their community in governing decisions (see Figure 3.2). That decision should take into account many individual and situational factors that can affect the ultimate success of the effort. Comfort with group process is often a determining factor for a local official, as is their understanding of how to manage such engagement.

The kinds of decisions that need to be made are a factor to be considered, but so are the community's history, options, and overall condition. But when conditions are really challenging and the risks are substantial, there may be no choice but to make inordinately difficult governing decisions with the help of the community. This chapter is written in recognition of present-day local problems that compel community involvement in decisions, and its focus is on understanding community culture as a key component of engagement.

Figure 3.2 **Engaging the Community: Questions to Consider**

- Are we good at the process?
- What decisions should include community input?
- Are conditions okay for gathering input?
- Are there any big risks?
- Are there any other options to get the community involved?

EXAMINING CHALLENGING LOCAL GOVERNMENT CONDITIONS

A few words about governing conditions at the local level are in order because of the seriousness of the issues surrounding the practice of community engagement. Like the rest of the country and its global counterparts, municipalities have weathered many financial setbacks in recent years. They have also experienced the turbulence of changes in technology and endured shifts in population and wealth. Localities also mirror larger governments in terms of management challenges, having complex, interrelated sets of problems. Cities in particular are historically multicultural, but now even some of the smallest municipalities can claim substantial cultural diversity. Taken together, these changes have intensified uncertainty and social distance, disrupted ways that citizens interact, and called into question the efficacy of conventional means for improving difficult situations.

Fiscal concerns in local governments have magnified existing problems, draining off resources and energy. The recession from which the nation is slowly recovering had a delayed impact on local governments but an exceedingly long tail. Even before the recession, the economic picture for municipalities was murky—services and employment costs were climbing and revenues were not keeping pace with obligations. Municipalities have few options for remedying difficult fiscal circumstances, as aid distribution and revenue-generating authority reside primarily with state and federal governments. As a result, local leaders have been left with some deeply unattractive prospects for financing essential services and dealing with social problems that have been aggravated by the prolonged economic malaise. For many local governments, the stakes are greater than difficult decisions about service restructuring. An unfortunate cross-section of municipalities now confronts issues of community survival, and many more face unwelcome and lasting shifts in the quality of life for their residents.

Some of the impacts of these overall conditions can be seen in the governing circumstances of three local governments in New York State (see Figure 3.3). The communities described in these examples have decidedly different conditions and risks in their situations, but each is at a crossroads that will require residents to participate in making decisions. Their elected officials cannot resolve these dilemmas alone. They will need the collective intelligence and consent of their respective communities to sort out the presenting problems and consider the choices available to them. Community members need to pinpoint the options they can live with and the options they cannot. And at the end of the process, these elected and appointed officials will make decisions that a majority of residents must back.

As an aside, it should not be adversity alone that propels government leaders toward greater public engagement. While the local environment is now roiling with challenges, there are possibilities for growth and transformation embedded in the turbulence. There are innovative decisions and choices being made every day that challenge conventional thinking and open communities to new possibilities. Local officials need public engagement to harness the positive in their midst as well as to help solve serious problems.

RESPONDING TO THE CHALLENGE: THE PROMISE AND PROBLEMS OF CITIZEN ENGAGEMENT

Citizen engagement offers one powerful but potentially problematic response to the challenges described above. The kind of engagement we have in mind is communal problem solving through give-and-take conversations in which the participants share perspectives, try to figure out what is really wrong, and consider choices open to them. There are different scales of engagement that vary with the decision-making power accorded to the participating citizens, as shown in Table 3.1. At the low end of engagement, citizens may be involved in focused discussion about an issue, and at the mid-range, citizens may be

Figure 3.3 **Three Local Government Circumstances from New York State**

Northern town	A town in the north of the state has tallied fewer residents in each of the last three censuses. Never having had more than a modest business community, the town's few remaining businesses are scraping by. In the last two years, the state has determined that the sewer system no longer functions within safe standards, and water quality has deteriorated and is no longer potable. Both systems need to be replaced, roughly estimated at a cost of 25 million dollars. Even if the town residents could afford to service the debt now, unless prospects improve, the funds may not be there in a year or two. Some residents and leaders question whether it makes sense for the town to try to stay in business.
Small waterfront city	A small city with a beautiful waterfront setting and proximity to a major urban destination has struggled with serious crime, gang activity, and poverty for decades. With the help of coordinated state and federal government agents, crime problems are more manageable but the community is still encumbered by dilapidated housing stock and high unemployment, making it difficult to capitalize on the gains made in reducing crime. As things stand, resources are scarce, citizen expectations are low, trust is mostly absent, and governing bodies are demoralized.
Rural town in a rural county	Most of the residents of a rural town in the southern tier are employed elsewhere in the county, and the recession left many families facing unemployment for stretches of time. There are only a handful of businesses in the town, and the saving grace for the town has been an increase in the number of part-time, second-home residents who buy and build, or renovate properties. As welcome as these new part-time residents are to the community, their ideas about amenities and services are leading to costly new commitments that run counter to local notions about the community. Although the new part-time residents are willing to pay their share of the new taxes needed to undertake this work, such decisions would obligate the original residents to services they neither want nor can afford.

Table 3.1

Levels of Citizen Interaction

Purpose of interaction	Ways officials handle the interaction
• Inform citizens • Raise awareness • Assemble backing for an action	• Make announcements at public meetings, in newspapers, or in posts on the government Web site • Send letters to residents
• Gather citizen input • Raise public interest in an issue • Increase public understanding of an issue	• Send surveys • Invite comments through a Web site form • Use a public session to elicit comments from citizens
• Allow citizens to choose a course of action • Promote broad understanding and acceptance of subsequent actions	• Allow citizens to create and carry out a set of initiatives • Authorize a task force to make recommendations or binding decisions

asked to make formal recommendations. At the high end of engagement, citizens may be given the authority to make a decision on behalf of a group or the community. Engaging citizens in local governing decisions is not the equivalent of holding information sessions, conducting public hearings, or doing surveys. Although valuable for some governing purposes, these activities are largely one-way forms of communication. Citizen engagement involves dialogue and deliberation among participants to find common ground.

More interactive forms of citizen engagement open many more possibilities, but also raise important questions. When we examine citizen engagement more closely, we find several puzzles that require attention. What does the process achieve that makes it so fitting for difficult community decisions? What dynamics in the process make citizen engagement more rewarding? More challenging? How do we think about citizen engagement more productively?

What does the process achieve? Interactions with government officials and other citizens allow participants to understand an issue and its importance across the larger community, not merely in terms of their self-interest. The engaged citizen assumes the role that democracy anticipates—direct public involvement in matters that affect the common good (Frederickson 1997). In this sense, citizens are not simply acting as the customers of government, partaking of a service, or filing a complaint. Nor are citizens acting as partners in service delivery as they do when they take part in a neighborhood crime watch. In those situations, citizens are stakeholders representing their special interests. Engagement, by contrast, opens the possibility for broadening perspectives and gaining a more nuanced understanding of an issue through the give and take of deliberating with others (Thomas 2010). The aim of citizen engagement is to find common ground in the interest of the public well-being, and the reward is authentic participation in governing.

The next question—What makes citizen engagement challenging?—can be answered from many angles. The challenges in the social and institutional environment are many: complex, often high-stakes decisions, competing interests, conflicting goals, stresses in the community, poor understanding of the community's history and diversity, policy constraints, and limited resources in the governing environment. On top of these challenges, the process of collaborating, which is the focus here, has its own set of hurdles that can confound and sidetrack deliberative activity.

CONSIDERING HURDLES IN THE CITIZEN ENGAGEMENT PROCESS

Effective citizen engagement builds on the results of the sense-making and weighing activities participants move through during discussion and deliberation. In sense-making, community members are absorbing and sorting out new information to grasp its significance. This information consists of whatever has been shared by members of the group, the factual information introduced throughout their interactions, and the experience of the interaction itself. Weighing activities incorporate information from sense-making and balance it against other ideas and thoughts. Sense-making and weighing occur continuously as participants move from thought to thought and action to action. For instance, in each group encounter participants will decide what is most important to remember and value among new bits of information, ponder how the information connects to previous information, and choose what questions to ask. Participants weigh what to do or say next in the group, and weigh and choose how to prioritize options that grow out of group deliberation.

Deliberative activity, with its repetitions of sense-making and weighing, is a natural part of social functioning, but is influenced and complicated by dynamics embedded in group decision making and other interactions. These factors include the influence of various cost and resource concerns, and the powerful role of culture.

Transaction Costs

The processes and outcomes of community engagement and collaboration can be influenced by costs incurred in the interactions, what we call *transaction costs*, and by certain attributes of resources of interest in the deliberation. Transaction costs are incurred in an interaction or exchange and make that process easier or more difficult. Resource attributes are the set of considerations about a resource or service that influences how parties value them, and what modifications they can accept. We examine a few of these factors in the context of citizen engagement.

Transaction costs can be a significant issue in the kinds of citizen engagement and collaboration we are concerned with (Williamson 1999). The process of engaging with citizens lacks the bureaucratic structures and controls of ordinary government actions and the constraints associated with working under legally binding contracts. The citizen engagement process also lacks the simplicity of most market interactions, where the value and the terms of the transactions are clear. Collaboration is messy and uncertain much of the time. That increases the costs to participants in terms of gathering and interpreting information, evaluating the behavior of others, and protecting their own interests.

One transaction cost concerns *information*, and is related to the ease with which parties in a deliberative process can acquire the information they need to feel comfortable moving ahead (Feiock 2009). Early in a collaborative effort the parties—local officials, members of the business community, neighborhood representatives, unaffiliated citizens, community organization members, and others—need to be fairly certain about what the other members want and what their motivations are. If any party feels that he or she has incomplete information about these things, or is concerned that the other party or parties are withholding information, it can undermine trust and confidence in their ability to succeed as partners. It is also essential to prevent information from becoming lopsided among the partners, causing those with incomplete information to feel blindsided, left out, or powerless in the group. Information costs can complicate both sense-making and weighing in the deliberative process.

A second transaction cost is related to an aspect of social relationships known as *agency*. An agency relationship consists of an *agent*—an individual or group acting on behalf of someone else in a transaction. In citizen engagement, a local official is typically seen as an agent acting on behalf of all of his or her community. Similarly, community members who are part of a deliberative body may be acting on behalf of a neighborhood or a business group, families in a school or an ethnic community, or some other affiliated group. Agency becomes a cost to the deliberative body if the agent is acting in ways that depart from the preferences of those they represent (Feiock 2009). If this happens, the agent's ability to get the group they represent to consent to or live with the agreements reached by the deliberative body may be in greater doubt. When this is the case, the weighing process is more difficult, participation becomes more costly, and successful outcomes are jeopardized.

Resource Attributes

How community members feel about the resources or services that are involved in the deliberation can influence any decisions to alter them. At times service or resource attributes like functionality and tangibility may be only dimly perceived by participants, further complicating sense-making and weighing activity.

One of the attributes we consider is *functionality*, which refers to the usefulness of a resource or service to a member or group. Here, the partners consider how critical the resource is, how much of the resource is actually available in the environment, and whether alternatives to the specific resource are available (Balakrishnan, Sunder, and Sivaramakrishnan 1999). There is also consideration given to the *importance* of the resource or service and the ways in which the resource might be affected by sharing it. A valuable resource might be improved or diminished by sharing it. For example, sharing data sets could add to the total amount of information available to each party in collaboration and increase the value of the initial asset. Conversely, a donor or volunteer list that is shared could lead to donor or volunteer fatigue, thereby diminishing its overall value (Tschirhart, Amezcua, and Anker 2009). A third possibility is that the resource could be transformed by sharing it. For example, one local government may have a substantial store of social capital in a relationship with a firm, an agency, or a network. Sharing this resource by adding another party to the relationship could change the original relationship, especially if something goes wrong (Tschirhart, Amezcua, and Anker 2009).

Tangibility refers to the degree to which a resource has a physical existence. When making decisions about tangible assets, it is usually easy to measure, count, and divide the resource. It is also important that both the use of that resource and the benefits that each party receives from the resource can be known. With intangible resources, like knowledge sharing for instance, it is harder to know what each partner is giving and receiving (Tschirhart, Amezcua, and Anker 2009).

These issues regarding resources attributes, inherent in group processes and decision making, can be managed through effective collaboration. However, collaboration across the many different groups and cultural perspectives in a community is a major challenge to citizen engagement. If the community can build a collaborative process, the prospects for successful problem solving are much brighter. Therefore we look in some depth at culture as a central aspect of collaboration and citizen engagement.

CULTURAL FACTORS: WHY CAN'T WE ALL JUST GET ALONG?

> Collaboration is an unnatural act between non-consenting adults. . . . We all say we want to collaborate, but what we really mean is that we want to continue doing things as we have always done them while others change to fit what we are doing.
>
> —*Former Surgeon General Jocelyn Elders*

Differences in culture are arguably the main reason why, for local government, collaboration across groups and organizations is seen as an unnatural act. What seems natural is predominately a matter of culture, and government exists in a multicultural environment.

If all local governments ran their services exactly the same way and served homogeneous communities where everyone shared the same visions, values, and beliefs, collaboration would certainly seem more comfortable and natural. But our histories, work practices, expectations, and, most importantly, attitudes and beliefs seldom align across community and organizational boundaries. And so those who seek the benefits of service sharing and consolidation face a host of challenges beyond the many financial, policy, or technical problems. This chapter focuses on the particular challenges that arise from trying to create new ways of working and interacting that cut across the different ideas, values, actions, and beliefs that have special relevance to citizens and groups—that is, what makes up culture. These elements of culture are what connect people with their shared past and future. Culture is the fabric of meaning and identity that ties people to a community, group, or organization, and what sets them apart from others.

It is not always clear why differences in culture present a problem. The idea of reaching out across parts of a community to collaborate with local governments has the same intuitive appeal as the desire for people of all backgrounds and interests to "just get along." The benefits of collaboration often appear quite obvious and substantial. Government officials are often urged to engage the community in governance. The professional literature and local government consultants extol the virtues of sharing with appealing success stories and sensible-sounding prescriptions for how to engage stakeholders to get everyone "on board." And there are in fact impressive examples of local governments achieving real benefits from collaboration.

The full story, however, is not quite so bright. Local officials are likely to be highly sensitive to the challenges of gaining community consensus and building collaboration around shared services or other goals. Experienced officials recognize that local governments exist in a highly complex web of relationships, rules, competing interests, and the deeply rooted ways of working, relating, and understanding, that is, culture. They also recognize that any attempts to make meaningful changes in services, operations, policies, or investments will face resistance of many possible kinds. They are aware that "the community" is not a monolithic thing but rather a patchwork of diverse groups often with conflicting interests, visions, and values. Ignoring these kinds of culture-based sources of resistance can be a direct path to failure; recognizing and working through cultural challenges can form a foundation for successful collaboration. Knowing more about the nature of cultural differences is an important step in that direction.

WHAT DO WE MEAN BY CULTURE?

To help focus this discussion, we will use a basic definition of "culture." This is just one among a long list of ways to define culture, not all of which are particularly relevant to our goals here. The definitions that seem the most useful come from anthropology and organizational studies, so we begin there. The anthropologist Clifford Geertz's definition is a good starting point:

> [The culture concept] denotes an historically transmitted pattern of meanings embodied in symbols, a system of inherited conceptions expressed in symbolic forms by means of which men communicate, perpetuate, and develop their knowledge about and attitudes toward life. . . . (1966, 89)

The important parts of this definition tell us that culture is:

- *historical*: it develops and persists over time, is rooted in the past
- about *meanings*, that is, how people think about and understand life
- embodied in *symbols* that carry meaning and significance
- shared and communicated among people
- composed of knowledge and attitudes

Though the study of culture started with social groups and societies in the late nineteenth and early twentieth centuries, it became clear that organizations can have distinctive cultures as well. Thus we have definitions of organizational culture. They vary from short and direct, "The way things get done around here" (Deal and Kennedy 2000), to more formal ones that mirror definitions from anthropology (above). They tend to reflect the same basic ideas: organizational culture consists of basic patterns of thinking and interacting that are considered valid and that serve to integrate the organization. The core idea across these definitions is that culture matters, whether we're looking inside organizations or at communities and societies. Culture shapes how people understand their social environment, how they act in it and on it.

Note that as used here, *culture* never refers to the superiority of one form of artistic or aesthetic expression over another. Someone who does not like or listen to classical music, for instance, is no more or less "cultured" than someone who does. We say instead that the creation of and preferences for distinctive forms of music, art, food, and so on are typical aspects of a culture, with no suggestion that one is higher or lower than the other.

CULTURE AS A CHALLENGE TO COLLABORATION: "WE COME FROM DIFFERENT TRIBES"

Culture, first of all, is about groups, what we loosely refer to here as "tribes."[1] Collaboration across local government agencies will almost certainly involve many different tribes, both within and outside government. Culture is thus about human beings in the aggregate and what is distinctive about these aggregations. What aspects of culture we may see in an individual person's ideas or cultural objects or behavior depend on context. Since people can belong to many groups, cultural influences on individual behavior will be linked to the cultural context of the group and to the person's place in it. There is, for example, a recognizable law enforcement culture; we would expect a deputy county sheriff to generally behave as a member of this group. But he or she can also be a weekend drummer in a rock band. There would likely be little resemblance between the deputy's behavior and appearance in a Monday morning roll call and onstage Saturday night.

To understand the importance and impacts of the differences across culturally defined groups, it helps to go a bit beyond casual conversation in which culture is often the catch-all explanation for why things do not work as planned. "Oh, it's just the culture," is often a glib way of accounting for lack of cooperation that stalls an initiative or the rise of unexpected and unexplained conflicts. Calling it "culture" may actually be an accurate observation, but without deeper analysis it is not very helpful. Instead, we prefer a more analytical approach that unpacks the concept of culture in ways that facilitate building effective collaboration in the complex setting of local government.

Building Collaboration Among Tribes

If collaboration is an unnatural act, then building collaboration entails finding ways to make it more natural. Cultural differences can be a big part of what feels unnatural, so we turn our attention to what those difference are and what they have to do with collaboration. Since culture can be a very complex and confusing topic, we will start with a simple but powerful way to describe how the elements of culture can vary across groups, or "tribes," in ways that affect collaboration.

This way of describing culture, developed originally by Edgar Schein (2004), is to group different elements into three basic levels: *artifacts, espoused values*, and *basic underlying assumptions* (Schein 2004). Artifacts of culture, the top level, are what you can see, hear, taste, and directly experience, including objects, activities, styles of dress and decoration, symbols, music, ceremonies, stories, architecture, and so on. Espoused values, in the middle, are the ways people talk about or otherwise describe their beliefs, attitudes, value propositions, and ideals, such as justice, honesty, spirituality. At the lowest, least visible level, we find basic underlying assumptions. They are more abstract, deeply held, and even unconscious dispositions about such issues as collectivism (valuing the achievement of the group above persons) versus individualism; value of competition versus cooperation; whether to apply more egalitarian versus meritocratic values; gender equality; treating time as flexible and personal versus rigid schedules and deadlines, and

Figure 3.4 **Levels of Cultural Elements**

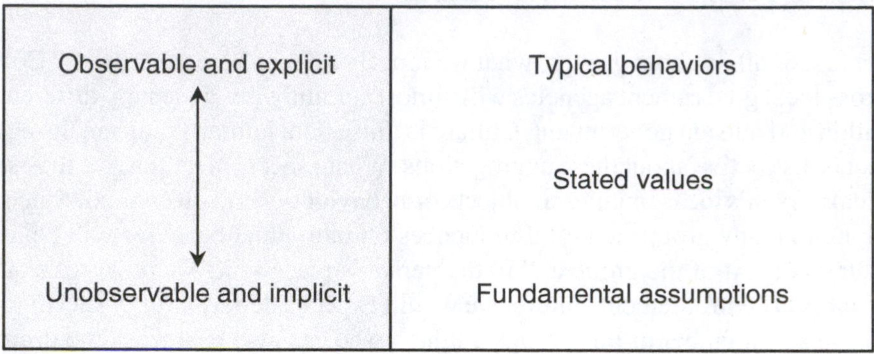

Note: The label "Typical Behaviors" represents Schein's artifacts.

so forth. The levels are sometimes compared to an iceberg, with much of the "mass" below the surface. What you see on the surface as indicators of culture do not tell the whole story (Figure 3.4).

As challenges to collaboration, differences at the deeper levels of culture are the most important and the least accessible or open to change. What feels unnatural about collaboration can be caused by cultural differences at any level, but the deeper ones are usually the most problematic. Asking people to accept someone with a different style of dress or musical preference is one thing. Expecting people to change their basic beliefs or simply accept interacting in ways they consider deeply wrong or improper is quite another. The latter can be a direct challenge to their identity, status, or acceptance by their own tribe. Fundamental assumptions can be rooted in family and ethnic identity, or lengthy professional training and experience, spiritual values, or even unconscious conditioning.

Separating elements of culture by these levels can be a useful analytical way of describing culture, but it does not reflect the way the differences play out in life. The levels are not separate at all in that sense. Cultural identity is linked to symbols, stories, and other artifacts as well as to values and assumptions. Symbols and other artifacts matter because they remind people of their cultural identity, reinforce solidarity with the group, and often highlight differences and boundaries between groups. Thus, anything that takes on symbolic significance can become important in ways that are unrelated to the superficial details. The Paris Peace Conference to end the Vietnam War, for example, was famously delayed for months, reportedly over lack of agreement about the shape of the negotiating table. The underlying issue was the unwillingness of either side to symbolically acknowledge the legitimacy of all parties on the other side by giving them equal seating positions. Other symbols, such as the New York State Muffin (apple cinnamon), are trivial and not relevant to government activity or any underlying value or assumptions (New York State Department of State 2014). Building collaboration requires finding the important cultural differences and dealing with them.

Where Collaboration Meets Culture

Cultural issues are important for collaboration because the kind of community engagement we are discussing is primarily eclectic, voluntary, and informal. Participants engage with varied motives, interests, and goals. They may be invited or self-selected. They may not know much about each other, about the workings of government, or about the issues at hand. They may come and go as they choose. There is no guarantee that all participants will accept or even understand any initial structures or rules for agenda setting and decision making. They will likely vary widely in age, level of education, and experience with collaboration. This is not a recipe for quickly building effective collaboration.

In facing these challenges to new or enhanced community engagement, local government officials have limited tools. They do not have the authority to legislate or coerce collaboration, that is, a hierarchical approach. They can only rarely encourage collaboration with financial incentives, a market-type approach. That leaves only persuasion and other voluntary, consensual methods of engineering collaboration, which depend not just on effective leadership, but on the willingness and capabilities of participants. Ultimately, effective collaboration depends on good communication and trust, agreement on goals, compromise when necessary, sharing power, knowledge, and other resources, and previous experience with successful collaborations. In short, members of different groups have to be willing and able to work well together. The main elements in the view of collaboration we have in mind are shown in Figure 3.5.

Figure 3.5 **Collaboration in the Cultural Context**

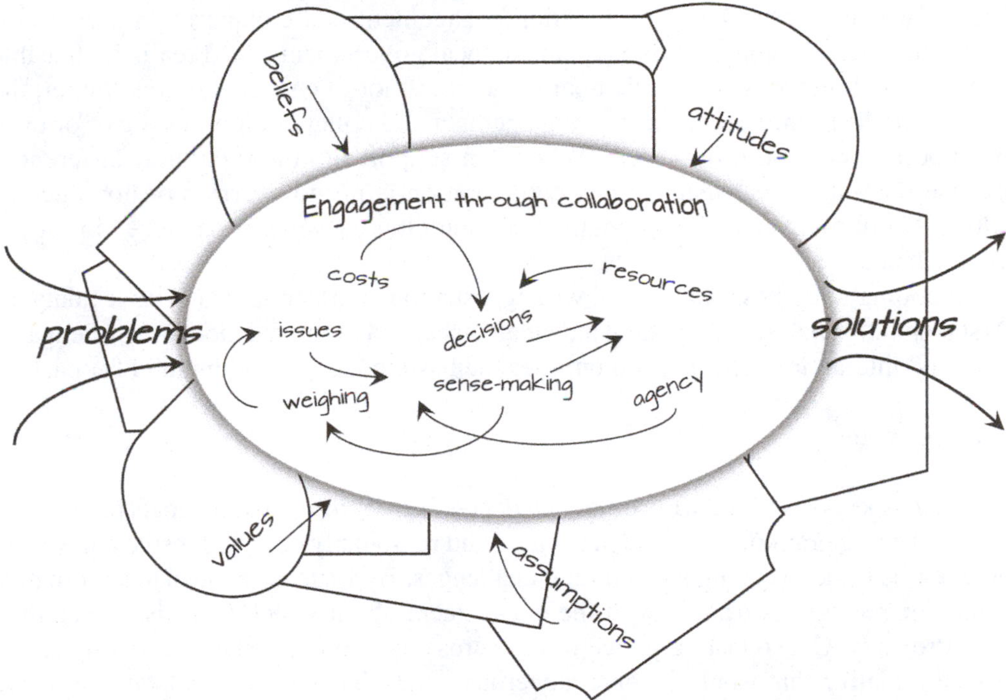

Working well together depends to a significant degree on the ideas and values people bring to the table, which is where the effects of cultural similarities and differences come into play. To explore how those effects can occur, we focus on common underlying assumptions and espoused values that can strongly impact voluntary collaboration and work relationships. Since there is no standard or complete list of such cultural assumptions, we have chosen several that have clear links to how well people can work together. The list in Table 3.2 includes assumptions that would likely differ among groups in any local government's community. Differences in more superficial aspects of culture, clothing, symbols, vocabulary, and so forth may be sources of some minor friction, but assumptions and values like these are more critical to effective collaboration. Implications for collaboration are listed for each assumption or value. The items on the list are phrased in terms of polar opposites to emphasize the differences in group member beliefs about what it means to be correct or appropriate perspectives or behavior.

The list could go on. Students of culture have identified other assumptions and value propositions that could be added to this list, such as respect for age, or the centrality of family. But the basic idea would be the same: It is important to identify and respond to the differences among cultures that matter when it comes to engagement and collaboration. The next section speaks to that point.

COPING WITH THE CULTURE CHALLENGE: A FOUR-PART STRATEGY

Though it may appear daunting, building engagement and collaboration across cultural differences is quite possible. To do so, local governments need realistic, feasible strategies and methods. The basic goal is therefore not to change cultures; rather, the goal should be to initiate and sustain engagement and collaboration in spite of or even in support of cultural differences. We say "in support of" these cultural differences because the goal of engagement and collaboration is not to override or homogenize culture. Cultural diversity is a strength of communities as well as a challenge in certain circumstances.

For coping with these challenges, we suggest a four-part strategy: (1) issue analysis, (2) stakeholder analysis, (3) cultural reconnaissance, and (4) mixed modalities of engagement and interaction. This section outlines the basic concepts and method for each.

Analyze Issues

Different aspects of culture will be relevant depending on the issues and goals for engagement and collaboration. Therefore, a detailed and reasonably comprehensive analysis of the issues is basic to coping with cultural challenges. By issues, we mean the alternative actions or policies associated with the engagement about which there is any conflict or controversy. Consolidating police forces across two communities, for example, is a service initiative that would involve numerous issues. They would include alternative arrangements for financing the new police force, and questions of how to consolidate

Table 3.2

Meaning and Implications of Cultural Assumptions

Assumption or Value	Meaning and Implications
Individualism vs. collectivism	Individualistic thinking values personal achievement over that of the group. Collectivists give priority to group success over their own. Collaboration is much more difficult among highly individualistic groups. Conflict is also likely in mixed groups.
Low vs. high deference to authority	Low deference to authority prompts frequent and persistent challenges to authority figures, disruptive to process. High deference suppresses challenges to bad information or poor decisions from authoritative figures.
Polychronic vs. monochronic time	Polychronic: time is flexible, fluid, and subordinate to interpersonal relations; work and personal time are integrated. Monochronic: time is inflexible, schedule is rigid and controlling; work time separate from personal time. Poor coordination likely in polychronic groups; schedule conflict expected in mixed groups; morale and creativity affected by highly monochronic styles or time conflicts.
Competition vs. cooperation	Competition: values success over others. Cooperation: values success with others. Similar to individual versus collective orientation. Collaboration difficult in highly competitive groups. Competition can promote creativity and motivation.
Egalitarian vs. meritocratic value	Meritocratic orientation: personal value and worth depends on achievement; rewards to winners. Egalitarian orientation: humans are fundamentally equal in value and social worth. Engagement over social programs often brings these differences to the surface; not readily reconcilable.
Gender equality vs. traditional roles	Equality: women and men equal in status, leadership roles, assertiveness, value. Traditional: women lower status, deferential, subordinate, follower roles. Interaction and communication between women and men can be strongly facilitated or blocked by their underlying attitudes about gender roles. Also, many government programs and policies have gender-related issues that can engage these differences and disrupt collaboration.
Conflict embraced vs. avoided	Conflict avoidance can lead to glossing over and failing to resolve important issues. Conflict seeking disrupts collaborating processes and social relationships.
Wide vs. narrow personal space; physical contact	What is a comfortable distance between persons varies widely across ethnic and national cultures. These preferences are easily violated. Unwanted closeness and physical contact can lead to discomfort, tension, even hostility.
Future vs. present orientation	Future orientation seeks clear plans and delayed gratification, expectation of progress, decisions based on imagined futures. Present orientation focuses on the current state, immediate goals and gratification. Cooperative planning across these differences is challenging.
High vs. low power distance	High power distance accepts hierarchy, autocratic and paternalistic leadership; low power distance expects more equal distribution of power, more democratic decision making, closer relations with superiors. Collaborative leadership must adapt to the power distance mix of groups, not apparent in early stages. Low power distance participants will not accept autocratic leadership.
High vs. low context	High-context communication: information is in the context and nonverbal signals as much or more than in the words; is implicit, relational, unnecessary to spell everything out. Low-context communication; information is in the words; is explicit, linear, logical. The two styles do not mix well in collaborative groups and can be difficult to adjust.
Direct vs. indirect expression	Direct communication seeks clarity, obviousness, puts ideas and feeling into words; indirect employs hints, acting out of messages or feelings. Direct styles risk conflict and damage to relationships; indirect risk misunderstanding and incomplete information. Matching the choice of style to the group and situation builds collaboration.

administrative leadership, merge personnel policies, reassign staff, integrate information systems, adjust patrol and response protocols, as well as many other concerns. Creating the issue map for the significant issues is a core element in planning engagement and collaboration strategies.

Preparing an issue map requires both internal and external inquiry. Internally, professional government staff can identify technical and policy alternatives, assemble data, and prepare arguments on the relevant sides of the issues. There should also be an external analysis of the question of how individual citizens and groups will align themselves with the issue alternatives. This requires combining staff knowledge with outreach to citizens familiar both with the issues and with their parts of the community and cultural groups. This latter is a kind of preliminary low-level engagement necessary to gather information for planning the larger initiative. The issue map helps ensure that the engagement plan covers the range of concerns that citizens and groups will bring to the process.

If better general engagement and collaboration with government is the goal, the task is more difficult if there is no specific issue or problem identified. In that case, the analysis should include the array of current issues that have generated significant controversy or other public attention in the community. These are likely to be salient in any efforts to enhance general engagement.

Engaging in Stakeholder Analysis

Not all members of a community will be interested in or relevant to the planned engagement and collaboration efforts. The issue analysis is preliminary to consideration of stakeholders because it identifies what is at stake and for whom, thus what persons and groups will likely want a role or voice in the collaboration. Once those stakeholders are identified, it is useful to assess the kind of role they might play in the engagement and the kinds of influence they may be able to exert.

Identifying stakeholders depends on knowledge of the community and the context of the initiative, such as the programs and services involved. The quality and usefulness of the analysis will typically depend on input from a mix of staff with relevant knowledge of the larger context. This is essential, and continuing reference to the nature of the initiative and impact mechanisms will produce the needed focus and detail.

The basic methods of the analysis are simple, based on identifying stakeholders and mapping them in a way that reflects their importance, means of influence, and gives guidance for estimating the way in which the initiative will impact their interests. The mapping example (see Figure 3.6) from Williams and Lewis (2008) identifies appropriate strategies for involvement of stakeholders according to their level of interest and ability to influence the initiative.

This form of mapping gives a rough impression of relative importance of stakeholders and is adequate for many situations. The usefulness of the analysis will depend on those doing the mapping having ample knowledge of the political and organizational context (Meyer and Hollerer 2010). All the requisite knowledge may not be found inside the

Figure 3.6 **Stakeholder Map**

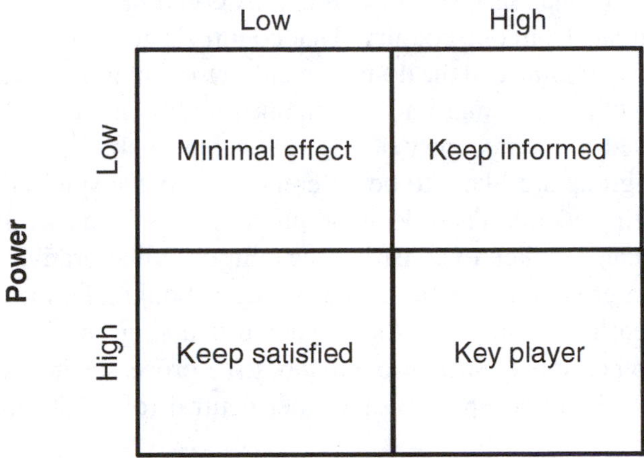

Source: Williams and Lewis, 2008.

agency; external participants and environmental scanning may therefore be a necessary part of the analysis.

This influence mapping provides only one part of stakeholder analysis. An additional, essential element is identifying the substance of the stakeholder interests involved and how those interests link to the goals and operations of the initiative. This additional level of complexity in the stakeholder analysis is not necessarily more demanding of effort since familiarity with stakeholders is likely to include some idea of their substantive interests as well as their salience.

Cultural Reconnaissance

The issues and stakeholders identified in those analyses will help indicate the kinds of relevant groups and sources of cultural diversity to take into account and plan for. The cultural reconnaissance will help identify the range of cultural diversity in the community and how that diversity is reflected in groups and organizations. One key source for this information, where available, is experience from previous collaborations or other engagements; tapping into that knowledge base is a good starting point. Other sources of cultural information about the community are leaders in local institutions and government agencies that have regular contact with local citizens and organizations. These include school administrators, clergy, social service staff, health-care organizations, law enforcement, news organizations, and even local merchants. Leaders in such organizations can identify a wide range of ethnic, social, political, and advocacy groups that may bring cultural differences and issues to a community engagement. This kind of reconnaissance does not involve gathering information about individuals, only about groups and organizations of potential relevance. The resulting picture of cultural diversity can then be used to anticipate how those differences may have important impacts on the engagement.

Cultural differences can emerge in many ways, but some can be anticipated. For example, the cultural reconnaissance in one community could show a significant decade-long increase in immigrants from one country. That country's government is known to be an autocratic, repressive regime and the dominant culture maintains traditional gender roles. A large proportion of those immigrants live in one neighborhood, and it has acquired an informal name based on their country of origin. It is reasonable to expect, therefore, that persons from that group are likely to be deferential to, but suspicious of, authority and uncomfortable with leadership and decision processes in which women take nontraditional roles. Care can be taken to construct meaningful collaborative relationships with members of such a group. However, such a strategy should take into account the issue of agency raised earlier, namely whether a person is acting on his own or as an agent of others. It is also possible to structure collaborative processes in ways that model and guide interaction to build acceptance of gender-neutral roles and other nontraditional styles of behavior.

The same kind of logic can be applied to other cultural differences where they arise, and it will help lay the groundwork for more successful engagement. However, this kind of information gathering can cause trouble as well, as it presents a serious risk of stereotyping individuals and groups, based on overgeneralization, that can provoke angry responses and undermine collaboration. That risk can be largely mitigated by training and monitoring to ensure that all involved treat the cultural information about groups as *only* imperfect descriptions of the group that may not apply to individual group members.

Ensuring Engagement via Multimodality

A variety of modes of engagement and facilities for collaboration are available to help mitigate problems arising from cultural differences. Community engagement and collaborative initiatives can range from small groups in intense face-to-face interactions lasting months, to hundreds or even thousands participating once or twice in brief social media exchanges, to open-ended opportunities for interaction via a government Web site.

The Boynton Beach, Florida, Police Department's Web-based engagement process is an example of multiple modalities in combination. The department created a mobile app called MyPD for a variety of engagement activities. These include chats with the police chief, voting on issues through the department's Facebook page, submitting tips, and Twitter notifications. This department has a large Web presence in addition to the app, and has made a significant investment in this form of interaction and community engagement.

This kind of digital engagement avoids many of the cultural issues linked to face-to-face interactions. However, these kinds of online interactions offer little opportunity for engagement and collaboration except for decisions manageable by simple online voting. Moreover, reliance on mobile apps to elicit engagement risks excluding those who either cannot afford smart phones or choose not to use them.

Cultural differences are more likely to surface in face-to-face meetings and large or small groups, especially when planning and decision making about important issues are involved. Digital media provide ways to avoid or limit this form of interaction, but only for some issues. Where face-to-face meetings are the preferred mode, preparation and extra resources are necessary. This includes identifying the salient cultural differences that are likely to emerge and identifying ways to mitigate the possible disruptive impacts. It also means that those in charge of the process become thoroughly familiar with the problematic cultural issues and participants. The venue for meeting should be chosen to be culturally neutral, comfortable, and allow for flexible kinds of interactions—small groups, side conversations, breakouts, and so on. Amenities such as food and drinks and allowing time for informal interaction can allay anxieties and ease participants into substantive interactions. Professional facilitation can also be an effective way to ensure a smoother and more productive process (Schuman 2005).

Local officials may not have much experience or training in the skills necessary for launching and maintaining collaborative engagements. If some officials have the relevant training and experience, extending that resource to others should be part of the preparation. Similar training or technical assistance may be available from other local governments or from state agencies. It also may be advisable to employ the services of skilled facilitators in cross-cultural meetings and to model the behaviors needed by staff for their interactions with the public. Information about facilitation is available on the International Association of Facilitators Web site (International Association of Facilitators 2013). Where the need for community involvement is heightened, local officials should consider recruiting expert help in this process among the residents, nonprofit organizations, businesses, regional governance groups, and state agencies in their midst.

CONCLUSION

We began this chapter by noting that community involvement in matters dealing with service restructuring and consolidation decisions is commonplace. We also noted that the cases in which the community was involved in a planned and deliberate manner were few in number. Community involvement is admittedly challenging, and this chapter offers some insight into its contours. Citizen engagement is a messy process that operates outside of the hierarchical structures that regulate organizations and the acceptable modes of exchange that govern the business world. Citizen engagement is complicated by transaction costs and cultural factors that intrude into discussion and deliberation. Even so, citizens can productively contribute to decisions that affect their lives and well-being, and add rich and detailed information to a problem-solving effort. Citizens who participate in governing decisions may not always agree with the outcomes, but they have a better understanding of the nature of the dilemmas and trade-offs that were involved. Local decisions, particularly the thorny and painful decisions of distressed communities, require an engaged community, and public officials need to learn how to manage the process with careful analysis and sensible facilitation. Though difficult, citizen engagement harnesses the common interests of the public and the power of communal fate to help deal with the most difficult governing decisions.

KEY POINTS

- Community involvement is crucial to successful local government restructuring or consolidation.
- Citizens can offer perspectives that help sort out the sources and size of problems and help choose among strategies to resolve difficult situations.
- Engagement strategies should be tailored to local conditions and resources.
- Engagement should be a process of give and take, learning, and weighing alternatives.
- Culture matters—organizational and group cultural differences are a challenge to effective engagement.

NOTE

1. We use "tribe" in a generic sense to identify a group with distinctive cultural characteristics, not in the more specific sense as identifying a group with an historical, kinship, and even legal status, such as Native American tribal communities.

REFERENCES

Balakrishnan, Ramji, Shyam Sunder, and Shiva Sivaramakrishnan. 1999. *Granularity, Time and Control of Economic Resources.* Yale SOM Working Paper No. AC-03, February.

Deal, Terrence E., and Allan A. Kennedy. 2000. *Corporate Cultures: The Rites and Rituals of Corporate Life.* New York: Perseus Books.

Feiock, Richard. 2009. Metropolitan governance and institutional collective action. *Urban Affairs Review* 44(3): 356–377.

Frederickson, H. George. 1997. *The Spirit of Public Administration.* San Francisco: Jossey Bass.

Geertz, Clifford. 1966. *The Interpretation of Cultures.* New York: Basic Books.

International Association of Facilitators. 2013. Web site. www.iaf-world.org/index.aspx.

Meyer, Renate E., and Markus A. Hollerer. 2010. Meaning structures in a contested issue field: A topographic map of shareholder value in Austria. *Academy of Management Journal* 53(6): 1241–1262.

Schein, Edgar H. 2004. *Organizational Culture and Leadership.* 3d ed. San Francisco, CA: Jossey-Bass.

Schuman, Sandor, ed. 2005. *The IAF Handbook of Group Facilitation.* San Francisco, CA: Jossey-Bass.

New York State Department of State. 2014. *New York State Symbols.* Retrieved from: www.dos.ny.gov/kids_room/508/symbols2.html.

Thomas, John Clayton. 2010. Citizen, customer, partner: Thinking about local governance with and for the public. In *The Connected Community: Local Governments as Partners in Citizen Engagement and Community Building,* ed. James H. Svara and Janet Denhardt. Phoenix, AZ: Alliance for Innovation.

Tschirhart, Mary, Alejandro Amezcua, and Alison Anker. 2009. Resource sharing: How resource attributes influence sharing system choices. In *The Collaborative Public Manager: New Ideas for the Twenty-First Century,* ed. Rosemary O'Leary and Lisa Blomgren Bingham, 15–30. Washington, DC: Georgetown University Press.

Williams, Wil, and Duncan Lewis. 2008. Strategic management tools and public sector management. *Public Management Review* 10(5): 653–671.

Williamson, Oliver E. 1999. Public and private bureaucracies: A transaction cost economics perspective. *Journal of Law, Economics, and Organization* 15: 306–342.

Additional Sources of Guidance for Local Officials

Jandt, Fred E. 2010. *An Introduction to Intercultural Communication: Identities in a Global Community*. Thousand Oaks, CA: Sage Publications.

Schmitz, Joerg. 2006. *Cultural Orientations Guide: The Roadmap to Cultural Competence*. 5th ed. Princeton, NJ: Princeton Training Press.

Kettering Foundation. 2011. *Working Through Difficult Decisions*. Dayton, OH. http://kettering.org/publications/working-through-difficult-decisions/.

Part II

Municipal Shared Services and Consolidation in Practice

4

Service-Level Consolidation and Sharing Arrangements

Michael R. Hattery

Local government leaders and managers operate in an environment of change. The need for change in local government management, structure, and service provision is ongoing and linked to changes in the economy, demographics, technology, and other factors that help determine public service need and scale. These forces that drive the need for change in order to provide efficient and effective local services will continue. States, regions, local governments, and citizens have a continuing need to find ways to facilitate and encourage a flexible framework for service delivery and service provision adjustments. Local leadership and management play an important role in maintaining a dynamic and innovative mindset in local government organizations. We are not facing a unique historic moment that calls for a "one-time house cleaning" in service delivery patterns, but rather the mindset of an ongoing improvement program with the certainty that service delivery adjustments will continue to be needed over time. Maintaining the efficiency and effectiveness of local service delivery in a dynamic environment is essential for local economic health and revitalization.

The need for service delivery change may be dynamic, and the mechanics of assessing the need for change, evaluating alternative service delivery arrangements, and negotiating and implementing such alternative arrangements can be challenging if not daunting. While there are always voices questioning the efficiency of current service delivery practices, experience requires caution because current service characteristics and patterns are often highly valued by citizens and other recipients. Proposals for service sharing or consolidation occur in historic context; they do not arise in a vacuum. Current service delivery patterns represent choices and adjustments made over time to tailor service delivery to local community needs and preferences within the constraints of available resources. The perceived threat of change or loss of service will usually quickly mobilize service recipients, and this potential leads to the stability of current arrangements and a cautious approach to exploring change.

Considerations of service sharing and consolidation have a number of important dimensions. Perhaps most important is a general perspective for local and regional service delivery systems. A public choice perspective is outlined below to help frame the overall discussion on interorganizational service delivery. This overview is followed by sections on: motivations for changing service delivery, a general process for evaluating the opportunity for service delivery change, important factors involved in the process of service change, barriers to service delivery change and overcoming them, capacity issues in assessing and implementing service change, and some concluding thoughts on the importance of flexibility in providing services among local governments.

FRAMING THE DISCUSSION WITH A PUBLIC CHOICE PERSPECTIVE

The public choice approach suggests a path to local public service efficiency and effectiveness within the context of local home rule in state, regional, and local governance systems. The core ideas in the public choice perspective are: the distinction between provision and production in service delivery; the idea of a local-regional public economy; and the principle of fiscal equivalence (Oakerson 1999, 2–4). Each of these concepts is introduced below.

Considering Provision and Production

Instead of producing services "in house," local governments are increasingly contracting with other public, nonprofit, and private organizations to "produce" services for citizens. Contracting and joint provision serve as an avenue for the efficient "production" of public services. Local governments are in the business of providing services that their constituents need or demand, but need not produce these services themselves with their own personnel, equipment, and so forth. Unhooking "provision" from "production" of public services opens up an array of possibilities for achieving scale efficiencies. In fact, with the varying economies of scale across services, no single local government is "right sized" for producing all the public services and public service bundles that are demanded or expected by citizens. This variation in efficient size or scale frustrates attempts to identify "optimally" sized local governments.

In a similar fashion, in most service areas, there really exists a "bundle" of service activities that combine to constitute a municipality's service. For example, policing services include road patrol, investigation, citizen education, and communication/dispatching and other services. While there are complementarities among these activities, each may have a different efficiency scale based on geographic size, population, or other characteristics. As a consequence, Kodrzycki (2013) has identified cost-saving opportunities for regional communications and dispatching among small- and medium-sized policing units in northeastern states. This cost-saving proposal does not require or advocate the consolidation of all police services in regions, but only one element of the service bundle based on the relatively larger population size or geographic area that may be served efficiently.

Regional Public Economies

In any region, whether metropolitan or nonmetropolitan, there exists a variety of public, nonprofit, and for-profit organizations that work in concert through a system of contracts and agreements to provide the public goods and services demanded by citizens. This constellation of organizations constitutes a regional public economy in which various local governments "buy and sell." Depending on the changes in demand for particular services, the technology for providing them, and other factors, the makeup of this regional public economy will *need* to change over time. Within this context, "consolidation" of services, service activities, or governments is one of a number strategies that may make sense, depending on service delivery needs and circumstances.

Maintaining Fiscal Equivalence

In financing local public services it is important to maintain the link between who pays and who benefits, whenever feasible and appropriate. This helps both citizens and local officials to better understand the price of particular public services and the demand for them. However, fiscal equivalence is a general principle that does not apply in all circumstances, for example, when local governments want to assure that all citizens receive a service regardless of their ability to pay.

The public choice approach provides an important perspective in assessing opportunities for service change in the local government system. This approach emphasizes the importance of flexibility and effectiveness in considering revenue alternatives, innovation, regional approaches, and management in reforming local government. Consolidation is viewed as one of a number of options for local governments to pursue in maintaining efficient and effective service delivery.

WHY CHANGE?

Forward-looking elected leaders and managers actively consider the need for change in the way things are currently done. There are a number of factors that provide an impetus to reassess service delivery. Fiscal constraints are perhaps the most constant factor providing pressure to reassess current service arrangements (Krueger and Bernick 2007). Budget pressure from competing demands on limited resources always exists, yet recessions and fiscal downturns stimulate a harder look at current practices (Ferris 1986). But there are other factors that cause managers and leaders to look at alternative service provision options. Serious local efforts to consider capital needs and investment plans highlight budgetary needs and provide a stimulus for reevaluating local service delivery practices to reduce operating costs (Hattery 1996a). Service delivery innovators highlight opportunities and provide stimulus for changing the way things are done. Other organizations, including the state and federal government, private firms, and municipal associations, often support and promote specific strategies or opportunities to change service delivery for cost saving, regulatory compliance, or service improvement.

Changes in service supply and demand factors also create pressure for modifying service delivery. On the demand side, flux in the composition of municipal residents will influence demand for services in a variety of ways. Many communities are faced with new service economies because of either population loss or the influx of new residents with a different profile of service preferences. On the supply side, an increase in the cost of equipment, materials, fuel, or other important components can tip the balance and lead to a reassessment of the current service method or scale of production.

THE PROCESS OF CHANGING SERVICE DELIVERY ARRANGEMENTS

Managers and elected leaders are often in a position to consider change in service provision. In many cases, this change involves a consideration of moving from solely in-house service production to arrangements that involve service sharing or contracting with other public and private organizations. This consideration consists of a series of steps (not necessarily linear) to arrive at a decision about whether or not to change, and if change is preferred, how to ensure a satisfactory new arrangement and monitor it over time. Figure 4.1 lists those steps, which will be outlined in more detail below.

Figure 4.1 **Considering Service Delivery Change**

1. Assess current service delivery
2. Evaluate service delivery alternatives
3. Negotiate and implement an alternative
4. Monitor service delivery

Assessing Current Service Delivery

Understanding current service delivery is the starting point for considering change. We often take our knowledge of the status quo for granted. A clear profile of the municipality's current service delivery will provide a factual basis for comparing current arrangements with potential alternatives. Without an accurate current profile, the consideration of alternatives is difficult, inefficient, and risky. But a careful specification of current service delivery can make the consideration of change much more straightforward. Current service delivery has at least three important attributes: activities, cost, and characteristics (frequency, response time, coverage).

Service Activities

Public services most often represent clusters of service activities. A service activity is one component of the public function that citizens view as a "public service." Service activities vary in their cost, direct impact on citizens, efficient size or scale, importance, and other characteristics. Differences in the attributes of these activities are important in considering alternatives for service delivery. For example, law enforcement or police services include the following activities:

- Road patrol
- Investigation
- Communication
- Safety education

Service activities are often provided by a group of employees and delivered in a manner that makes it difficult to separate them out and carefully assess them distinctly. In other situations, service activities are highly separable and distinct.

Service Cost

Municipal budgeting and financial reporting vary significantly in the extent to which service costs can be clearly identified. The identification or estimation of service and service activity costs is important for clearly specifying current service delivery (Michel 2004). It is an essential metric in comparing options for alternative service delivery. In many cases the costs of particular services or service activities are difficult to estimate with current financial record keeping. Contracting out a service or service component is sometimes the first occasion on which local leaders have monitored or evaluated directly the service cost in question. Improved service costing is a critical component in considering service alternatives. Careful assessment of fixed and variable, short- and long-term cost relationships can be a key factor in making decisions about service sharing and consolidation. Distinguishing between these cost elements carefully is important in effectively comparing the cost of other alternatives. For example, excluding fixed costs that will not change when considering contracting out can make a critical difference in selecting the lowest-cost option among alternatives.

Service Characteristics

Within a single service, like sanitation, service delivery characteristics vary from community to community. Public services vary along a number of important dimensions, including frequency, response time, and service coverage. For example, sanitation services include the service activity of garbage pickup. Its frequency can vary. The service may have qualitative differences: Is refuse picked up at curbside or is it picked up behind the house? The coverage of the service may vary: Are types of customers (business, multifamily, single family, etc.) included or not, and how do fees differ for different types of customers or refuse volume? Response time is usually not a critical feature of refuse removal but it is an important characteristic of most public safety and emergency services. Clearly outlining these service component characteristics is important in considering alternative options for provision. Service characteristics are sometimes expressed in terms of quality and quantity attributes.

In summary, characterizing a service that is under consideration for contract or shared service arrangements requires a clear delineation of major service activities. Once activities are delineated the cost of service activities and their characteristics should be documented.

For example, in the recent assessment of policing services in New England, Kodrzycki (2013) argues for cost saving and service improvement by regionalizing call centers (communications) for emergency services in New England. This analysis did not propose regionalizing police services, fire services, or emergency medical services in their en-

Figure 4.2 **Criteria for Evaluating Alternative Service Delivery Options**

1. Service activities	How do the proposed service activities correspond with those currently provided?
2. Service cost	Per unit and total costs for alternative provision options in comparison with current provision costs on an activity-by-activity basis. It is also important to consider the potential transition costs and the cost of contract monitoring and administration.
3. Service characteristics	How do the service characteristics (frequency, response time, etc.) compare on an activity-by-activity basis?
4. Continuity	Any loss of service capability and the capacity to restart the service in-house (with municipal resources) in the future has to be considered both for its importance to local officials and for the difficulty of restarting and impediments that would exist should this need arise.

tirety, but only one activity in the service bundle that is shared by all three service areas. Detailed multistate evaluation of the size economies of cost per call and service quality considerations provided the basis for the recommendation.

Evaluating Service Delivery Alternatives

Today's local government structures are the result of problem solving by local managers, citizens, and their leaders in the past (Parks and Oakerson 2000). When municipalities are considering service alternatives there is usually a limited number of proximate organizations to work with in sharing a service or in contracting out service delivery. As the service delivery setting moves from urban to rural on the density gradient, the number of available organizations to work with usually declines. In reviewing the available alternatives, it is critical to base the review of potential alternatives on the assessment of current service delivery. Proposed service alternatives have to be compared using the same important criteria (see Figure 4.2).

As indicated in Figure 4.2, alternative service delivery options should be assessed for the service activities that will be provided and how they compare with current activities. Since the cluster of new service activities may vary (e.g., only one or more service components may be candidates for joint or contract service provision), it is important that costs for alternative service arrangements be compared at the level of service activity. Important changes in service characteristics under proposed service alternatives should be noted, and, any loss of capability to provide the service in-house needs to be weighed. Shared and contract service arrangements can cease or become problematic for a variety of reasons. The future cost of restarting the service should be considered. A related consideration is the impact of proposed alternatives on other current service activities and the ability or flexibility to address special service needs. For example, a move from internal provision of police dispatching and communications services to a regional approach may reduce core staff in administration. Will this reduction impinge on other administrative needs? There may be similar cross-service impacts from assumed changes in equipment or personnel that are used for multiple service activities.

Public service operating costs are usually a central concern for managers, local elected officials, and citizens (Vojnovic 1998). Operating costs for alternative service arrangements need to be estimated using a metric that can be easily compared with current costs for the average citizen taxpayer. Depending on the community, the relevant metric could be cost per household or the change in property taxes for the median property value in the community.

The bundle of services that will result from any contracting or organizational change should be articulated as clearly as possible (Hattery 1996a). Will residents receive the same level of service (e.g., will police road patrols remain the same or increase)? Will the quality of service improve or stay the same (e.g., will emergency response times be quicker)? Answers to these kinds of questions help local leaders and citizens understand how projected costs are linked to service delivery changes. Differences in service quality and quantity often have a direct linkage with community characteristics that citizens want to maintain and protect. For example, residents of small cities and villages may value a well-maintained and extensive sidewalk network to ensure a "walkable" community environment. Initiatives to integrate public works services with a surrounding "open country" town or county government would need to address this preference for community sidewalks that differentiates the more densely populated area.

Another important factor to consider is governance control (Toft 1986). Proposed changes need to be assessed with respect to real and perceived loss of governance or local control. This reflects the degree to which the current community of interest will have access and influence on decision makers and elected officials under proposed changes. By specifically addressing governance issues, leaders and citizens can consider directly their concerns about loss of control. In some cases the loss can be mitigated or at a minimum its impacts more clearly understood.

The service activities affected, their cost, service characteristics (quantity and quality), and governance control are primary considerations to managers, citizens, and local leaders in weighing their support for municipal options. Approaches that help evaluate such criteria in a common framework are needed to provide more efficient public choices. Table 4.1 provides one example of combining these factors in comparing municipal service and organizational alternatives.

Changes in service delivery or local government organization often involve significant costs that are incurred as a part of the process of change or transition (Brown and Potoski 2003 use the term "transactions costs"; here we use "transition" and "transaction" interchangeably). Transition costs can include legal fees, infrastructure (e.g., for water and sewer interconnections), equipment purchases, administrative costs for combining financial and other record-keeping systems, and so on. It is valuable to consider at least the general magnitude of these costs in comparison with any projected savings in future operating costs. For example, Vojnovic (1998) found, for Canadian local governments, that transition costs for a regional consolidation of governments ran in the millions of dollars and as high as $75 per capita. Vojnovic also found that these transition costs were higher on a per capita basis for larger municipalities.

A variety of factors will influence the future impacts of changes made in the current period. Many studies calculate financial projections or forecasts as a means of providing

Table 4.1

Comparison of Homeowner Costs, Service Delivery Changes, and Degree of Local Control for All Options

	Option 1	Option 1	Option 2	Option 3	Option 4	Option 5
Characteristic	Village current	Village current constrained	Co-terminus option	Contracting with the City of XYZ	Village dissolution	Merger with the City of XYZ
Annual homeowner cost	$3,795	$4,232	$3,874	$3,852	$4,056	$3,742
Increase or decrease from current village costs	$0	$438	$79	$58	$261	–$52
Change in service delivery						
General administration	No change	No change	No change	No change	Decline	Mixed
Police	No change	No change	No change	Improvement	No change	Improvement
Fire	No change	No change	No change	No change	No change	Improvement
Emergency medical	No change	No change	No change	No change	No change	No change
Water	No change	No change	No change	No change	No change	No change
Sewer	No change	No change	No change	No change	No change	No change
Solid waste	No change	No change	No change	No change	No change	Improvement
Streets and sidewalks	No change	No change	No change	No change	Decline	Improvement
Change in local control for current village residents	No change	No change	No change	No change	Decline	Decline

a sense of the future fiscal implications of service delivery and organizational changes (Schroeder 1987). Often there are known factors that will impact service and financial conditions in the future. These include items like termination clauses in current service contracts as well as planned changes in state aid and regulatory arrangements. Planning, land use, and development patterns and trends often have important service delivery implications but are sometimes neglected in shared service considerations. It is valuable to identify these factors and to provide estimates of their impact, where feasible, in evaluating proposed changes.

Negotiating and Implementing an Alternative

The evaluation of service alternatives may lead to a decision to change current service provision. If change is desired, then an agreement governing the arrangement needs to be drafted and a transition plan developed. Toft (1986) identifies implementation as a key indicator or aspect of governance capacity. It is valuable to identify at least preliminary implementation steps for potential service delivery or organizational changes.

It is important to build in adequate transition time for transfer of knowledge about current operations, for staffing changes and the purchase of needed equipment, and so forth. The transition may involve higher-than-normal costs as personnel and equipment might need to be duplicated or overlapped to ensure an effective continuity of service provision. Performance criteria and objectives to guide service delivery should be developed and communicated as clearly as possible, and contract language should indicate how objectives and performance criteria will guide the administration of the contract, the payment of funds, and so on (Brown, Potoski, and Van Slyke 2006).

It should also be clear who will be responsible for monitoring service delivery and contract performance. Depending on the level of history with such agreements, language describing the process for modifying the contractual agreement between the parties should be clear. Service changes and contract modifications often need to be made and providing a pathway to making these adjustments with ease is important (Henderson, Whitaker, and Altman-Sauer 2003).

Changing service arrangements is not something that is done easily or quickly, but it is good to identify what conditions or criteria will trigger a reconsideration of a contracted or shared service arrangement. This is usually based on performance criteria like service delivery quality, service cost, or other conditions set in the agreement.

Monitoring Service Delivery

The key elements of monitoring a new alternative service delivery approach should be addressed in the process of negotiating and implementing the new approach. It is critical, however, that service delivery monitoring happen and that the responsibility for monitoring be clear. In some instances a separate governance group is created to oversee a joint or shared service activity, and in some cases this is a legal requirement. The person or group that oversees a contractual, shared, or joint service delivery arrangement should have both accountability for service performance and the authority to make the changes needed to ensure ongoing performance.

MORE THAN A PROCESS: INFLUENTIAL FACTORS

The process of exploring and implementing opportunities for service change is influenced by a number of factors. Below I introduce some of these factors, including: local leadership, citizen engagement, venues for cooperative discussion, use of consultants, larger organizations working with smaller ones, supporters of change, the value of starting with simpler opportunities, and working with groups of municipalities on an opportunity. The discussion of factors below benefits from a review of successful and unsuccessful cases of service sharing and consolidation in New York State (Benjamin, Hattery, and John 2007).

Local Leadership

Previous efforts have demonstrated that elected officials and administrative staff in local government generally take initiative in identifying opportunities and pursuing alternatives for interlocal cooperation. Without this initiative and action, opportunities remain unexplored. Previous studies have also shown the importance of a shared, mutually respectful involvement of elected and staff leadership in successful collaborations. Governing board members often take a leadership role, but generally, staff with the dedicated and clear responsibility to review options, assess cost, negotiate terms, and so on are required to make progress toward decisions to pursue change and choose between available options.

Citizen Engagement

Changes in service delivery vary in the extent to which they directly impact citizens. There is often reticence about contracting out services with a high degree of visibility and direct citizen contact, such as policing. Previous research has shown that collaborations are most successful for services consumed collectively (e.g., parks), or accessed impersonally without direct citizen contact with a government worker (e.g., highway maintenance), as well as those for which the government itself is the customer (e.g., equipment maintenance, specialized infrastructure). They are less frequently successfully launched for services that are directly delivered to citizens and consumed individually (e.g., police protection, education). Communication with citizens and businesses is important, especially when change will directly affect citizens or at least their perceptions.

In these instances, municipal officials can foster an environment to address concerns and questions and help frame the value or benefits of change in service delivery (Potapchuk et al. 1998). This engagement can help local managers and leaders link proposed action to the underlying problems of current service delivery, cost, taxation, and benefits for community members. Engagement can help address the common responses from citizens that local leaders are "presenting a solution where there is not a problem" or that "cost savings are overestimated" or that "they will yield unacceptable changes in the services delivered." In most instances the citizens will have the final say, either sooner (referenda) or later (future elections of local leaders or retention of managers).

Citizen surveys can be a valuable tool, depending on the cost and salience of the service change anticipated. Other tools for direct citizen input, like public information meetings and focus groups, can provide valuable, more detailed insights about the impacts of proposed changes and unanticipated affects. These tools often do not provide an accurate picture of the broad-based level of citizen support or opposition to proposed service changes. Well-designed, accurate citizen survey results can provide valuable information for both managers and local elected leaders (Hattery 2008). Citizen surveys can be affordable, depending on the approach and purpose.

Create a Venue Where Service Collaboration Is a Core Focus

The venue may be a regular meeting of officials from several governments to discuss common problems and seek shared solutions or the formation of a formal organization—a council of governments or collaboration council. Even when there are not immediate opportunities, such a venue provides the opportunity to build relationships and understand the needs and capabilities of potential local partners. These kinds of linkages, and regular communication over time, make it possible to take advantage of opportunities that may arise from regulatory pressure, production cost changes, or a joint need for new equipment or facilities.

Use Consultants and Experts Carefully

Third-party experts can be important in pursuing intergovernmental service delivery. Properly used, consultants may disarm the argument that one or another of the local officials involved in seeking change is pursuing a personal agenda. A key potential role of the outsider in these efforts, and one that has been less specified, is as a neutral stipulator of facts. In contrast, it is also important to insist that consultants report in a manner that is not preemptive of local choice. As we will discuss below, many nonmetropolitan communities need short-term assistance from a consultant or staff from a regional organization in order to have the professional capacity required to work through the data collection and evaluation needed when assessing service sharing or consolidation. The key is to carefully identify the role for this outside help and monitoring project goals as you proceed.

Larger Organizations Need to Collaborate, Not Control

Larger jurisdictions often have the resources to lead. For example, school districts and counties often have larger budgets and staff than the localities with which they seek to collaborate on initiatives for shared or consolidated services. But disparities in size and capacity may raise fears about being subordinated. Larger governments must be mindful that successful collaborations can only result if the process is neither actually nor apparently controlled by the larger partners. There are a number of existing cases where larger partners were willing—as an act of enlightened self-interest—to spend their own resources to help create and launch a collaborative structure. For example, Tompkins County, New York, invested significant staff resources in helping to foster the Greater Tompkins County Municipal Health Insurance Consortium. The goal of the consortium, which is an outgrowth of the county's council of governments, is to stabilize the growth in the cost of health insurance for municipal partners. Formed in 2010, the bulk of the consortium's benefits have flowed to the smaller local government members within the county.

Whether larger or smaller, the failure to consult and gain agreement can be a fatal blow for working together, even when action is urgent. Make time your friend—use it to prepare, plan for change over time, and mitigate potential opposition to change from those most affected.

Identify Constituencies for Change

Initiatives for service delivery change can be legitimized through the support of key community players. Chambers of commerce and other business groups and local media, for example, are usually enthusiasts of service consolidation or collaboration because of what they regard as its self-evident economic logic. The positive effects of collaboration may reach far beyond the jurisdictions actually entering into a formal agreement. For example, two or three municipalities may see the practical need and benefit of investing in a joint fueling facility, but a variety of local public and state units will benefit as well, albeit as minor partners in the effort. Consider who those other beneficiaries might be and draw them into a supportive role when communicating the project concept to the public.

Pick Low-Hanging Fruit

Look for win-win opportunities that minimize change and conflict, and have a demonstrable impact or benefit. Some service sharing and consolidation opportunities carry bigger benefits in terms of potential cost savings or service improvements. These larger benefits often carry with them more inherent conflict or controversy. It is often wise to use successes in lower conflict and benefit efforts to build trust and understanding for bigger and more difficult-to-achieve opportunities in the future.

Get Started and Avoid Veto Situations

Requiring that all potential partners sign on before collaboration begins gives any single municipality veto power. For example, announcing that "we won't do this unless every local government in the county (or region) agrees to participate" gives any local partner veto power over something that could benefit many governments and citizens. On the other hand, if the most committed jurisdictions get started, others may join later. As we will see below, two-party agreements are most common; multiparty actions are most difficult.

Previous research in the downstate New York metropolitan area showed that most reported collaborations were between two or three municipalities, with the difficulty of mounting intergovernmental collaborative efforts growing as the number of involved governments increased (Benjamin and Nathan 2001). Moreover, reported collaborations were most common where governments were layered (or nested) geographically, that is, where some of the people served by the jurisdictions seeking to collaborate were citizens (and could vote) in two or more of them. These overlap and adjacency factors were confirmed by a review of over 200 municipal cooperative agreements in western New York (Foster 1998).

OVERCOMING BARRIERS TO CHANGE

There are a variety of barriers to changing service delivery through the sharing or consolidation of services. Some persistent barriers are discussed below with suggestions for overcoming them.

Identify Relevant Requirements in the State Constitution or Law

New York State has a broad statute permitting shared and consolidated service delivery among local governments (Carpinello and Salkin 1990). Yet local governments in New York have often been frustrated by a variety of more specific state requirements that can serve as a barrier to local collaboration (Briffault 1990). For example, state law requires a local referendum to shift an office from elected to appointed. Changes in service structure inevitably lead to a shift in necessary roles, which may trigger a need for a referendum. In a number of instances this provision has frustrated town and village attempts to contract or consolidate highway and public works service operations. It is important to have a legal assessment of proposed options before moving too far down the road on intermunicipal service options and to develop strategies for working with perceived legal barriers. For example, in at least one New York town, the position of elected town highway superintendent was not eliminated but the salary was dramatically reduced, creating a position that chiefly monitors contracts and advises the governing board on contract performance and renewal with other municipal service providers.

Fiscal Fairness When Jurisdictions Are Not Coterminous

School district boundaries in New York State are often not coterminous with those of other general purpose governments (counties, cities, towns, and villages). Village boundaries may cross county or town lines. A service delivery collaboration with a few municipalities within a school district might be seen as unfair if no benefits accrue to the other parts of the district, but the "other parts" are being called upon to share costs. In such instances, it is important to make the anticipated costs and benefits of collaborative efforts clear and fair. Communicating them early and clearly to all affected parties is also essential.

Potentially Disadvantaged Individuals and Groups Will Resist

In a set of cases of proposed service sharing or consolidation reviewed in New York State, the most vigorous resistance came from leaders and employees who feared the loss of their jobs—and organizations that represented them (e.g., employee unions). This opposition must be anticipated, and a plan developed to address concerns and minimize the often short-term costs of change to achieve the longer-term benefits. In particular, remember that local employees find protections in civil service law and collective bargaining agreements. These legal protections need to be understood and respected in seeking change.

Respect the Community and the Idea of Community

Governance structures whose overt purpose is to deliver public service also may be at the center of the social and cultural life of a place; for many residents these structures are at the core of community identity. Faced with the economy/community trade-off, people will rarely opt for the former over the latter. That is why proponents for change are wise to clearly distinguish an idea of collaborating on delivery of a service or consolidating a single function from a threat to the continued existence of a general purpose government or school district, and—most often—to disavow the latter.

CAPACITY ISSUES IN ASSESSING SERVICE CHANGE

Effective service sharing and consolidation require significant capability on the part of local governments to evaluate options, initiate and consummate agreements, and manage and monitor performance. The smaller the unit of government (in terms of population size, number of employees, and fiscal resources), the thinner will be the resources and capacity to accomplish these important management tasks. A significant literature exists on "management capacity building" to address the effectiveness problems of nonmetropolitan governments, based upon the understanding that these governments lack the management capacity of their metropolitan counterparts (see, for example, Honadle and Howitt 1986). Gargan (1981) has defined management capacity as the ability or extent to which a local government can do what it wants to do (or what it knows it should do). This capacity includes the ability to:

- Anticipate and influence change
- Make informed, intelligent decisions about policy
- Develop programs to implement policy
- Attract and absorb resources and manage them
- Evaluate current activities to guide future action
- Innovate and adopt new methods and technology that reduce cost or improve service

Management capacity is demonstrated in the successful execution of financial functions such as budgetary control and purchasing, and the successful implementation of decisions to revise service provision, maintain facilities, purchase needed equipment or build a new building. A critical aspect of management capacity is the ability to generate and acquire the information and the analysis needed to carry out these functions. Nonmetropolitan governments often have a great number of service sharing and consolidation options to consider, but a thin capacity to effectively assess them. A variety of strategies have been tried to help address this deficit (Hattery 2012). Regional and state strategies need to be considered in helping address this need among nonmetropolitan governments.

CONCLUSION

Service sharing and consolidation arrangements among municipal partners are many-faceted and ongoing. With the environment of change surrounding local governments, service delivery needs and priorities continue to push local officials to assess the need for change in service arrangements and to explore new local organizational partners in the production of local services. Nonmetropolitan governments may need capacity assistance from consultants and other regional organizations to continue the process of service alignment over time. While local managers and governing board members have to approach change cautiously and in consultation with service partners and citizens, they must remain flexible in how services will be provided to ensure an efficient and effective public sector.

KEY POINTS

- Even in stable communities, factors are at work changing what constitutes "effective and efficient" public service delivery for local citizens. Local government leaders need to conscientiously oversee their service system for potential changes.
- Assessing change begins with a sound understanding of current service delivery activities, costs, and characteristics.
- The consideration of alternatives involves additional factors, including the importance of governance control, linkage with other service activities, the cost of transition, and the medium- and long-term consequences of change.
- A variety of factors influence the consideration and success of service delivery change, including: local leadership, citizen engagement, existing relationships among local governments, the number of involved organizations, the support of community actors, and others.
- The administrative capacity to effectively characterize current services and soundly assess potential alternatives is critical for a government's ability to serve its citizens and make essential changes for future community health and well-being. For smaller communities, local leaders may have to be creative in accessing the capacity for this administrative need.

REFERENCES

Benjamin, Gerald, Michael Hattery, and Rachel John. 2007. Lessons on sharing services from the first two years of the SMSI program: The highlights. *Government, Law and Policy Journal* 9(2): 69–77.

Benjamin, Gerald, and Richard Nathan. 2001. *Regionalism and Realism*. Washington, DC: Brookings Institution Press.

Briffault, Richard. 1990. *The Law of Local Government Restructuring and Cooperation in New York.* A manuscript prepared for the Local Government Restructuring Project. Albany: Nelson A. Rockefeller Institute of Government, State University of New York.

Brown, Trevor L., and Matthew Potoski. 2003. Transaction costs and institutional explanations for government service production decisions. *Journal of Public Administration Research and Theory* 13(4): 441–468.

Brown, Trevor L., Matthew Potoski, and David M. Van Slyke. 2006. Managing public service contracts: Aligning values, institutions, and markets. *Public Administration Review* 66: 323–331.

Carpinello, George F. and Patricia E. Salkin. 1990. *Legal Processes for Facilitating Consolidation and Cooperation Among Local Governments: Models from Other States*. Albany, NY: Government Law Center of Albany Law School.

Ferris, James M. 1986. The decision to contract out: An empirical analysis. *Urban Affairs Quarterly* 22(2): 332–344.

Foster, Kathryn A. 1998. *Municipal Cooperative Agreements in Western New York: Survey Findings.* Buffalo: Institute for Local Government and Regional Growth, University of Buffalo, State University of New York.

Gargan, John. 1981. Consideration of local government capacity. *Public Administration Review* 41: 649–658.

Hattery, Michael R. 1996a. *Contract for Street Maintenance and Repair Between the Town and Village of Bergen, Genesee County, NY*. Cooperative Highway Services Case Study Report Number 1. Ithaca, NY: Local Government Program, Department of Applied Economics and Management, Cornell University.

———. 1996b. *Enhancing Cooperation in Highway Services: Summary Report of Case Study Findings and Recommendations for Legislative and Regulatory Change.* Cooperative Highway Services Case Study Report Number 8. Ithaca, NY: Local Government Program, Department of Applied Economics and Management, Cornell University.

———. 2008. *Morristown Shared Services Study Survey of Citizen Satisfaction with Public Services and Support for Change.* A report prepared for the joint Town and Village of Morristown Shared Services Committee, supported by the New York State Local Government Efficiency Grant Program.

———. 2012. The state and its localities. In *The Oxford Handbook of New York State Government and Politics,* ed. Gerald Benjamin, 455–481. New York: Oxford University Press.

Henderson, Margaret, Gordon P. Whitaker, and Lydian Altman-Sauer. 2003. Establishing mutual accountability in nonprofit-government relationships. *Popular Government* 69(1): 18–29.

Honadle, Beth Walter, and Arnold M. Howitt, eds. 1986. *Perspectives on Management Capacity Building.* Albany: State University of New York Press.

Kodrzycki, Yolanda. 2013. *The Quest for Cost-Efficient Local Government in New England: What Role for Regional Consolidation?* Research Report 13–1, New England Public Policy Center. Boston: Federal Reserve Bank of Boston.

Kreuger, Skip, and Ethan Bernick. 2007. *Hierarchy and Selection: The Impact of State-Level Rules on Interlocal Cooperation Choice.* A paper presented at the Sixty-Fifth Midwest Political Science Association National Conference, Chicago. April 12–15.

Michel, R. Gregory. 2004. *Cost Analysis and Activity Based Costing for Government*. Chicago: Government Finance Officers Association.

Oakerson, Ronald J. 1999. *Governing Local Public Economies: Creating the Civic Metropolis.* Oakland: Institute for Contemporary Studies.

Parks, Roger B., and Ronald J. Oakerson. 2000. Regionalism, localism, and metropolitan governance: Suggestions from the research program on local public economies. *State and Local Government Review* 32(3): 169–179.

Potapchuk, William R., Jarle P. Crocker, Dina Boogaard, and William H. Schecter. 1998. *Building Community: Exploring the Role of Social Capital and Local Government.* Washington, DC: Program for Community Problem Solving.

Schroeder, Larry. 1987. Local government multi-year budgetary forecasting: Some administrative and political issues. In *Crisis and Constraint in Municipal Finance,* ed. James H. Carr, 146–159. New Brunswick, NJ: Center for Urban Policy Research.

Toft, Graham S. 1986. Building capacity to govern. In *Perspectives on Management Capacity Building,* ed. Beth Walter Honadle and Arnold M. Howitt, 242–267. Albany: State University of New York Press.

Vojnovic, Igor. 1998. Municipal consolidation in the 1990s: An analysis of British Columbia, New Brunswick, and Nova Scotia. *Canadian Public Administration* 41(2): 239–283.

5

Lessons Learned from the Nonprofit–Government Relationship for the Municipal Government Manager

Lauren Miltenberger

Local governments are currently looking to both the shared services and consolidation models as ways to reduce public costs while continuing to deliver high levels of service. The benefits of sharing or consolidating the delivery methods include an increase in the market-based advantages of economies of scale and consequently a reduction in costs and inefficiencies. This model is gaining in popularity, as many local governments are currently being forced to make difficult decisions to cut costs and squeeze budgets. Therefore, this volume is extremely timely, as local government managers need practical guidance in defining and creating effective shared service and consolidation arrangements. The purpose of this chapter is provide guidance specifically for the shared service model. This will be accomplished by highlighting specific lessons learned from the nonprofit–government experience, as they have been sharing services for more than 50 years. Reviewing how the nonprofit–government shared service system has evolved and discussing the best practices in the nonprofit–government relationship is a useful way for municipal managers to plan effective shared service arrangements.

Both the nonprofit–government relationship and the municipal shared service relationship utilize the contract as the basic blueprint for the way service delivery systems are created. This is due to the fact that the majority of shared service arrangements are formed when partners agree to a contract that names one of them as the lead agency responsible for producing the service, and the other(s) as the agency that receives the service (Holzer and Fry 2010). A similar scenario applies to the nonprofit–government relationship, whereby the government contracts out public human services to nonprofit organizations.

There is a robust literature that describes the interactions between nonprofits and government and it is applicable to the municipal shared service dialogue. A look toward the nonprofit–government contracting literature can reveal lessons learned. A review of how the government contracts with nonprofits in the delivery of human services and a discussion on the current best practices can provide a firm foundation for the municipal shared service model. This type of review can stimulate a dialogue about how best to structure the municipal shared service system so that it produces effective and efficient public services. Due to the similarities in service provision, reviewing the development of the nonprofit–government relationship via human service contracts can be useful for the municipal manager. The focus of this chapter is to discuss current best practices in the nonprofit–government relationship and glean from the review five strategies that can help the municipal government manager structure the shared service system.

This chapter is formatted to first provide a brief review of the nonprofit–government relationship. Next, the chapter provides a synopsis of current best practices in the nonprofit–government relationship, focusing primarily on collaboration. Then, a five-point typology is proposed to share specific lessons learned with the municipal government manager on how to influence the creation of collaborative partnerships. The five-point typology then provides the basis for a successful model in a shared service initiative.

A BRIEF INTRODUCTION TO THE HUMAN SERVICES SYSTEM

There has been a more than 30-year trend of privatization in the public sector that has resulted in government contracting out many of its services to the private sector, both for-profit and nonprofit. Some have called this the "hollowing out of government" (Milward and Provan 2000) or "third-party government" (Salamon 1995). This is especially the case in the field of human services, where these trends have effectively transformed parts of the nonprofit human services sector. Nathan (1996) explains that this has resulted in an extensive, complicated pattern of "nonprofitization," a linking of government and nonprofits in a new kind of relationship that goes beyond typical contracting arrangements because of the very nature of human services. "Nonprofitization" has created a system of human service provision in the United States that is a hybridized mix between the public and private sectors. Nonprofit social service agencies depend on the funding received from the government and governments have come to rely on nonprofits for the delivery of social services, with many public agencies not directly providing services to constituents anymore. In fact, a study by the Boris et al. (2010) found nationally that human service organizations, on average, depend on government funding for 65 percent of their total budgets. This nonprofit–government relationship is one where both sectors are mutually dependent on the other (Gilbert 1983; Hall 1992; Smith and Lipsky 1993; Nathan 1996; Abramovitz 2002; Gronbjerg and Salamon 2002; Lynn 2002; Denhardt et al. 2008; Baines 2010).

The system of contracting for human services carries with it certain challenges. A study of this phenomenon by Boris et al. (2010), the first-ever national study on this topic, has produced comprehensive data on the structure, results, and scope of this relationship. A major finding from their research is the complex nature of this system and the obstacles that nonprofits must face. They found that nationally, 76 percent of the nonprofit respondents indicated that the complexity and time required for reporting on contracts and grants was a problem (Boris et al. 2010). They also found that 75 percent indicated that the application process was too complex and time consuming. Analysis of data from Urban Institute's national survey of 2,497 human service organizations indicates that organizations are likely to face late payments, changes in contract terms, and even contract cancellation, all of which lead to organizations being more likely to have to reduce salaries, lay off employees, or raid financial reserves. This hollowing out of organizational capacity can have serious implications for how the system delivers its services.

Contracts are the products of a complicated federal block grant system where different human services are funded and directed by the federal government. The federal government then provides the funds to the states and turns over the responsibility of service delivery to the states. Certainly, there are some problems with the current system guiding the nonprofit–government relationship. There are incompatibilities and deficiencies in how the system is structured that lead to inefficiencies, frustrations, and failure to utilize information to improve performance. There are questions about whether the state is paying the full cost of providing the services for which they are contracting. If they are not paying the full cost, there is every reason to expect this will detract from achieving higher levels of performance because front-line service providers will serve administrative functions or others will expend valuable resources in seeking funding elsewhere to fill the gap left by the state.

Over time this service delivery "system" has evolved through a fragmented process, mainly due to the structure of the funding of the contracts. Many nonprofits are currently facing extremely difficult circumstances whereby they must serve more clients as funding for programs and services is being diminished (Boris et al. 2010). The strain in the government–nonprofit relationship has implications for nonprofit organizations, government agencies, the clients they serve, and the public at large. This stems from a lack of information exchange and coordination, and a failure of government to consistently deliver coherent messages about policies, programs, requirements, and expectations to its nonprofit contractors (Van Slyke 2003; Alexander et al. 2001). Creating collaborative structures will increase the likelihood that these impediments to service provision are reduced.

BEST PRACTICE REVIEW: THE CALL FOR COLLABORATION

Even within the constraints of the contracting system, a hopeful sign for the future is in a stream of research demonstrating that obstacles seemingly inherent to the contracting system can and should be overcome (Van Slyke 2003; Suarez 2011). In fact, a key conclusion in the research on the nonprofit–government relationship is the move toward a collaborative approach to governance (Austin 2003; Brown and Troutt, 2005; Milward and Provan, 2000; Poole 2003; Suarez 2011). Due to fragmentation in the structure and funding of human services, current research on the nonprofit–government relationship recommends the collaborative governance paradigm.

The human service delivery system operates most effectively when designed using a collaborative governance framework. However, for every mention of a collaborative benefit there is a discussion of the difficulties inherent in the collaborative process. Collaboration is a difficult undertaking in any context because it lacks a structured hierarchy to formally organize the process. Collaboration between nonprofits and the government in the delivery of human services is a unique situation in which collaboration can be even more difficult than normal. In fact, some researchers do not think it is possible to create a partnership within the contracting model. Gazely and Brudney (2007) investigate the problems associated with partnership within the contracting arrangements. They use a definition of collaboration, adapted from Wood and Gray (1991), that defines it as a voluntary, autonomous relationship where partners agree to common rules using shared decision-making powers and they have some transformational purpose to increase the capacity of their operating systems by using shared resources. Under this general definition they conclude, "collaboration between local governments and nonprofit organizations would exclude purely contractual relationships, in which power is not shared" (Gazely and Brudney 2007, 389). However, they found that there was a willingness on the part of public managers to develop a collaborative framework to guide the government–nonprofit partnership (Gazely and Brudney 2007).

Empirical studies on this topic provide evidence that contracts for human services are best implemented when focused on creating partnerships and collaborations between nonprofits and government. Current issues related to contracting for social services—like Temporary Assistance for Needy Families (TANF) programs, job assistance, and childcare—reflect less of the old principal–agent dimensions of privatization and more of the community building and networking dynamics of partnership development (Austin 2003). Another study finds that, rather than assuming the traditional arm's length role of service delivery, state agencies overseeing human service contracts can accomplish more by adopting a partnering role with local nonprofit organizations (Poole 2003). Milward and Provan (2006) state that evidence shows that stability and collaboration are key elements of effective relationships between government and nonprofits. Lastly, researchers in Canada found that high levels of trust, respect, and collaboration produced positive outcomes. It was discovered that a participatory process with significant input from nonprofits into the establishment of standards, structure, and design diminished problems and contributed to a trusting and collaborative relationship in which both parties worked together smoothly to fulfill the common mission of providing services (Brown and Troutt 2004).

Effective collaboration between nonprofit organizations and government agencies is the ideal way to structure the human services system. Collaborative efforts are based on trust and stability, and require both partners to communicate regularly. Stability supports effective performance because it promotes coordination of services within a complex system. A stable system allows the different providers of services time to work out issues and agree on how to manage the system. Stability also allows the government to have enough time to learn how to "govern" the system, which includes getting to know the service providers and establishing the means to effectively monitor and evaluate services (Milward and Provan 2006). There is also evidence that a partnership approach to contracting has achieved much higher levels of performance in some federal contracting arenas (Denhardt 2003). In sum, attempting to bring into reality the expressed desire of both sectors to function through an integrated, collaborative partnership can result in significant performance improvements.

The advantages of collaboration are also being recognized in practice, as cities and states are creating collaborative contracting relationships with their nonprofit partners. New York, New Jersey, and Connecticut are a few examples of states that are currently designing new systems to guide a collaborative relationship. Making these systems work demands enormous investments, informal adjustments, and the building of trust among diverse state agencies, different levels of government, service providers, and community organizations (Austin 2003). In fact, nine states in the United States have realized the advantages of collaboration and have created state-level task forces to begin to discuss the collaborative relationship. The National Council of Nonprofits is working with these nine states to understand how these relationships are forming on the ground. One of the states leading the collaborative movement is Connecticut, with its creation of a Human Services Cabinet and a Nonprofit Liaison to the Governor. It is one of the first states to establish these positions and structures to guide the human services system and move it toward collaboration.

It is clear that there are many advantages of collaborative partnerships as a means of achieving public policy goals. Specifically, collaborative advantage involves creating synergies between organizations to enable them to achieve their objectives better than if they were acting alone (Huxham 1993). The idea of collaborative advantage presents an attractive alternative to the market, quasi-market, and contractualized relationships that have dominated the public management reform movement internationally in the past decade (Lowndes and Skelcher 1998, 313). Understanding the way that collaborative approaches may provide value is therefore an essential element in understanding how best to structure the shared service system. An important contribution to comes from the collaborative systems in the United Kingdom

The United Kingdom provides an example of how a model of partnership may be utilized in practice to achieve this lofty goal of "collaborative advantage." The public sector in the United Kingdom has been promoting the use of partnerships with private agencies for public service delivery for 15 years. Many organizations in the United Kingdom not only endorse the partnership idea but actively employ it as a programmatic tool for adapting to what they perceive as changing needs and circumstances (Linder 1999). Innovation in the United Kingdom has come in the form of strategies to develop interrelationships, trust, and collaborations in an environment of resource scarcity where organizations would typically be oriented to protect and defend themselves behind their walls of bureaucracy (Lowndes and Skelcher 1998). These innovative practices have produced an intersectoral partnership agreement called the Compact.

The above review of the nonprofit–government relationship provides the context and background of the human services system in the United States. This review has also clearly demonstrates the need for collaboration as best practice. Local government leaders have had considerable experience developing collaborative networks (Graddy and Chen 2006; Purdy 2012). This prior experience is extremely useful and will benefit the development of a shared service agreement. Also, municipal government managers will benefit from reviewing five lessons learned from the nonprofit–government experience. The five-point typology described below attempts to minimize obstacles to collaboration and maximize opportunities for successful shared service initiatives.

SHARING LESSONS LEARNED WITH THE MUNICIPAL GOVERNMENT MANAGER: THE FIVE-POINT TYPOLOGY IN COLLABORATIVE LEADERSHIP

Upon review of the nonprofit–government relationship, the major lesson learned is that collaboration is needed in the design of the contracting system. Collaboration is a difficult undertaking in any context because it implies a lack of structured hierarchy to formally organize the process. In collaborative settings, people organize differently due to the network structure of the environment. They also communicate and cooperate in different ways than in formal organizations. They share information, harmonize operations and activities, share resources, and enhance each partner's capacity (Gardner 1999; Lawson 2003, 2004). Most importantly, in effective collaborations, participating entities realize they are interdependent. For this reason, effective collaboration is characterized by relationships built on reciprocity, trust, mutual commitment, and a strong sense of joint ownership of positive outcomes. The lack of structure to guide the process can be a hurdle for municipal government managers to overcome, especially since this is quite different from the standard structure of government bureaucracies. Therefore, in order to effectively collaborate, municipal government leaders need specific skill sets that will help them achieve success in their shared service initiatives. This five-point typology is a useful framework for the local government manager because it identifies five issues that need special attention for collaboration to thrive in this unique environment.

1. Trust Is an Important Antecedent to Effective Collaboration

This is obvious, yet its importance cannot be underestimated. Trust has been found to be a precursor in most effective collaborations (Ansell and Gash 2008; Emerson, Nabatchi, and Balogh 2006) and also within the human services contracting system. It is possible for nonprofits and the government to have a lack of trust due to the different conceptions about sector differences. However, an effective collaboration must be mindful of the importance of trust in the relationship. In a study in New York, interviews conducted with public managers revealed the impact of trust on an effective partnership again and again. This study found that trust development can reduce costs; "[It] is affected by time, how power is shared, and the manner is [*sic*] which conflict is managed; and is an outcome based on a range of inputs and activities. . . . But trust development is also derived and therefore achieved based on the party's attitudes, values, and beliefs about exchange, reciprocity, resources, and the degree to which they are aligned. This issue of alignment is especially the case for contract relationships" (Van Slyke 2009, 151). Local government leaders can use this as a guiding post in how they select their partners; that is, they can choose to work with other municipalities with which they already have a working relationship or where know the agency staff well. Or if a shared service agreement is forced upon two governments, the leaders involved must identify ways in which trust can be built into the relationship.

2. Examine Your Shared Service Initiative as Connected to a Broader System

In addition to cultivating trust in a relationship, municipal managers involved in the creation of shared services can increase collaborative efforts by viewing the process through a systems lens. How will this shared service affect other agencies in the community, whether public, nonprofit, or private? A study on community health collaboration (Alexander et al. 2001) found that the best leaders were the ones who formed collaborative competencies that viewed the entire system and not just their individual contract. Nonprofit leaders who have a systems mindset and who can cultivate a systems perspective can and will operate more effectively than those who do not. The opposite of this is to view the nonprofit–government relations as dyadic—existing between just one nonprofit organization and one government agency. However, the municipal government leader who views contracts as just the starting point for the whole system of contracting will have a broader perspective on the collaborative and an increased capacity to work within the system as a whole.

3. Create a Very Specific Agreement That Makes the Roles and Responsibilities Clear

After testing a number of propositions from the literature about what should lead to effective collaborative service—such as the perceived trustworthiness of partners, the openness of decision making, information and resource sharing—Graddy and Chen (2006) concluded that the best predictor of success is the presence of a written formal contract that defines "the roles and responsibilities" of the different entities involved. Leaders can begin to advocate for this and communicate how it will help both parties work together better. This process will also highlight any structural or funding mechanisms that can create problems when trying to share services. Parties to the contract should know at the outset that there will be structural constraints due to funding arrangements, but should work though these problems to overcome barriers to effective collaboration. Both parties must remember that they are mutually dependent on each other and a document that clearly outlines their specific roles and responsibilities will reinforce this mutual dependence. Using this framework, local government leaders can use their power to engage and communicate with their counterparts in an effective and productive way.

4. Utilize a Pragmatic and Empathetic Approach to Your Partner's Unique Situation

There are structural, environmental, and cultural differences between nonprofits and the government. For example, certain constraints exist that are mostly due to the way block grants are designed from the federal to state to local government. These issues can create oversight and structural reporting requirements that are due to the block grants and not the state or local government agency. When viewed by nonprofit leaders empathetically, items that could cause conflict in the relationship are instead understood as items of structural rigidity and constraint. An effective partner views the situation from a pragmatic perspective, understanding that certain rules and structures can exist to constrain the working relationship. In addition, the partners must also empathize with the structural, environmental, and cultural differences that may exist. It is important for each partner to understand the unique contributions of the other partners and to also know that there are unique realities that create their partners' situation. Municipal government leaders who are both pragmatic and empathetic to the issues facing their partners will be more successful in creating a lasting collaboration.

5. Understand the Importance of Communication Between Frontline Workers and the Municipal Managers

The contracting environment changes the communication and feedback loops that exist within government agencies. In a traditional service delivery system where the government agency provides the service, there are institutional systems that foster and influence communication between those on the front lines and those in leadership positions. This institutional design is disrupted when services are contracted out. For example, in a study analyzing the street-level performance of nonprofits in contracted programs, Sandfort (1999) finds that social policies are actually enacted through the interpretations of staff and their interactions with policy clients. Rather than being externally imposed through formal arrangements or rules, she finds that structure is more fluid and dependent on the internal social culture of the organizations. In this way, collaboration must be viewed as a continual process and feedback must be sought through every channel possible. Municipal government managers will create a more effective shared service arrangement when new feedback and communication channels are constructed.

Municipal managers need to develop a unique set of collaborative leadership skills when they operate within their shared service arrangements. One agency has power because they are the principals in the contract—they provide the funding, scope, and types of services. However, the partnering agency, or the agents in the contract, must realize that they too have power in this relationship as they are the direct service providers. Planning is of vital importance to ensure that the shared service arrangements are properly designed in a collaborative fashion. The plan needs to include important concerns such as the role of trust and communication, the overall impact of this arrangement on the region, and clarity on the specific roles and responsibilities of each partner. These are not easy accomplishments and great care must be taken to design the agreements with as much foresight and consideration as possible. This five-point typology specifically reinvents issues that could become obstacles to collaboration, and remakes them into opportunities for the public manager to prepare for the challenges of collaboration. By understanding these five issues and their importance to creating collaborative frameworks, the municipal government manager can craft a more effective system of shared services.

Table 5.1

Framework for Building a Successful Shared Service Initiative

1.	The importance of cultivating trust	How can the structure of the shared service relationship focus on building and maintaining trust? Are there specific ways in which the partners can identify the current level of trust? Are there certain partners that should be considered or not be considered because of existing trust or lack of trust?
2.	Broader regional/ systemic issues considered	How does this individual shared service arrangement impact the region? What other services are being shared? How does the vision of the shared service initiative connect to the broader strategic goals for this region?
3.	Roles and responsibilities need to be clear	How are the roles of the principal different from those of the agent? What are the specific responsibilities of each? How can these be identified and communicated effectively?
4.	Empathy is needed	How can the leadership from each government agency promote empathy and understanding about the unique constraints and opportunities that exist for both partners? How can these be effectively and efficiently identified?
5.	Communication channels are important	How can the front-line service providers communicate most effectively with all parties involved? How can the partners design a system that includes effective and efficient communication channels? How does the implementation of effective communication systems impact service delivery?

CREATING A SUCCESSFUL SHARED SERVICE INITIATIVE

Creating and facilitating collaborative partnerships is the best way to craft the relationship between nonprofits and government. Creating a shared service agreement using a collaborative governance design also is the ideal way to craft these arrangements. However, collaboration is an extremely difficult undertaking. Much of the difficulty comes from the fact that there is a lack of structured hierarchy in collaboration. Therefore, developing a shared service arrangement in a collaborative way can be a daunting task for the municipal government manager. Lessons learned from the nonprofit–government experience with collaboration become instructive and can be quite useful to the municipal manager who is about to start a shared service agreement or is already involved in one.

The above five-point typology can be a starting point in helping government leaders craft successful shared service initiatives. These five issues have been identified as a way to begin to think about collaboration. The next step is for the municipal government manager to consider how each of these five issues impacts their unique circumstances. Table 5.1 provides a framework for the municipal government manager to help build a successful collaborative shared service arrangement.

CONCLUSION

The purpose of this chapter is to discuss lessons from the nonprofit–government relationship that can be used as a guide in creating a shared service relationship. Nonprofits and government have been sharing services through the use of contracts for many years. Very often, shared service arrangements are provided through the use of contracts. Therefore, reviewing lessons learned in the nonprofit–government relationship is a useful exercise in crafting shared service arrangements. Nonprofit–government best practice recommends that partners in this service delivery system approach it using a collaborative framework. This lesson can and should also be applied to the municipal government managers who are designing shared services.

Collaboration is a uniquely challenging enterprise within the contracting environment. Municipal managers can learn how to avoid certain obstacles to collaboration by heeding advice from the nonprofit–government experience. Rather than be passive agents in the shared service system, municipal government managers can take an active role and begin to create a framework that prepares them for effective collaboration. When embarking on a new shared service initiative, local government leaders should pay careful attention to not only *what* services should be shared but also *how* the system for sharing the services is designed. In so doing, they will assure that the shared service model has greater likelihood for success and, equally important, that effective services will result for their constituents.

KEY POINTS

- Specific lessons can be learned from the nonprofit–government experience, as they have been sharing services for more than 50 years. Reviewing how the nonprofit–government shared service system has evolved and discussing the best practices in the nonprofit–government relationship is a useful way to for municipal managers to plan effective shared service arrangements.
- Current best practice in the nonprofit–government relationship focuses primarily on collaboration and creating effective partnerships. Collaboration is a uniquely challenging enterprise in any environment, and particularly difficult when using contracts. Municipal managers can learn how to avoid certain obstacles when creating a collaborative shared service contract by heeding advice from the nonprofit–government experience.
- A five-point typology is proposed to share specific lessons learned with the municipal government manager on how to influence the creation of a collaborative shared service partnership. This typology attempts to minimize obstacles to collaboration and maximize opportunities for successful shared service initiatives.
- Five important issues for the municipal government manager to consider are included in the typology. These are (1) the importance of cultivating trust, (2) ensuring that broader regional/systemic issues are considered, (3) making certain that roles and responsibilities are clear, (4) realizing that empathy is needed in the collaboration, and (5) focusing on the creation of effective communication channels.

REFERENCES

Abramovitz, Mimi. 2002. *In Jeopardy: The Impact of Welfare Reform on Nonprofit Human Service Agencies in New York City*. New York: Task Force on Welfare Reform, New York City Chapter, National Association of Social Workers.

Alexander, Jeffrey A., Maureen B. Comfort, Bryan J. Weiner, and Richard Bogue. 2001. Leadership in collaborative community health partnerships. *Nonprofit Management and Leadership* 12(2): 159–175.

Ansell, Chris, and Alison Gash. 2008. Collaborative governance in theory and practice. *Journal of Public Administration Research and Theory* 18(4): 543–571.

Austin, Michael. 2003. The changing relationship between nonprofit organizations and public social service agencies in the era of welfare reform. *Nonprofit and Voluntary Sector Quarterly* 15(1): 97–114.

Baines, Donna. 2010. Neoliberal restructuring, activism/participation and social unionism in the non-profit social services. *Nonprofit and Voluntary Sector Quarterly* 39(1): 10–28.

Boris, Elizabeth, Edward de Leon, Katie L. Roeger, and Milena Nikolova. 2010. *Human Service Nonprofits and Government Collaboration: Findings from the 2010 National Survey of Nonprofit Government Contracting and Grants.* Washington, DC: The Urban Institute Center on Nonprofits and Philanthropy.

Brown, Laura K., and Elizabeth Troutt. 2004. Funding relationships between nonprofits and government: A positive example. *Nonprofit and Voluntary Sector Quarterly* 33(2): 5–27.

Denhardt, Kathryn. 2003. The procurement partnership model: Moving to a team-based approach. New Ways to Manage Series, IBM Endowment for the Business of Government. Retrieved from: www.businessofgovernment.org/sites/default/files/ProcurementPartnership.pdf.

Denhardt, Kathryn, Deborah Auger, Maria Aristigueta, and Lauren Miltenberger. 2008. Forward together project: Research report. Newark: University of Delaware.

Emerson, Kirk, Tina Nabatchi, and Stephen Balogh. 2011. An integrative framework for collaborative governance. *Journal of Public Administration Research and Theory 22* (1): 1–29.

Gardner, S. 1999. *Beyond Collaboration to Results: Hard Choice in the Future of Service to Children and Families.* Tempe and Fullerton: Arizona Prevention Resource Center and the Center for Collaboration for Children, California State University.

Gazely, Beth, and Jeffrey Brudney. 2007. The purpose (and perils) of government-nonprofit partnership. *Nonprofit and Voluntary Sector Quarterly* 36(3): 389–415.

Gilbert, Neil. 1983. *Capitalism and the Welfare State: Dilemmas of Social Benevolence.* New Haven, CT: Yale University Press.

Graddy, Elizabeth, and Bin Chen. 2006. Influences on the size and scope of networks for social service delivery. *Journal of Public Administration Research and Theory* 16(4): 533–552.

Gronbjerg, Kirsten, and Lester M. Salamon. 2002. Devolution, marketization, and the changing shape of government-nonprofit relations. In *The State of Nonprofit America*, ed. L.M. Salamon. Washington, DC: Brookings Institution Press.

Hall, Peter D. 1992. *Inventing the Nonprofit Sector and Other Essays on Philanthropy, Voluntarism and Nonprofit Organizations*. Baltimore, MD: Johns Hopkins University Press.

Holzer, Marc, and John Fry. 2010. Shared services and municipal consolidation: Pursuing careful assumptions and grounded studies. *Friends of Local Government Policy Paper* 2(1). Trenton, NJ: NJLM Educational Foundation.

Huxham, Chris. 1993. Pursuing collaborative advantage. *Journal of the Operational Research Society* 44(6): 59–78.

Lawson, Hal. 2003. Pursuing and securing collaboration to improve results. In *Meeting at the Hyphen: Schools-Universities-Communities-Professions in Collaboration for Student Achievement and Well Being,* ed. M. Brabeck and M. Walsh, 45–73. (Yearbook of the National Society for the Study of Education). Chicago: University of Chicago Press.

———. 2004. The logic of collaboration in education and the human services. *The Journal of Interprofessional Care 18*(3): 225–237.

Linder, Stephen H. 1999. Coming to terms with the public-private partnership. *American Behavioral Scientist* 43(1): 35–51

Lowndes, Vivien, and Chris Skelcher. 1998. The dynamics of multi-organizational partnerships: An analysis of changing modes of governance. *Public Administration* 76(2): 313–333.

Lynn, Laurence E. 2002. Social services and the state: The public appropriation of private charity. *Social Service Review* 76(1): 58–82.

Milward, H. Brinton, and Keith Provan. 2000. Governing the hollow state. *Journal of Public Administration Research and Theory* 10(2): 359–379.

———. 2006. *A Manager's Guide to Choosing and Using Collaborative Networks*. Washington, DC: IBM Center for The Business of Government.

Nathan, Richard P. 1996. The "nonprofitization movement" as a form of devolution. In *Capacity for Change? The Nonprofit World in the Age of Devolution,* ed. D.F. Burlingame, W.A. Diaz, and W.F. Ilchman and Assoc. Indianapolis: The Center on Philanthropy at Indiana University.

Poole, Dennis L. 2003. Scaling up CBO's for second-order devolution in welfare reform. *Nonprofit Management and Leadership* 13(4): 325–341.

Salamon, Lester M. 1995. *Partners in Public Service: Government-nonprofit Relations in the Modern Welfare State*. Baltimore, MD: Johns Hopkins University Press.

Sandfort, Jodi. 1999. The structural impediments to human service collaboration: Examining welfare reform at the front lines. *Social Service Review* 73(3): 314–339.

Smith, Steven R., and Michael Lipsky. 1993. *Nonprofits for Hire: The Welfare State in the Age of Contracting.* Cambridge, MA: Harvard University Press.

Suarez, David F. 2011. Collaboration and professionalization: The contours of public sector funding for nonprofit organizations. *Journal of Public Administration Research and Theory* 21(2): 307–326.

Van Slyke, David M. 2003. The mythology of privatization in contracting for social services. *Public Administration Review* 63(3): 296–314.

———. 2009. Collaboration and relational contracting. In *The Collaborative Public Manager: New Ideas for the Twenty-First Century,* ed. Rosemary O'Leary and Lisa Blomgren Bingham, 137–156. Washington, DC: Georgetown University Press.

Wood, Donna J., and Barbara Gray. 1991. Toward a comprehensive theory of collaboration. *Journal of Applied Behavioral Science* 27(2): 139–162.

6

Managing Interlocal Contracts and Shared Service Relationships

Eric S. Zeemering

When municipalities decide to share, contract, or consolidate services with other local governments, the adoption of an agreement and the implementation of the new service model represent the culmination of months or even years of analysis, bargaining, and staff work. Officials are eager to report immediate successes related to service cost or quality. Soon, the new and innovative service model becomes the routine method of service delivery. As managers and policymakers turn their attention to other pressing problems, interlocal relationships run the risk of atrophy, decay, and underperformance if systems are not in place for oversight, evaluation, and adjustment. Local government officials should think about interlocal agreements as relationships that require active management and regular oversight. Practical and theoretically grounded approaches are available to help officials maintain strong interlocal relationships.

This chapter explains why interlocal relationships require active oversight and maintenance. Research on shared service delivery and contract management provides a foundation for thinking about shared services as relationships that require ongoing maintenance, and additional insights can be drawn from political science research on legislative and democratic oversight of public agencies. This chapter also augments what we already know from existing studies with some descriptions of how interlocal cooperation is maintained by cities in the San Francisco Bay Area. On the one hand, being a good manager of shared services may entail what Steven Kelman (2011) labels being a good "plain-vanilla manager." In this line of thinking, local government managers concerned with the success of shared services should give attention to the same areas that might get attention if the service was provided by their jurisdiction alone. For example, performance measures, budgets, and financial management may require managerial oversight even if a service is obtained through a contract relationship. On the other hand, shared service management requires local governments to engage in good management practices *with partners*. Managing with partners may involve tackling new challenges related to trust, communication, and political control of the bureaucracy. Local government officials must invest in the ongoing monitoring of shared service relationships and work with their partners to adapt services to changing conditions and expectations. The promised benefits of interlocal cooperation and shared services can only be achieved with ongoing management and the tending of cooperative relationships.

THE ECONOMICS AND POLITICS OF INTERLOCAL AGREEMENTS

Interlocal contracts and formal agreements for shared services between two or more local governments are the focus of this chapter, and the term "interlocal agreements" will be used to refer to this class of relationships. Interlocal agreements have a rich history in communities across the United States (e.g., Stewart and Ketcham 1941; Friesema 1971; Miller 1981; Stein 1990). While the direct in-house delivery of a service remains the most popular method of service production by municipal governments, recent data from the International City/County Management Association (ICMA) suggest interlocal contracts are growing in popularity, with high levels of interlocal contracting in areas such as health and human services, transit, libraries, and tax assessment (Warner and Hefetz 2009). Contracting with other governments may be a popular option for services that entail some risk of contract failure, making a government vendor a preferred option to a private sector service provider (Brown 2008). Local government leaders may also be seeking new and innovative service delivery models. While limited research has been conducted to evaluate the outcomes of interlocal agreements, local officials tend to report satisfaction with these arrangements (Chen and Thurmaier 2009; Wood 2008).

The growth of interlocal agreements is important because this cooperative interaction helps us better understand economic and political choices in local communities. Economic considerations are salient among the public officials negotiating interlocal agreements. Vincent and Elinor Ostrom (1965) encouraged scholars to think about local government service provision using an industry model. The division of local government authority among many municipalities within a metropolitan area has the potential to yield many competing service providers, each striving to provide efficient service. Public agencies seek to maintain their funding and satisfy mobile residents who may choose to move elsewhere if public services do not meet with their expectations. In any given service or industry, incentives may exist to work across local government boundaries in order to take advantage of different technologies, economies of scale, or specialized information. Interlocal contracts and service sharing agreements provide mechanisms to adjust services to meet the economic needs of local communities.[1] If industry structure and market factors are at the forefront of concern, the management of interlocal agreements requires ongoing evaluation of production costs, evaluation of service quality and customer satisfaction, and comparison of service and work processes to other industry competitors. In this line of thinking, local government managers responsible for managing interlocal agreements should invest in skills that will help them evaluate the market of municipal service providers, craft clear language in service contracts, and design performance measures and reports that will help their city judge the quality of services provided by other governments. However, this would not be sufficient preparation to manage interlocal agreements.

Interlocal agreements also involve political choices and intergovernmental relations. In *Governing Local Public Economies: Creating the Civic Metropolis*, Ronald Oakerson (1999) explains that different communities make different judgments about the appropriate scale of service production and the appropriate number of local government units to provide services. "Different communities arrive at different trade-offs. This means that some parts of a metropolitan area may provide services in one way, while others' [*sic*] parts choose different arrangements," writes Oakerson (1999, 117). Oakerson asks us to consider how public preferences for service delivery shape the design of municipal services. In order to identify areas in which local governments can work together, we would not only need to understand their technical capacity to provide the service, but also the underlying political preferences about how that service should be delivered. Thurmaier and Wood (2002) explain that interlocal agreements have the potential to tie metropolitan areas together in networks of cooperation. In order to achieve this cooperation, politicians and the general public may need to recognize common interests with their neighbors and come to consensus on shared values in public service delivery.

To successfully manage interlocal agreements, local government officials must make explicit the values that guide service delivery within their communities. While officials may claim that efficiency or cost effectiveness are their most important priorities in service delivery, public administration scholars have emphasized that a wide range of additional values inform decision making in a democratic polity (Bozeman 2007). Public sentiment about working with neighboring governments shapes both the opportunity and the ongoing challenges for shared services. Public managers responsible for the oversight and maintenance of interlocal agreements must be aware of the political support that was necessary to move toward a shared service model. Politicians and public managers may make explicit in written agreements the unique concerns of participating communities, but often this is not the case. As a result, public managers responsible for shared services must develop skills as an intergovernmental liaison, brokering a common understanding of service goals and expectations among the participating political jurisdictions. This may require more dialogue with politicians or the general public than is expected of the managers of in-house services. Maintaining interlocal agreements requires not only technical skills and contract management capacity, but also attention to the political support necessary to maintain cooperation.

Along with the expanded use of interlocal agreements has come the development of stronger theoretical frameworks for analyzing cooperative local governance. Local governments engage in interlocal cooperation through various mechanisms with different degrees of formalization and different consequences for the conduct of joint action (Ostrom, Parks, and Whitaker 1999; Feiock 2009; Feiock and Scholz 2010). The institutional collective action (ICA) framework articulated by Richard Feiock (2007, 2008) and his research collaborators provides one important theoretical foundation for analyzing cooperative local governance. The ICA framework draws from transaction cost economics and focuses attention on the costs and benefits associated with organizing and maintaining cooperation. This theoretical framework is helpful for students and practitioners because it highlights factors that are critical to the management of cooperative relationships among governments. Two factors are highlighted in this chapter on the management of interlocal agreements—the selection of mechanisms that join governments together, and the social network connections among governments (see Figure 6.1).

First, different mechanisms or tools can be used to join municipalities together in

Figure 6.1 **Areas of Focus for Interlocal Agreement Management**

1. Mechanisms

Local governments choose different mechanisms of cooperation to work together and share services. State laws outline the specific approaches local governments can use for cooperation on service delivery. Common approaches to cooperation include:

- Contracts to buy or sell a specific service
- Establishment of a special-purpose government or authority
- Networks of independent agencies working together

2. Communication

Ongoing patterns of communication among public officials, or social networks, can help governments identify new opportunities to share services and coordinate ongoing cooperation. Government officials communicate regularly through various channels, including:

- Direct one-on-one conversations with public officials from other local governments
- Local meetings of all city managers or mayors in a county or region
- Professional working groups for department managers, such as police chiefs or public works directors
- Statewide associations of city or county officials

cooperation, each with distinct cost and benefit structures for the participating governments (Feiock 2009). For example, two cooperative mechanisms are commonly used by local governments in California—contracts for service and joint powers agreements (Margo 1992). Contracts between governments formalize a buyer–seller relationship, in which one government pays a fee for service to another government that is responsible for producing, staffing, and managing the service. While the terms of the contract may be renegotiated periodically, the government purchasing the service may have limited involvement in day-to-day decision making about the service. In contrast, the establishment of a joint powers authority (JPA) allows two or more governments to create a quasi-independent public entity that is jointly governed and managed by the participating governments. This mechanism for cooperation more closely approximates the joint production or sharing of a service than the buyer–seller relationship established under a contract for service. The participating governments may favor this mechanism if they hope to maintain more direct involvement with the governance and management of the service. While interlocal agreements may be beneficial to a set of municipalities at one point in time, we must be aware that the balance of costs and benefits can shift over time, or that officials might prefer to change the mechanisms used for cooperation in order to achieve different results.

Second, research under the ICA framework also shows that the social networks of public officials have the potential to bridge communities in cooperation by serving as a conduit for information and reducing uncertainty (e.g., Carr, LeRoux, and Shrestha 2009; Feiock, Steinacker, and Park 2009; Feiock et al. 2010; Shrestha and Feiock 2009). With interlocal agreements comes ongoing dialogue among public officials. Understanding how public officials and municipalities are tied together in social interaction and in other cooperative governance relationships can help us better understand how they monitor and maintain shared services. City managers and elected officials within a county or metropolitan area may meet on a regular basis to discuss shared challenges that spill over municipal boundaries. Other local government professionals, like police chiefs or public works directors, also talk with their counterparts in neighboring cities. Good working relationships among government officials can help city officials identify problems with interlocal agreements before they escalate to a point at which relationships are damaged. Studying the frequency of intergovernmental communication, and knowing which officials maintain strong intergovernmental networks, can help us better understand the social links that support the management of interlocal agreements.

SHARED SERVICE OVERSIGHT: AN EXAMPLE FROM THE SAN FRANCISCO BAY AREA

Before outlining some principles city officials should consider when structuring the management and oversight of interlocal agreements, we might hope for some evidence about the extent to which city officials currently check up on interlocal agreements. The San Francisco Bay Area provides an opportunity to examine the scope of shared service oversight. In order to better understand how communities oversee and maintain interlocal agreements, I collected an array of data on local government service delivery from cities in the San Francisco Bay Area between 2008 and 2011. California cities have extensive experience with interlocal agreements, making the nine-county San Francisco Bay Area an ideal region in which to investigate the ongoing dynamics of interlocal cooperation (Sonenblum, Kirlin, and Ries 1977; Joassart-Marcelli and Musso 2005). Through in-depth interviews with city managers and a survey of elected officials, I asked local government officials about how they oversee services provided through interlocal agreements.

City managers in the metropolitan region report a variety of approaches to monitoring services provided to their governments through interlocal contracts or through California's JPA mechanism.[2] Most commonly, city managers report checking up on shared services with department heads, reviewing performance data, or directly observing work—the same methods that city managers might use to oversee services directly produced within their own jurisdictions. For shared services managed by a JPA, managers also report attending meetings and reading JPA board meeting minutes as methods of monitoring services. Consistent with the ICA framework's attention to social networks, city managers also reported communications with other city managers, either directly or through countywide meetings of local managers, as important approaches to keeping tabs on shared services. These social network approaches to service monitoring were more frequently mentioned for services that were multi-jurisdictional in nature, in contrast to services shared by only two units of government. Future research should more systematically scrutinize how city managers use their social networks to oversee or obtain information about shared services.

Some scholars express concern that the move toward multi-jurisdictional problem solving has attenuated the accountability relationship between formal government institutions and public policy (Catlaw 2009). Based on these concerns, we can hypothesize

Table 6.1

Manager Reports of Public Feedback about Service Delivery

	Low (1–2)	Medium (3–5)	High (6–7)	Mean
Police				
City Production	18.2% (6)	57.6% (19)	24.2% (8)	4.15
Interlocal/External	25% (2)	75% (6)	0% (0)	3.50
Fire				
City Production	14.3% (2)	64.3% (9)	21.4% (3)	3.68
Interlocal/External	37% (10)	48.1% (13)	14.8% (4)	3.39
Parks and Recreation				
City Production	8% (2)	68% (17)	24% (6)	4.32
Interlocal/External	25% (1)	50% (2)	25% (1)	4.20
Library				
City Production	16.7% (1)	50% (3)	33.3% (2)	4.00
Interlocal/External	46.2% (12)	46.2% (12)	7.7% (2)	2.92

Note: The frequency or number of responses in each category is listed in parentheses below the percentage.

that city managers will report less public feedback about services that their jurisdiction provides through an interlocal agreement. City managers were asked how frequently they hear feedback from the public, and they offered their responses on a Likert scale ranging from infrequently (1) to very frequently (7). The frequency of public feedback for four services is reported in Table 6.1. For police, fire, parks and recreation, and library services, managers appear to receive medium levels of feedback from the public, the modal category in Table 6.1. This is true for services produced directly by the city or through an interlocal agreement or external service provider, such as a special district. Comparing the mean level of feedback for internal production versus interlocal agreement for each service, managers appear to receive similar levels of feedback. The only service with a statistically discernible lower level of citizen feedback to city managers is library service, a service for which county governments are the primary service providers, with cities often providing and maintaining facilities but not operations. While interlocal agreements may channel citizen feedback away from city managers for some services like libraries, we cannot conclude that service production through interlocal agreements uniformly reduces levels of public feedback.

What role do local elected officials play in the oversight of interlocal agreements? In an effort to better understand how local elected officials monitor and evaluate shared service relationships on an ongoing basis, a survey of city council members and mayors in the

San Francisco Bay Area asked respondents several questions about their cities' existing shared service relationships.[3] City council members seek information from formal channels within city hall, but also use their social networks and relationships outside of the city to learn more about shared service delivery. On a seven-point Likert scale, respondents attributed a high level of importance to the information they receive about shared services from the city manager (6.6), department heads (6.1), and staff reports and government documents (6.0). Colleagues on the city council (5.6) and countywide meetings of elected officials (5.5) were also assessed as important sources of information.

The survey asked, "How likely are you to check up on or conduct oversight of services that your city shares or contracts with other local governments?" Over 74 percent of respondents reported they are very likely to oversee shared services, with only about 5 percent reporting that they were somewhat or very unlikely to monitor shared services. This high level of reported oversight in part may reflect a social-desirability affect in survey research, with elected officials viewing a positive response as consistent with their job responsibilities. Additional questions help us probe deeper into the level of monitoring by elected officials. The survey respondents were asked to identify an example of a service shared by their city government, and then were asked, "As a city council member or mayor, have you ever suggested a change to this contract or JPA relationship?" Only 37 percent of respondents indicated that they had requested a change to an existing shared service relationship. This number probably more accurately reflects the proportion of elected officials giving detailed attention to shared service relationships.

In order to better understand the adjustments that elected officials seek in shared service relationships, respondents were asked to explain what changes they had requested to their shared service relationship, and why they requested that change. Among the elected officials who requested a change, 32 percent expressed interest in reviewing other options for service delivery. Within this category, a few officials reported that they were involved with the initial move to a shared service model and expressed support for working with intergovernmental partners on service delivery. However, interest in reviewing methods of service delivery also hints that elected officials do not view shared service models as permanent or unchangeable. Several reported interest in seeing analysis of whether or not a return to jurisdiction-based service production would yield better service. Other officials report an interest in expanding existing shared services by bringing in new partners.

Related to the elected officials' concerns about service delivery methods is concern about governance. Of those reporting a request to change an existing shared service arrangement, about 18 percent asked for changes to the terms of governance. Governance concerns included requests for the reporting of information about shared services to elected officials, as well as requests for the involvement of elected officials in decision making. For example, one official expressed concern that an elected official should represent the city on the JPA board, rather than an administrative official from the city. About 20 percent of the elected officials requesting a change to a shared service arrangement identified concerns about the distribution of costs, or cost escalations over time. These survey responses suggest that some elected officials seek to evaluate and influence the implementation and ongoing work of shared service arrangements. Future research should investigate the range of methods elected officials use to monitor shared services, and scrutinize the range of activities that fall between the survey respondents who report monitoring a service and the smaller number who report requesting specific changes to their city's shared services.

From cities in the San Francisco Bay Area, we have a tentative sketch of the scope of interlocal agreement oversight by city managers and elected officials. Both public managers and elected officials have roles to play in the oversight of interlocal agreements, and research in public administration and political science illuminates areas in which public officials can focus their efforts.

DEVELOPING MANAGEMENT CAPACITY AND DEMOCRATIC OVERSIGHT

Local government officials who seek to improve their interlocal agreements can focus attention on two key areas. First, public managers must give attention to the capacity of government to manage contract relationships. Second, both managers and elected officials must design pathways of feedback so that governments can assess public satisfaction with services delivered through interlocal agreements.

Creating Contract Management Capacity

Local governments, especially those within metropolitan communities, have long known the importance of intergovernmental cooperation with neighbors (Gulick 1962; Williams et al. 1965; Wright 1973). Government reform trends at work around the globe in the late twentieth century pressured more municipalities to consider which tasks or services could be delivered through market-based approaches (Osborne and Gaebler 1992; Kettl 1997; Peters and Pierre 1998; Ruhil et al. 1999). With expanded contracting, scholars have attempted to develop better explanations of contracting behavior. Municipal contracting research is now often theoretically grounded in transaction cost economics. Transaction cost economics draws attention to the costs associated with maintaining economic exchange (Williamson 1981). When municipalities contract for service delivery, the up-front costs of investing in assets or the costs of monitoring a vendor may figure into the overall estimation of the benefit of contracting for a service versus producing the service directly within the municipal bureaucracy (Brown and Potoski 2003b). Municipalities engaged in interlocal agreements must consider the transaction costs associated with this form of service delivery, and must be especially attentive to the costs of developing the capacity to manage interlocal agreements on an ongoing basis.

In *Governing by Contract*, Phillip Cooper (2003, 101) writes, "Good contract administration is about building and maintaining a positive and effective working relationship that ensures a good deal for the public in the operation of the contract and not just in the selection of a bidder or the drafting of the contract." What is contract management capacity? While definitions and measures of this concept vary across studies, contract management capacity commonly refers to the ability of governments to (1) determine whether a service should be produced internally or through a contract with another party, (2) assess the market of potential service providers, (3) negotiate and develop a contract, (4) work with selected contractors to deliver a service and make adjustments as needed over time, and (5) evaluate the performance of the service and the satisfaction of goals associated with the contract (c.f., Brown and Potoski 2003a, 2004; Brown, Potoski, and Van Slyke 2006; Cooper 2003; Curry 2010; Johnston, Romzek, and Wood 2004).

Using contract management capacity as a framework for thinking about research on interlocal agreements, existing research provides insight into which municipalities adopt interlocal agreements and for which services these tools are used (e.g., Carr, Gerber, and Lupher 2009; LeRoux and Carr 2007; Morgan and Hirlinger 1991; Wood 2006). Following an industry metaphor, scholars frequently conceptualize metropolitan areas as a market of service producers (Ostrom, Tiebout, and Warren 1961; Parks and Oakerson 2000). Municipalities appear to be adroit at assessing opportunities to directly produce or purchase services from another provider (Sonenblum, Kirlin, and Ries 1977; Stein 1990; Oakerson 1999), though the professional and academic literatures do not provide clear guidelines or recommendations for systematically analyzing these choices. So, while we still might want to know more about how municipalities make choices about service production and local service markets, public administration scholars do give attention to these aspects of contract management capacity as applied to the use of interlocal agreements.

The implementation and ongoing administration of interlocal agreements are aspects of contract management capacity that have not received much scrutiny. In short, what makes interlocal agreements work on a day-to-day basis? In a study of state agency contract implementation, Romzek and Johnston (2002) conclude contract effectiveness will be enhanced when adequate resources are provided for the contract task, when careful planning occurs for contractor performance measurement, when staff responsible for contract management receive intensive training, and when contractor staff capacity is carefully evaluated, among other factors. Developing collaborative implementation relationships based on trust between the government buyer and seller may be critical to the long-term performance of contract relationships (Van Slyke and Hammonds 2003; Yang, Hsieh, and Li 2009). While research on contract implementation is limited, the advice that partners working together should develop trust through regular interaction is strongly supported by interdisciplinary research on other types of cooperative interaction. For example, experimental methods in economics and agent-based modeling have demonstrated that cooperation is improved through repeated interaction (Axelrod 1984; Ostrom and Walker 2003). Face-to-face interaction has also been shown to improve cooperation more than indirect communication (Ostrom, Gardner, and Walker 1994). These findings are robust not just in the laboratory, but also in field settings around the globe (Poteete, Janssen, and Ostrom 2010). When managing interlocal agreements, local managers can take these research findings seriously by instituting regular executive-level meetings to review the performance of shared services. While a municipality may eliminate or reduce service delivery staff, department heads or city executives may need additional training or support to monitor the intergovernmental service provider. Agreements can also designate department-level staff to serve as intergovernmental liaisons to help contract service providers better understand their community's geography, unique constituency demands, or past problems in service delivery. Establishing both executive and staff-level communications around interlocal agreements may ensure long-term success by giving attention to problems or unexpected service variations as they arise.

Governments may not develop sufficient contract management capacity, explains Cooper (2003), because agencies do not adequately budget for contract management and too few public employees have specialized training in contract management. Dissatisfaction with past contracting experiences, high transaction costs, and political conflict may prompt local government to improve contract management capacity (Brown and Potoski 2003a). Studies by Marvel and Marvel (2007, 2008) show local governments report lower levels of monitoring for services provided by other governments than for services provided through contract with private firms; and, municipalities are less likely to contract with other governments for services that require high levels of monitoring. Municipalities appear to adjust their contract management capacity over time. Joaquin and Greitens (2012), using ICMA survey data, found that over a 10-year period local governments reported lower capacity for some contract management activities, but higher capacity for contract evaluation. These studies might prompt municipalities with interlocal agreements to reconsider if they have adequate staff and structures in place to review services obtained from other governments. At the same time, municipalities may contract out performance monitoring or other management functions along with service delivery, resulting in an overestimation of the extent to which contracting reduces government management capacity (Brown and Potoski 2006). Interlocal agreements should specify what role, if any, the service provider will play in service monitoring and oversight.

In sum, the practices prescribed in the contract management literature provide local government managers with a foundation to maintain their interlocal agreements. From scrutinizing the market of potential service providers to maintaining performance measures to evaluate existing relationships, the capacities necessary to manage contract relationships with private firms are also relevant to intergovernmental relationships. Yet, interactions with neighboring governments within a political community are not fully parallel to economic exchange in the market.[4] Municipalities may prefer to think of interlocal agreements as cooperative, rather than competitive market interactions (e.g., DeHoog 1990). Additional theoretical lenses can shed more complete light on the challenges of maintaining interlocal relationships.

Understanding Legislative and Democratic Oversight

Existing research in public administration tends to describe public managers as the key players in interlocal cooperation. H. George Frederickson (1999), for example, advances a theory of administrative conjunction, arguing that the professional connections of city managers help identify opportunities for interlocal cooperation, bridging jurisdictional boundaries to solve complex regional problems (see also Matkin and Frederickson 2009; LeRoux, Brandenburger, and Pandey 2010). However, many interlocal agreements, especially those involving visible public services, require a vote of a local legislative body for approval. City councils express interest in the development of shared service agreements, often making inquiries about the distributions of costs and benefits, the consequences of shared services for city employees and employment policies, and the mechanisms available for governance and future service change (Zeemering 2008, 2012). We have good reasons to believe that municipal legislative bodies play a role in overseeing and ensuring the long-term success of shared services. If, as Oakerson (1999) suggests, the underlying preferences of the public help shape patterns of interlocal cooperation, then we should investigate areas in which these preferences might be articulated, including the work of elected officials. Both researchers and practitioners would benefit from a clearer understanding of the ongoing role of local elected officials in shared service efforts.

Extensive political science research describes how legislative bodies choose to exercise their oversight responsibilities over the bureaucracy (e.g., White 1945; Calvert, McCubbins, and Weingast 1989; Aberbach 1990; Wood and Waterman 1994; Huber and Shipan 2002), though few empirical studies explore how local legislative bodies monitor local government services. Research on legislative oversight and bureaucratic design in the U.S. national government highlights at least two lines of inquiry relevant to our understanding of interlocal agreements.

First, are shared services designed to maximize political control by elected officials, or to insulate services from political interference? When legislative bodies authorize the bureaucracy to implement public laws, they may grant varying degrees of discretion to the agencies based on the expertise present in the bureaucracy, political and policy uncertainty in the future, and the probability of change in the legislative coalitions that allowed authorization (Epstein and O'Halloran 1994; Bawn 1995; Balla 1998; Huber, Shipan, and Pfahler 2001). When adopting interlocal agreements to obtain services from another municipality or share services among multiple units, local officials must, explicitly or implicitly, make decisions about bureaucratic discretion and the extent to which local legislative bodies will be able to influence or shape the interlocal agreement through implementation or future policy change. Local legislative bodies may be less attentive to questions of bureaucratic discretion because they lack the professionalism of state or national legislative bodies (Krebs and Pelissero 2003), or because the professional norms of local government, especially in cities operating under the council–manager form of government, discourage legislative involvement in administration (Nalbandian 1991; Montjoy and Watson 1995). Those responsible for designing interlocal agreements should be aware that the design and implementation of the service delivery model has consequences for the level of discretion exercised by the bureaucracy and how public managers interact with politicians in the participating governments.

Second, how do local legislative bodies conduct oversight of shared services? McCubbins and Schwartz (1984) distinguish two types of congressional oversight—police patrols in which legislative committees actively investigate the bureaucracy's implementation of programs by conducting hearings and other investigations, and fire alarms in which programs are designed to provide opportunities for constituents or organized interests to alert legislative officials to problems when they occur. These forms of oversight are widely referenced in political science, yet are not employed in discussions about the oversight of interlocal agreements. One explanation for this gap is a general lack of attention to the design of oversight mechanisms for interlocal agreements by both scholars and practitioners. A better explanation might be that the performance management movement in public administration generally casts oversight as a managerial activity, even though many performance measures are designed for the consumption of legislative bodies and external constituencies (Behn 2003). For the future, careful discussions about the design of legislative oversight for interlocal agreements might benefit municipalities. Local elected officials should have some understanding of how they will be able to monitor and obtain information about the success or failure of shared services.

Finally, shared services may be held accountable to a democratic public through forums other than local legislative bodies. As policy development and public program implementation have moved into complex multi-organizational networks, some scholars express concern that the traditional institutions that bind collective policy decision making to the public, like legislatures, lose the capacity to ensure accountability (Catlaw 2009; Sørensen and Torfing 2005, 2007). When a municipality provides a service through an interlocal agreement, local officials must be able to explain to their residents how a service will remain accountable to their preferences even when provided by agencies and staff that are not directly under their municipality's control. Municipalities participating in shared services may create new institutions to anchor the service to the public in all participating communities. For example, a citizen advisory committee with representation from each participating jurisdiction may provide valuable feedback for public managers and may provide the public with a better working understanding of how shared services are implemented. Alternately, public managers may use citizen feedback surveys to evaluate public service satisfaction, comparing responses across units participating in the shared service. Whether democratic accountability of shared services comes through legislative or public oversight, municipalities should give careful thought to how their shared service models will be responsive to the public.

CONCLUSION

With an eye toward best practices for interlocal relationship management, successful management of interlocal relationships might entail what Kelman (2011) labels good "plain-vanilla management." For municipalities concerned about maintaining strong interlocal contract and shared service relationships, developing a strong capacity to manage contracts should be a primary concern. The latest research on contract management suggests municipalities develop specialized capacity in areas ranging from the analysis of which services are best delivered through contracts to the evaluation of contract relationships. Cities engaged in shared services should give special attention to the management capacity required to establish strong implementation relationships, in which the service buyer and seller develop patterns of communication and trust. However, the literature reviewed in this article and my research on shared services in cities from the San Francisco Bay area lead me to believe that the public officials who oversee interlocal service relationships need more than good management skills for their shared services to succeed.

Interlocal agreements bind local political communities together in economic exchange and political dialogue. Public administrators and elected officials recast services to serve multiple jurisdictions with different constituencies. Public officials would benefit from understanding how social networks tie their communities together and provide information channels to monitor their cooperative work. Municipalities participating in shared services should also consider how governments can demonstrate accountability to the public and elected legislative bodies in the participating jurisdictions.

With the growing importance of interlocal contracting and shared service models, scholars and practitioners should work together to develop robust evaluations of shared service management practices in order to scrutinize and share effective approaches to service oversight. Investigating interlocal cooperation can advance our understanding of the work of public managers as well as our theoretical understanding of the scale and operation of local governance. As we work together to evaluate shared service management, we must be attentive to the economic and managerial concerns associated with the delivery of municipal services, the operation of urban service industries, and the capacity of staff to manage contracts. We must also develop tools and approaches to assess how shared services shape collaborative governance relationships among communities, and how shared services remain democratically accountable to distinct local political communities.

KEY POINTS

- To successfully manage shared services, local governments must develop contract management skills within public agencies *and* develop plans for democratic oversight by elected officials and the public.
- Contract management capacity includes the ability to analyze whether a service should be provided internally or through an interlocal agreement. Contract management capacity also includes the ability to work with a contract partner over time to modify and improve the working relationship.
- Developing trust through regular, face-to-face interaction is important for successful contract management.
- Local governments must clarify the role for elected officials and the general public in providing oversight for a service no longer managed by one government alone.
- The public accountability of shared services may be improved through public forums and other plans to share information with and obtain feedback from the public.

NOTES

1. While our recent discussions of interlocal cooperation assume local governments adjust service provision to gain efficiencies or service improvements, Ostrom and Ostrom (1965), under the industry model, also discuss challenges related to collusion and information asymmetries, pointing to the possibility that the public might not always benefit from public service consolidation. While this concern was taken seriously in their subsequent research (e.g., McGinnis 1999, see Parts III and IV), recent studies of interlocal cooperation have not done enough to evaluate this important concern.

2. My research on interlocal cooperation in California involved the collection of secondary data from state government reports, in-depth interviews with city managers, and a mail survey of elected officials. Over 40 interviews were conducted with city managers in the San Francisco Bay Area between 2008 and 2011, inquiring about how a list of common local government services are organized, how managers monitor those services, and whether any changes were being considered to the organization of services. The semi-structured interviews provided an opportunity for the managers to discuss current service challenges in an open-ended format, but collected uniform data on how services are monitored and how often the managers receive feedback about the service from various constituencies. The interview approach for this project was a hybrid of practices recommended by Dexter (1970) and Aberbach, Chesney, and Rockman (1975). Additional details and the interview question list are available by request.

3. The survey was sent to 554 local elected officials in the 101 cities of the nine-county San Francisco Bay Area in California. The officials received an initial contact by postcard, followed by the survey, a reminder postcard, and a replacement survey for nonrespondents, following standard mail survey procedures (Dillman 2000). The data include responses from 153 elected officials (27.6 percent response rate) representing 76 different cities.

4. Indeed, ties among local governments may help compensate for some types of market failure, such as information asymmetries. For example, see Brown and Potoski's (2004) study of public management networks and refuse disposal in the Columbus, Ohio, metropolitan area.

REFERENCES

Aberbach, Joel D. 1990. *Keeping a Watchful Eye: The Politics of Congressional Oversight.* Washington, DC: Brookings Institution.

Aberbach, Joel D., James D. Chesney, and Bert A. Rockman. 1975. Exploring elite political attitudes: Some methodological lessons. *Political Methodology* 2(1): 1–27.

Axelrod, Robert M. 1984. *The Evolution of Cooperation.* New York: Basic Books.

Balla, Steven J. 1998. Administrative procedures and political control of the bureaucracy. *American Political Science Review* 92(3): 663–673.

Bawn, Kathleen. 1995. Political control versus expertise: Congressional choices about administrative procedures. *American Political Science Review* 89(1): 62–73.

Behn, Robert D. 2003. Why measure performance? Different purposes require different measures. *Public Administration Review* 63(5): 586–606.

Bozeman, Barry. 2007. *Public Values and Public Interest: Counterbalancing Economic Individualism.* Washington, DC: Georgetown University Press.

Brown, Trevor L. 2008. The dynamics of government-to-government contracts. *Public Performance & Management Review* 31(3): 364–386.

Brown, Trevor L., and Matthew Potoski. 2003a. Contract-management capacity in municipal and county governments. *Public Administration Review* 63(2): 153–164.

———. 2003b. Transaction costs and institutional explanations for government service production decisions. *Journal of Public Administration Research and Theory* 13(4): 441–468.

———. 2004. Managing the public service market. *Public Administration Review* 64(6): 656–668.

———. 2006. Contracting for management: Assessing management capacity under alternative service delivery arrangements. *Journal of Policy Analysis and Management* 25(2): 323–346.

Brown, Trevor L., Matthew Potoski, and David M. Van Slyke. 2006. Managing public service contracts: Aligning values, institutions, and markets. *Public Administration Review* 66(3): 323–331.

Calvert, Randall L., Mathew D. McCubbins, and Barry R. Weingast. 1989. A theory of political control and agency discretion. *American Journal of Political Science* 33(3): 588–611.

Carr, Jered B., Elisabeth R. Gerber, and Eric W. Lupher. 2009. Explaining horizontal and vertical cooperation on public services in Michigan: The role of local fiscal capacity. In *Sustaining Michigan:*

Metropolitan Policies and Strategies, ed. R. Jelier and G. Sands. East Lansing: Michigan State University Press.

Carr, Jered B., Kelly LeRoux, and Manoj Shrestha. 2009. Institutional ties, transaction costs, and external service production. *Urban Affairs Review* 44(3): 403–427.

Catlaw, Thomas J. 2009. Governance and networks at the limits of representation. *American Review of Public Administration* 39(5): 478–498.

Chen, Yu-Che, and Kurt Thurmaier. 2009. Interlocal agreements as collaborations: An empirical investigation of impetuses, norms, and success. *American Review of Public Administration* 39(5): 536–552.

Cooper, Phillip J. 2003. *Governing by Contract: Challenges and Opportunities for Public Managers.* Washington, DC: CQ Press.

Curry, William Sims. 2010. *Government Contracting: Promises and Perils.* Boca Raton, FL: CRC Press.

DeHoog, Ruth Hoogland. 1990. Competition, negotiation, or cooperation: Three models for service contracting. *Administration & Society* 22(3): 317–340.

Dexter, Lewis Anthony. 1970. *Elite and Specialized Interviewing*. Evanston, IL: Northwestern University Press.

Dillman, Don A. 2000. *Mail and Internet Surveys: The Tailored Design Method.* 2d ed. New York: John Wiley.

Epstein, David, and Sharyn O'Halloran. 1994. Administrative procedures, information, and agency discretion. *American Journal of Political Science* 38(3): 697–722.

Feiock, Richard C. 2007. Rational choice and regional governance. *Journal of Urban Affairs* 29(1): 47–63.

———. 2008. Institutional collective action and local government collaboration. In *Big Ideas in Collaborative Public Management*, ed. L.B. Bingham and R. O'Leary. Armonk, NY: M.E. Sharpe.

———. 2009. Metropolitan governance and institutional collective action. *Urban Affairs Review* 44(3): 356–377.

Feiock, Richard C., In Won Lee, Hyung-Jun Park, and Keon-Hyung Lee. 2010. Collaboration networks among local elected officials: Information, commitment, and risk aversion. *Urban Affairs Review* 46(2): 241–262.

Feiock, Richard C., and John T. Scholz. 2010. *Self-Organizing Federalism: Collaborative Mechanisms to Mitigate Institutional Collective Action Dilemmas*. New York: Cambridge University Press.

Feiock, Richard C., Annette Steinacker, and Hyung-Jun Park. 2009. Institutional collective action and economic development joint ventures. *Public Administration Review* 69(2): 256–270.

Frederickson, H. George. 1999. The repositioning of American public administration. *PS: Political Science & Politics* 32(4): 701–711.

Friesema, H. Paul. 1971. *Metropolitan Political Structure: Intergovernmental Relations and Political Integration in the Quad-Cities.* Iowa City: University of Iowa Press.

Gulick, Luther Halsey. 1962. *The Metropolitan Problem and American Ideas*. New York: Knopf.

Huber, John D., and Charles R. Shipan. 2002. *Deliberate Discretion: The Institutional Foundations of Bureaucratic Autonomy.* New York: Cambridge University Press.

Huber, John D., Charles R. Shipan, and Madelaine Pfahler. 2001. Legislatures and statutory control of bureaucracy. *American Journal of Political Science* 45(2): 330–345.

Joaquin, M. Ernita, and Thomas J. Greitens. 2012. Contract management capacity breakdown? An analysis of U.S. local governments. *Public Administration Review* 72(6): 807–816.

Joassart-Marcelli, Pascale, and Juliet Musso. 2005. Municipal service provision choices within a metropolitan area. *Urban Affairs Review* 40(4): 492–519.

Johnston, Jocelyn M., Barbara S. Romzek, and Curtis H. Wood. 2004. The challenges of contracting and accountability across the federal system: From ambulances to space shuttles. *Publius: The Journal of Federalism* 34(3): 155–182.

Kelman, Steven. 2011. If you want to be a good fill-in-the-blank manager, be a good plain-vanilla manager. *PS: Political Science & Politics* 44(2): 241–246.

Kettl, Donald F. 1997. The global revolution in public management: Driving themes, missing links. *Journal of Policy Analysis and Management* 16(3): 446–462.

Krebs, Timothy B., and John P. Pelissero. 2003. City councils. In *Cities, Politics, and Policy: A Comparative Analysis,* ed. J.P. Pelissero. Washington, DC: CQ Press.

LeRoux, Kelly, Paul W. Brandenburger, and Sanjay K. Pandey. 2010. Interlocal service cooperation in U.S. cities: A social network explanation. *Public Administration Review* 70(2): 268–278.

LeRoux, Kelly, and Jered B. Carr. 2007. Explaining local government cooperation on public works: Evidence from Michigan. *Public Works Management & Policy* 12(1): 344–358.

Margo, Randall N. 1992. Interlocal governmental cooperation: A growing trend among cities attempting to cut costs while maintaining services. PhD diss., Golden Gate University, San Francisco, CA.

Marvel, Mary K., and Howard P. Marvel. 2007. Outsourcing oversight: A comparison of monitoring for in-house and contracted services. *Public Administration Review* 67(3): 521–530.

———. 2008. Government-to-government contracting: Stewardship, agency, and substitution. *International Public Management Journal* 11(2): 171–192.

Matkin, David S.T., and H. George Frederickson. 2009. Metropolitan governance: Institutional roles and interjurisdictional cooperation. *Journal of Urban Affairs* 31(1): 45–66.

McCubbins, Mathew D., and Thomas Schwartz. 1984. Congressional oversight overlooked: Police patrols versus fire alarms. *American Journal of Political Science* 28(1): 165–179.

McGinnis, Michael D., ed. 1999. *Polycentricity and Local Public Economies: Readings from the Workshop in Political Theory and Policy Analysis*. Ann Arbor: University of Michigan Press.

Miller, Gary J. 1981. *Cities by Contract: The Politics of Municipal Incorporation*. Cambridge, MA: MIT Press.

Montjoy, Robert S., and Douglas J. Watson. 1995. A case for reinterpreted dichotomy of politics and administration as a professional standard in council-manager government. *Public Administration Review* 55(3): 231–239.

Morgan, David R., and Michael W. Hirlinger. 1991. Intergovernmental service contracts: A multivariate explanation. *Urban Affairs Quarterly* 27(1): 128–144.

Nalbandian, John. 1991. *Professionalism in Local Government: Transformations in the Roles, Responsibilities, and Values of City Managers*. San Francisco, CA: Jossey-Bass.

Oakerson, Ronald J. 1999. *Governing Local Public Economies: Creating the Civic Metropolis*. Oakland, CA: ICS Press.

Osborne, David, and Ted Gaebler. 1992. *Reinventing Government: How the Entrepreneurial Spirit Is Transforming the Public Sector.* Reading, MA: Addison-Wesley.

Ostrom, Elinor, Roy Gardner, and James Walker. 1994. *Rules, Games, and Common-Pool Resources*. Ann Arbor: University of Michigan Press.

Ostrom, Elinor, and Vincent Ostrom. 1965. A behavioral approach to the study of intergovernmental relations. *Annals of the American Academy of Political Science* 359: 137–146.

Ostrom, Elinor, Roger B. Parks, and Gordon P. Whitaker. 1999. Defining and measuring structural variations in interorganizational arrangements. In *Polycentricity and Local Public Economies: Readings from the Workshop in Political Theory and Policy Analysis,* ed. M.D. McGinnis. Ann Arbor: University of Michigan Press.

Ostrom, Vincent, Charles M. Tiebout, and Robert Warren. 1961. The organization of government in metropolitan areas: A theoretical inquiry. *American Political Science Review* 55(4): 831–842.

Ostrom, Elinor, and James Walker. 2003. *Trust and Reciprocity: Interdisciplinary Lessons from Experimental Research.* New York: Russell Sage Foundation.

Parks, Roger B., and Ronald J. Oakerson. 2000. Regionalism, localism, and metropolitan governance: Suggestions from the research program on local public economies. *State and Local Government Review* 32(3): 169–179.

Peters, B. Guy, and Jon Pierre. 1998. Governance without government? Rethinking public administration. *Journal of Public Administration Research and Theory* 8(2): 223–243.

Poteete, Amy R., Marco Janssen, and Elinor Ostrom. 2010. *Working Together: Collective Action, the Commons, and Multiple Methods in Practice.* Princeton, NJ: Princeton University Press.

Romzek, Barbara S., and Jocelyn M. Johnston. 2002. Effective contract implementation and management: A preliminary model. *Journal of Public Administration Research and Theory* 12(3): 423–453.

Ruhil, Anirudh V.S., Mark Schneider, Paul Teske, and Byung-Moon Ji. 1999. Institutions and reform reinventing local government. *Urban Affairs Review* 34(3): 433–455.

Shrestha, Manoj, and Richard C. Feiock. 2009. Governing U.S. metropolitan areas: Self-organizing and multiplex service networks. *American Politics Research* 37(4): 801–823.

Sonenblum, Sidney, John J. Kirlin, and John C. Ries. 1977. *How Cities Provide Services: An Evaluation of Alternative Delivery Structures.* Cambridge, MA: Ballinger.

Sørensen, Eva, and Jacob Torfing. 2005. The democratic anchorage of governance networks. *Scandinavian Political Studies* 28(3): 195–218.

———, eds. 2007. *Theories of Democratic Network Governance.* New York: Palgrave Macmillian.

Stein, Robert M. 1990. *Urban Alternatives: Public and Private Markets in the Provision of Local Services.* Pittsburgh, PA: University of Pittsburgh Press.

Stewart, Frank M., and Ronald M. Ketcham. 1941. Intergovernmental contracts in California. *Public Administration Review* 1(3): 242–248.

Thurmaier, Kurt, and Curtis Wood. 2002. Interlocal agreements as overlapping social network: Picket-fence regionalism in metropolitan Kansas City. *Public Administration Review* 62(5): 585–598.

Van Slyke, David M., and Charles A. Hammonds. 2003. The privatization decision: Do public managers make a difference? *American Review of Public Administration* 33(2): 146–163.

Warner, Mildred E., and Amir Hefetz. 2009. Cooperative competition: Alternative service delivery, 2002–2007. In *Municipal Year Book 2009.* Washington, DC: International City/County Management Association.

White, Leonard D. 1945. Congressional control of the public service. *American Political Science Review* 39(1): 1–11.

Williams, Oliver P., Harold Herman, Charles S. Liebman, and Thomas R. Dye. 1965. *Suburban Differences and Metropolitan Policies: A Philadelphia Story.* Philadelphia: University of Pennsylvania Press.

Williamson, Oliver E. 1981. The economics of organization: The transaction cost approach. *American Journal of Sociology* 87(3): 548–577.

Wood, B. Dan, and Richard W. Waterman. 1994. *Bureaucratic Dynamics: The Role of Bureaucracy in a Democracy.* Boulder, CO: Westview Press.

Wood, Curtis. 2006. Scope and patterns of metropolitan governance in urban America: Probing the complexities in the Kansas City region. *American Review of Public Administration* 36(3): 337–353.

———. 2008. The nature of metropolitan governance in urban America: A study of cooperation and conflict in the Kansas City region. *Administration & Society* 40(5): 483–501.

Wright, Deil S. 1973. Intergovernmental relations in large council-manager cities. *American Politics Quarterly* 1(2): 151–188.

Yang, Kaifeng, Jun Yi Hsieh, and Tzung Shiun Li. 2009. Contracting capacity and perceived contracting performance: Nonlinear effects and the role of time. *Public Administration Review* 69(4): 681–696.

Zeemering, Eric S. 2008. Governing interlocal cooperation: City council interests and the implications for public management. *Public Administration Review* 68(4): 731–741.

———. 2012. The problem of democratic anchorage for interlocal agreements. *American Review of Public Administration* 42(1): 87–103.

7

Do Shared Services Achieve Results?

The Performance of Interlocal Agreements

Daniel E. Bromberg

Jon Frederick's email managed to make me laugh on a cold New Hampshire morning as I was finishing my grading for the fall semester. Jon's email was nothing more than a quick "nice to meet you" after we had just met at a municipal managers meeting in Portsmouth, New Hampshire. The laughter was not from the content of the email, but Jon's title, in the signature below the content. It said

Jon Frederick, Town Manager
Mapleton, Castle Hill, & Chapman

Jon is the town manager of three towns. His position is the product of an interlocal agreement (ILA) that was informally put in place in 1947 between Mapleton, Maine, and Castle Hill, Maine. Chapman, Maine, joined the informal arrangement in 1974. In 1992 the three towns entered into a formal ILA. I asked Jon to describe the arrangement to me and he responded with this:

> The population of the three towns is just under 3,000. We have a Town Manager, Treasurer, Code Enforcement Officer, Road Commissioner and three highway operators, a Town Clerk and two assistant Clerks—10 total employees serving the three towns. Our Fire Department is all volunteer with an on-call Fire Chief and Assistant Fire Chief working for annual stipends. Two of our highway operators are also firemen, so our response time during the work week is much quicker. We also have several agreements with bordering towns to address snow plowing, road maintenance and fire coverage—basically, I scratch your back, you scratch mine type of arrangements. We have a very cooperative county up here.

It was funny to think of one town manager for three towns, but it seems that Mapleton, Castle Hill, and Chapman have implemented a viable option—viable enough to last for over 50 years.

While longevity might be one measure of success, it is certainly not a reason to enter into an ILA. According to a study conducted by Burns and Yeaton (2008), 22 percent of those involved in shared services initiated the efforts in order to save money. Warner (2011) found similar motivation in her analysis of data from the International City/County Managers Association (ICMA). Sixty-five percent of respondents noted that they formed cooperative agreements to save costs. Shared services are about providing services in a cooperative manner between multiple jurisdictions. Ideally, this will "help communities capture economies of scale, gain use of the latest technology and equipment that they (if acting on their own) would otherwise be unable to afford, eliminate duplicative efforts and achieve significant cost savings" (New York State, Office of the Comptroller n.d., 2). While the position of town manager is not the first function that comes to mind to reap such savings, it suggests that ILAs offer a range of possibilities.

Little empirical evidence is available to determine the effectiveness of ILAs and which functions are most apt to help communities find cost savings. As Zeemering (2012) notes, "Despite popularity and increased attention, we remain uncertain about the performance and benefits of ILAs for local government" (88). Andrew (2009) suggests that "[little] progress has been made in understanding the outcomes of using IJAs [interjurisdictional agreements]" (138). The current literature covers more descriptive data and does not address issues of performance (Andrew 2009; Zeemering 2012).

This chapter offers a first step toward addressing the lack of integration between performance and shared services. It introduces the basic building blocks to implementing a performance measurement system and how those concepts might apply in shared service provision. The literature suggests that the conditions necessary to successfully measure performance are very similar to the conditions necessary to successfully implement a shared service initiative. Therefore, it might benefit managers to consider establishing a performance measurement system at the inception of an ILA.

EXAMINING THE ROLE OF PERFORMANCE MEASUREMENT IN THE PUBLIC SECTOR

Performance measurement is an "advanced management tool" that enables public managers to track data to help determine the best way to utilize resources (National Center for Public Performance n.d.). At its most basic level a performance measurement system is a process or system of measures and procedures whereby organizations assess how well they are doing compared to their previous performance, compared to other organizations, or compared to previously established targets. It is made of a series of indicators most frequently captured as inputs, outputs, outcomes, efficiency, and productivity indicators (see Table 7.1).

According to Robert Behn (2003) there are eight reasons to measure performance:

1. To evaluate how well an agency is performing
2. To control subordinates within an organization
3. To budget resources appropriately
4. To motivate stakeholders (employees, citizens, partners, etc.) to improve performance

Table 7.1

Types of Performance Measurement Indicators

Indicator Type	Definition
Input indicators	Designed "to report the amount of resources, either financial or other (especially personnel), that have been used for a specific service or program. Input indicators are ordinarily presented in budget submissions and sometimes external management reports." (Government Accounting Standards Board)
Output/Workload indicators	Report units produced or services provided by a program. Workload measures indicate the amount of work performed or the amount of services received.
Outcome/Effectiveness indicators	Report the results (including quality) of the service. These measures answer the question "How well is the organization meeting its goals?"
Efficiency indicators	Report whether the desirable ends are achieved with minimal input of resources, or that the resources we employ bring the maximum amount of desirable goal attainment. Efficiency refers to the ratio of the quantity of the service provided to the cost, in dollars or labor, required to produce the service.
Productivity indicators	Combines the dimensions of efficiency and effectiveness in a single indicator. For example, the costs (or labor-hours) of faulty meter repairs as well as the costs of effective repairs are included in the numerator of such a calculation, but only good repairs are counted in the denominator—thereby encouraging efficiency and effectiveness of and by meter repair personnel. (Ammons 1996)

Source: National Center for Public Performance (n.d.).

5. To promote organizational priorities with stakeholders
6. To celebrate organizational accomplishment
7. To learn what works best
8. To improve performance

While many of these reasons might lead to overall productivity improvement, they also suggest that a performance measurement system might be in place to ensure accountability. Advocates of performance measurement suggest that utilizing performance as a tool for accountability is significantly more effective than utilizing traditional rule-based accountability systems. Behn argues that rule-based accountability systems inevitably lead to more time spent following these accountability schemes rather than focusing on agency performance. In return, it detracts focus from public managers' ability to perform their primary tasks, and consequently hurts performance (Behn 2001). Behn claims that systems of accountability should not be set up to deter behavior; they should be set up to provide incentives for behavior (2001).

If managers are provided with goals and results they must achieve, then their actions will be based on meeting those goals rather than sifting through red tape. Establishing a basic performance measurement system can help managers improve performance and create an environment of accountability. The challenge is often in determining the goals organizations must meet.

Public-sector goals are frequently ambiguous and composed of competing interests. For example, the mayor may have a different goal than the town council, or the public manager may have a different goal than the citizens. Each group offers a different perspective from which to evaluate performance and accountability. For example, let's suppose that lowering the crime rate is a goal that a city is looking to achieve. Then we must decide what factors might lead to a lower crime rate. Is a lower crime rate solely dependent on the number of police officers, or might income inequality be a determining factor? Ho (2004) suggests increasing citizen participation might solve many of these challenges. "Performance measurement requires a context in which the data is judged and used. Since elected officials often look to citizens when they make decisions, citizen participation provides the necessary context and political incentives to ensure the credibility and value of performance measures in the decision-making process" (Ho 2004, 11).

Developing consensus-based indicators is one of the most challenging aspects to initiating a performance measurement system. The challenge multiplies when attempting to reach consensus among multiple municipalities, cities, and or counties in an ILA. The literature on ILAs suggests that reaching such consensus might be necessary in achieving a high-performing shared service agreement. Therefore, we examine this literature to determine where intersection between the two frameworks might take place.

AT THE INTERSECTION OF PERFORMANCE AND SHARED SERVICES

Limited integration has been made between performance measurement and shared services. There are three studies that address this issue in a significant manner, examining effectiveness and efficiency (Chen and Thurmaier 2009), citizen perceptions (Morton, Chen, and Morse 2008), and political involvement (Zeemering 2012). These studies do not address the manner in which to measure performance; rather, they discuss what leads to high-performing ILAs.

The most relevant analysis conducted to determine if ILAs achieve outcomes was that by Chen and Thurmaier, whose "hypotheses deal with the relationships between various factors and the success of ILAs as measured by goal achievement, effectiveness, and efficiency" (2009, 541). The factors they examine in relation to success are reciprocity, equity, and impetus for collaborative action. The assumption is that reciprocity between collaborators builds trust, hence increasing the likelihood of a sustainable arrangement. Similarly, equity (fair distribution of costs and benefits) creates an environment of fairness in which parties are likely to reach their goals. Last, they hypothesize that a "shared understanding" of the goal and or problems is more likely to lead to accomplishing that goal (540). They find that:

> [E]quitable sharing of benefits is a consistent and significant factor in determining the perceived success of ILAs measured by goal achievement, efficiency, and effectiveness. Equitable sharing of costs is also significantly associated with goal achievement and ef-

> fectiveness. This finding confirms the importance of the norm of equity and reciprocity specifically in an interlocal setting. (545)

Chen and Thurmaier (2009) also find support for their hypothesis about goal congruence. They write, "Throughout the implementation of an ILA, public managers can invoke the primary reason for entering the agreement to focus partners' energy on achieving its primary goal. This is likely to produce a focusing effect to achieve its main mission" (547). These three factors that Chen and Thurmaier identify are foundational elements. That is, the factors must be present at the beginning of an initiative in order for it to succeed. Reciprocity, equity, and goal congruence create a set of building blocks upon which managers can construct a high-performing ILA. To establish these building blocks one might consider increasing the involvement of key stakeholders to ensure a joint understanding of program goals.

Zeemering captures this by looking at democratic performance of ILAs rather than service quality, efficiency, or effectiveness. Zeemering (2012) explains:

> Studying performance will direct some researchers' attention to financial outcomes and service efficiencies. The democratic anchorage and performance of ILAs must also be part of the discussion and research agenda. This investigation draws on theoretical insights about the democratic performance of networks to scrutinize how ILAs are linked to the expectations of the public in the individual cities participating in service sharing. (98)

Zeemering interviewed 47 elected officials, including city council members and mayors, to measure "the *content* of expressed concerns about ILAs" (2012, 92). His findings share similarities with frequently cited challenges associated with ILAs; namely, elected officials are concerned about costs, personnel, capacity, quality, assets, communication, and technology. Zeemering (2012) noted that many of these concerns are similar to those in the transaction cost literature and suggests that collaborating with politicians might reduce some of these transactional challenges thereby increasing performance. Zeemering (2012) writes, "Elected officials may help their communities anticipate points of disagreement and build enforcement mechanisms into ILAs when agreements are first negotiated and adopted" (97). Furthermore, he suggests that elected officials may help create increased transparency in ILAs and additional monitoring. Ultimately, the inclusion of elected officials may increase performance from a democratic perspective while overcoming some of the well-known challenges associated with collaborative arrangements that are often a hindrance to performance.

An alternative mechanism to assess an ILA is based solely upon citizen perception. As citizens are the main stakeholders in such agreements, their perception of success is a key indicator of service quality. Morton, Chen, and Morse (2008) examine whether or not the presence of an ILA has an effect on citizen perception of service quality. Their findings suggest that, in general (that is when all services are examined in an aggregate manner), there is limited difference in quality perceptions between direct service provision and services provided in a collaborative manner. However, when services are examined in a specific manner, a significant difference in perceived quality of service exists. The most substantial difference in perception is seen in the delivery of police services. Morton and colleagues write, "Our findings show higher citizen perceptions of quality with police services that are directly provided rather than those that are provided through interlocal agreements (which most often involve the small town contracting with the county sheriff's office)" (55). That is to say, there is a negative correlation between police services provided under an ILA and citizen perception of the quality of those services. Additionally, their findings suggest that there is a significant correlation between quality of emergency medical services, quality of streets, and quality of fire services in relation to direct service provision. However, they do not find a negative correlation between these services and ILAs. Overall this study suggests that perceived performance (by citizens) is connected to ILAs, but the perceptions are more nuanced than simply whether or not a town has an ILA.

Identifying the Key Factors

In sum, the literature identifies key building blocks to achieving high performance in ILAs. Building off of Chen and Thurmaier (2009), there are three factors critical to success: reciprocity, equity, and shared understanding of goals (see Table 7.2). Fundamentally, a sense of reciprocity translates into a sense of trust between collaborators. It answers the question, Can I trust you to fulfill your obligations? If trust is broken, rules of reciprocity create an understanding that there will be consequences. The second condition, equity, is straightforward. It is defined as the "equitable sharing of costs and benefits" (541). The last key factor found by Chen and Thurmaier (2009) is the concept of shared goals. They found, "Effectiveness as an impetus is significantly associated with a higher perceived level of effectiveness as an outcome," and, "Efficiency as an impetus is also significantly associated with a higher level of efficiency as the measure of success" (547). Chen and Thurmaier note that these findings indicate "the importance of . . . a shared understanding of the purpose of an agreement" (547). This concept of a shared understanding is echoed to some degree by Morton, Chen, and Morse (2008) along with Zeemering.

Morton, Chen, and Morse (2008) write, "For agreements to happen, these interlocal service-sharing arrangements must not only be financially desirable but also reinforce community ownership." Hence, even if managers can reach a "shared understanding of purpose" from a financial standpoint, citizens might be unable to reach a "shared understanding of purpose" from a community pride perspective. Therefore Morton, Chen, and Morse suggest that managers "might selectively choose nonvisible, routine portions of public services to share while directly providing those services that seem most important to their residents. Or, alternatively, they might consider how service-sharing arrangements might be more sensitive to community identity/control issues that fall outside professional understandings of effectiveness and efficiency" (59). Zeemering (2012) adds that one way to engage citizens and ensure investment for ILAs is to engage elected officials. Early engagement by elected officials can help shape the document in a manner that creates accountability. Zeemering writes:

Table 7.2

Factors Critical to Performance in ILAs

Condition	Meaning
Reciprocity	I can trust you to fulfill your obligations
Equity	I will benefit as much as you will benefit
Shared understanding of goals	We are striving to achieve the same goals

Source: Chen and Thurmaier (2009).

> Elected officials may call for mechanisms of cooperation and cost formulas that are transparent to the public and easy to understand. In the areas of service quality and capacity, elected officials might keenly monitor new ILAs to ensure their jurisdiction is receiving all promised benefits. When considering ILAs for service provision, local government managers should take time to consider how elected officials might provide a link of democratic accountability between the citizens within their city and the service provided through the ILA. (2012, 98)

The foundational factors necessary to develop a successful ILA are the same foundational factors essential to creating performance measurement system. In a sense, to develop a successful ILA a manager must do all of the heavy lifting required to develop a successful measurement system. Both frameworks are based upon the joint efforts of citizens, politicians, and managers to develop a shared understanding of the goals and the means with which those goals are achieved.

Avoiding Roadblocks

While garnering a sense of shared goals and creating an environment in which trust is established is essential to achieving high performance in a shared service initiative, there are a number of factors that can hinder an organization's performance. Transaction cost barriers are frequently cited as major challenges associated with collective action (Zeemering 2012). These are the added costs, beyond the good or service produced, to engage in a transaction. Williamson (1981) writes:

> A transaction occurs when a good or service is transferred across a technologically separable interface. One stage of activity terminates and another begins. With a well-working interface, as with a well-working machine, these transfers occur smoothly. In mechanical systems we look for frictions: do the gears mesh, are the parts lubricated, is there needless slippage or other loss of energy? The economic counterpart of friction is transaction cost: do the parties to the exchange operate harmoniously, or are there frequent misunderstandings and conflicts that lead to delays, breakdowns, and other malfunctions? (551)

Table 7.3

Other Factors Shaping ILAs

Factor	Meaning
State-level rules	Ensure state-level laws do not inhibit the agreement
Spatial and demographic characteristics of institutional units	Make certain that your organizations fit well together
Internal political structure	Politics needs to be considered to make an agreement successful

Source: Feiock (2009).

The costs associated with these "non-harmonious" exchanges increase the costs associated with the transaction. The production of some goods or services lends itself to harmonious exchanges, whereas other goods or services might inhibit harmony. Brown and Potoski (2005) write, "The costs of negotiating, implementing, monitoring, and enforcing contracts are higher when services have outcomes that are difficult to measure and when services require asset-specific investments that increase the likelihood of monopoly markets" (327). As ILAs are another form of collective public action (and a possible alternative to contracting), transaction cost concerns resonate in a similar manner to those of contracting.

In addition to these traditional transaction cost factors, Feiock (2009) suggests that factors such as "state level rules, the spatial and demographic characteristics of institutional units, and their internal political structure" specifically affect ILAs (368) (see Table 7.3). State-level rules are those that are imposed from the state level that either inhibit or induce collaborative action. These can be incentives to participate in an ILA or additional layers of bureaucratic oversight, which decrease the efficiency of the process (Feiock 2009). Spatial and demographic characteristics may similarly increase or decrease costs to collective action depending upon a number of factors. Shared borders and shared demographic makeup make it easier to align goals and form successful partnerships, whereas increased heterogeneity make may it challenging to agree to common goals (2009). Last, the internal political structure relates to things such as type of government and the personalities of those involved. Does the city council fear a loss of control or does a mayor see an opportunity for notoriety? Each of these moving parts will play a role in the cost and performance associated with collaborative action.

All of these factors may induce or inhibit higher results in a shared service initiative. The challenges associated with shared services will vary based on the communities involved and the services being provided. Therefore, performance and managers' ability to measure performance will likewise vary based on all of these factors.

TAX ASSESSMENT: AN OPPORTUNITY TO ACHIEVE RESULTS

Property tax assessment provides a useful case to explore for two reasons. First, one of the primary reasons to engage in a collaborative agreement with another jurisdiction is to save costs for the taxpayers. Therefore, the service must gain from economies of scale. There is evidence that tax assessment benefits from economies of scale (at least to a point). Sjoquist and Walker (1999) examine 138 county assessment offices in Georgia to determine if they benefit from economies of scale. They write:

> The results suggest that states should consider allowing consolidation of small assessment offices. However, our results also suggest that beyond 100,000 parcels, the economies of scale have been pretty well exhausted. For point of reference, in Georgia, the ten counties that contain more than 100,000 parcels have populations from 150,000 to more than 500,000. Thus, while our results suggest that consolidating assessment offices could result in substantial savings in Georgia and other states with similar size districts, the same would not be true in states with large assessment districts. (207)

In evaluating performance of tax assessment, Mehta and Giertz (1996) likewise find that economies of scale exist in tax assessment. Their findings suggest that if the quality of the assessment remains constant then an increase in number of parcels assessed results in "a reduction in the average per parcel cost of assessment (79). These findings point to the benefits a smaller municipality might gain from forming an ILA to provide tax assessment.

The second reason to examine tax assessment is because it presents a service that is moderately placed on the transaction cost scale developed by Brown and Potoski (2005). In the 64 services examined on a scale of 1 to 5, tax assessment falls close to a score of 3 in both in both ease of measurement and asset specificity (2.87 for ease of measurement and 2.93 for asset specificity). This mid-range score suggests that tax assessment is neither the most challenging service on which to collaborate nor the easiest. According to Warner (2011), as the transaction cost associated with a service increases, the likelihood of providing it through an ILA also increases. Both of these factors suggest that tax assessment is an ideal service in which to achieve results with an ILA.

Property Taxes in New Hampshire

Property tax plays a different role in every state. In New Hampshire, property taxes play a central role in financing government services. Without a broad-based income or sales tax, both local governments and state government rely on property taxes to fund a number of services. The New Hampshire state government utilizes property taxes to fund the state's portion of education. In 1999, the legislature passed a statewide property tax to help equalize education funding across the state. After a number of court cases and scrutiny from the legislature and the public, the process of property assessment became a formal one statewide. Prior to the statewide tax, property assessment had been completed in an ad hoc manner, leaving a great deal of discretion to municipalities.

The formality brought to this process compelled a number of municipalities to re-evaluate the manner in which they assessed their properties—cost being a major factor in revaluations. Three of those municipalities were the Town of Newbury, the Town of Sunapee, and the Town of New London. Each of the towns has populations under 5,000 people, with New London being the largest with a population of 4,116 people (State of New Hampshire 2013). The size of these towns is typical for New Hampshire, which has a total of 234 towns and cities. Twelve towns or cities have populations larger than 10,000 residents. The towns' municipal appropriations (not including education appropriations) were as follows: New London, $7,827,619; Newbury, $4,052,587; and Sunapee, $11,854,908. The three towns are located in the Dartmouth–Lake Sunapee region of the state. These towns are located in the southern section of this region and therefore do not benefit economically from Dartmouth College, which is located in the northern part of the region. The towns of Newbury, Sunapee, and New London all share the shoreline of Lake Sunapee, and the town of Newbury is home to the Mt. Sunapee ski resort.

In 2004, the town administrators (both Newbury and New London have town administrators) and the town manager of Sunapee began conversations about creating an ILA for a regional tax assessor.[1] Why tax assessment? Initially, according to the town managers, there was simply a desire to cooperate in service provision and a number of services were considered. However, with the changing regulatory environment emerging at the state level, tax assessment became an advantageous option. There were a number of shared goals that drove this decision, including cost, continuity (both internally and externally), better customer service, and a greater sense of control. In a press release issued in 2007, New London's town administrator, Jessie Levine, stated:

> All three towns have similar assessing needs, including lakefront property on Lake Sunapee, and because revaluations had not been done for many years, all three towns experienced sharply raised assessments after property updates. While none of us was in a position to justify a full-time assessor, we realized that the revaluation process would have been greatly enhanced if we had an experienced assessing staff on hand to handle questions and explain the increased assessments. (Town of Newbury 2007)

Prior to this, each town had utilized a private company to perform the town revaluation.

Chen and Thurmaier (2009) emphasize reciprocity and equity as two major components of achieving performance in an ILA. A sense of reciprocity was directly present in the forming of this agreement. Prior to forming an ILA the three managers frequently met to have lunch. Primarily, they met to share insights and get feedback from one another about making their towns work better. Some of the discussions were about tri-town issues, while other topics were unique to each of the towns. During these frequent luncheons trust was developed. Coincidentally, the state regulatory environment was changing rapidly and was a factor in forming an ILA, but it was the underlying trust that led to creating a formal ILA. The formal ILA that emerged "simply followed state statutes" and defined what the towns paid, noted one of the managers, but it was the underlying relationships that determined how the position would function. The trust that existed between the managers cultivated an environment in which a true sense of equity could arise—both formally and informally.

The equity of the cost distribution was primarily defined in the formal ILA. It was calculated based on a per parcel cost by each municipality. The agreement reads, "Apportionment shall be based on the percentage of total parcels as of April 1 preceding the fiscal year. For example, the three Towns had a total of 8,462 parcels as of on April 1, 2004 [*sic*]. Sunapee had 3,005 parcels, or 35.51% of the total, New London had 2808 parcels, or 33.18% of the total, and Newbury had 2649 parcels, or 31.31% of the total" (Towns of Newbury, New London, and Sunapee 2007). Clearly, this speaks to the shared costs of the arrangement, but as Chen and Thurmaier (2009) note, equity also refers to shared benefits. A logical arrangement for the benefits of the assessor's services would have been to apportion the assessor's time based upon the above percentages. The officials, however, did not view this as a practical solution. Rather, they specified in the agreement:

> The Towns recognize that due to revaluation, litigation, or other large projects, one town may require disproportionally more of the Joint Assessor's attention for a period of time, and that in the long run, use by all Towns should balance out. This is a chance that all Towns are willing to take and the Towns enter into this Agreement with that knowledge. (Towns of Newbury, New London, and Sunapee 2007)

Equity, in this case, is expressed by a much more sophisticated sense of practice than one might assume in framing an ILA. The willingness to take on added risk is only made possible by the sense of reciprocity already established. Furthermore, the three officials shared unified goals—one being customer service to the citizens. Therefore, even though the tri-town assessor might be in one municipality on specific day, he was encouraged to respond to the needs of the citizens from each of the towns based on level of importance, rather than an arbitrary schedule.

A shared understanding of goals is a major component that might inhibit or encourage performance (Chen and Thurmaier 2009). As noted above, some of the shared goals that drove this decision included cost, continuity in service provision, better customer service, and a greater sense of control. Prior to this ILA each town had utilized a private company to perform the town revaluation. Therefore, many of the goals in the ILA focused upon what the private companies were unable to provide. While cost was a major factor, the managers did not suggest it was the primary reason to establish this agreement; rather, there was clear desire that the assessor establish a deep knowledge of the region and a connection to the citizens. The managers all wanted local knowledge to be a part of the assessing process. One of the managers stated (about the private contractors): "There were no roots in their work . . . they came, they charge by the hour . . . they didn't own it." This local knowledge was exemplified in how the contractors versus the new assessor would examine lakefront property. As the managers spoke, I was reminded of the claim that Eskimos had many words for snow. The managers explained that the contractor only used two views to assess waterfront housing. They laughed at how ridiculous this was because those with local knowledge knew there were more than two. The new assessor used multiple views to assess property, including a lake view, a mountain view, a lighthouse view, and many others. It was this level of granularity that the managers were seeking—a more in-depth knowledge of the town's landscapes. Moreover, the lake was just one area of property with which the assessor had to be familiar.

Such in-depth knowledge also leads to better customer service—a second shared goal of the municipalities. The contracted assessors, according to the officials, typically set aside one day in which to meet with all property owners. They would schedule 20-minute meetings and try to answer the citizen concerns as best they could. The full-time assessor is a constant presence in the towns. He provides in-depth knowledge, along with a consistent face that does not change every time a new contractor is hired. The managers all noted that customer service was improved based on this position. One of the managers stated, "Citizens didn't love the contracted assessors we had—our citizens had a poor experience over the last few years so any change was welcome." Another manager noted that by utilizing a private contractor every few years, this essentially meant that there was no assessor—the position did not exist. If the citizens were not happy with the process, they had to talk to the town manager. Ultimately, one of the managers said, "We were bringing it [tax assessment] closer to them [the citizens]." While local knowledge and customer service were two main goals, the managers were well aware that lowering costs had to accompany improved quality.

There are two main costs associated with the assessment process. The first is the basic cost of the service. Traditionally, each of these towns hired a private contractor to accomplish the various tasks associated with assessment. Second are the costs associated with any legal ramifications emerging from the assessment process. This is how one of the managers described the process of determining the costs and benefits of the joint initiative:

> First, we calculated how much it currently cost each town for the simple tasks of regular assessment and pick-up work. We then factored in the additional time required to address abatements, taxpayer questions, field errors, and legal costs for appeals. We added the actual cost for abatements (overlay) as well as the capital reserve funds that each town had been putting aside for future revaluation or statistical updates. Finally, we added the town's administrative costs (time spent by managers and staff on assessing tasks). The estimated annual cost of the three towns' then-current assessing practice was $287,109. Our next task was to project the cost of a full-time assessing department. Originally, we thought the cost would have been significantly more than the expenses we had identified. As we broke down the assessing costs, we found that the budget for FY 2006 would be approximately $213,000. This included a second full-time employee to assist the assessor, and still provided a cost savings of approximately $75,000 total for the three towns. (Bernaiche et al. 2006)

While these initial costs were somewhat easily foreseen, there are a number of additional costs that might have been barriers to performance. According to the literature, the transaction costs might be greater than anticipated. As Williamson (1981) noted "non-harmonious" exchanges might increase costs to a greater extent than simply the cost of production. In this case, tax assessment was being provided by private contractors and the municipalities were bringing the service back in house. Warner (2011) writes, "We would expect cooperation to be higher in services where transactions costs are higher" (426). One of the managers expressed the challenges of working with a contractor rather than in-house personnel. The manager said that dealing with contractors is certainly easier at points than dealing with personnel in that you can always tell a contractor to "get in line," but you cannot say that to an employee. That being said, the manager went on to explain that even though the revaluation happens every five years, the work associated with hiring a contractor takes place more accurately every three years. The manager went on to say that "dealing with the community every time you have to revalue properties," explaining there might be a "strange guy" in their yard, is all a "part of the cost of the contractor." The manager continued, "and then at the end you have this really short process where the contracted assessors will be available in 20 minute stints" to meet with property owners. The manager summed up by saying, "that is all a lot more work and time and they [the contractor] don't care about the appraisal."

The three managers took additional steps to ensure risks arising from the ILA would not outweigh the benefits. While the managers did not need to make any additional capital investments, they did need to hire a person with a very specific skill set. Therefore, they added a very specific cost to their budgets—a nontransferable employee. That being said, the municipalities built in clauses for termination of the agreement that would limit any loss associated with the investment in personnel. Withdrawal from the agreement would have to be made in the second year of the collaboration and would go into effect after the third year. With one year's notice they could withdraw from the ILA with no penalty.

The second transaction cost that may hinder performance is the challenge of monitoring the assessor. To some degree, the ILA provided the managers with more control to monitor than they previously had with private contractors. As stated by one of the managers, why would you use a contractor "[i]f you can do the exact same thing with the money and have more control?" While the managers admitted that monitoring an in-house assessor was not an easy task, they suggested that there is a level of discretion granted to an employee that is not granted to a contractor. One manager stated, "This is a professional department head . . . they come to you when there is a big unusual situation . . . other than that they know what they are doing." Therefore, even if the managers' ability to monitor performance does not significantly improve from contractor to employee, there is a level of trust that is granted to an employee that is not granted to a contractor. Hence, the cost associated with monitoring an employee decreases in comparison to that of monitoring a contractor.

As both of these typical costs decrease, or stay constant, by bringing tax assessment in house, there are a number of other costs associated with ILAs that must be considered (Feiock 2009). Specifically, according to Feiock (2009), "state level rules, the spatial and demographic characteristics of institutional units, and their internal political structure" all must be considered as additional costs to ILAs. There are a number of state-level rules that might have increased costs associated with this ILA. The three managers, however, believe that the ILA actually decreased costs associated with complying with state-level rules. One of the initial steps taken by the managers was to consult with the state Department of Revenue (DRA). The DRA is responsible for implementing the new tax assessment standards. Prior to introducing the idea to their respective selectmen or citizens, the managers got buy-in from the state DRA. In their initial presentation to their boards of selectmen, a state DRA representative was present to endorse the ILA. Locally, this helped gain political support for the proposal. All of the other aspects of state laws remained the same—whether the revaluations were performed by an in-house employee or a private contractor. One of the managers said that the newly hired assessor "knew the laws well," so complying was not a problem.

The main challenge the newly hired assessor faced in terms of state law was the timing in which various reports and revaluations were due. There is a specific schedule as to what municipalities need to submit to the state and when. A number of documents and data are due on an annual basis and each municipality needs to be certified by the state once every five years. These dates are determined in consultation with municipalities in their revaluation contracts. As opposed to working for one municipality, the assessor had to comply with these deadlines for three municipalities. He therefore worked with the state to change the schedules in which the municipalities had to file certain documents. This compelled certain systems to be put in place that otherwise would not have been present.

Part of this reorganization of scheduling and systematizing meant that the new assessor had to change the manner in which the municipalities operated. These efforts also created a situation in which assessors were faced with the challenge of operating within the cultures of the different organizations, thus creating another cost associated with the implementation of this ILA. As one of the managers acknowledged, even if some systems overlapped, there "were three different ways of doing things." That, according to a different manager, was "dependent upon the assessor to handle." The assessor noted the challenges associated with different cultures in different towns. He wrote,

> The culture was different in each town and everyone had varying levels of responsibilities. The first thing I did was to determine the structure of each town and figure out how this new position fit in and what needed to be changed—immediately and long term—for this to work. (Bernaiche et al. 2006, 1)

The assessor went on to create a policy handbook that looked the same for each town. The handbook included state laws and various practices that were implemented in a uniform manner across the three towns (Bernaiche et al. 2006). He also increased communication by implementing online scheduling and requiring a bi-annual meeting between the three clerks that were providing administrative support. Ultimately, the assessor tried to standardize as much as possible by adopting the best practices from each community. Nevertheless, he allowed certain practices to remain different in each community so long as they did not conflict with state law or have a negative effect on the assessing process (2006).

Focusing on these organizational challenges does not necessarily alleviate the political challenges that might have arisen. There were two clear political challenges the tri-town assessor initiative would face. First, there was a financial concern. While there was no specific capital investment, there were two new personnel positions that had to be approved by the boards of selectmen. One of the managers said, "We can't hire people as an interlocal agreement. We can share, but we cannot hire." This meant that one of the three towns had to assume the gross cost for the two positions. Knowing the dynamics of their boards and their community members, the managers approached the town selectmen in Newbury, NH and asked them to take on the gross cost. The initiative was approved with little problem. The ILA reads:

> The parties agree that the Town of Newbury shall be the employer of record of the Joint Assessor and the measurer and lister, and shall be responsible for all employment-related expenses, including but not limited to payment of wages, benefits, retirement, payroll taxes and any applicable insurance coverage. However, the Town of Newbury has delegated all supervisory authority to the Joint Board, as described in Section IV, A, above, and neither the Joint Assessor nor the measurer and lister shall be subject to the personnel policies of the Town of Newbury. The Towns of Sunapee and New London shall reimburse Newbury for their respective shares of expenditures related to this Agreement within the first week of every quarter, beginning the week of July 1, 2005. (Towns of Newbury, New London, and Sunapee 2007)

Along with taking on the gross cost of the employees, the above agreement also stipulates that the Town of Newbury has to relinquish a good deal of control. The Town of Newbury did not hold supervisory authority over the employees nor were the employees subject to town personnel policies. This required a second political strategy by the town managers. In creating a joint board to supervise and hire the assessor, they established a bit of goodwill among their selectmen. The Joint Board was composed of "seven members: the Town Administrator or Town Manager from each of the three towns and two Selectmen and two at-large residents appointed to rotating two-year terms" (Towns of Newbury, New London, and Sunapee 2007). The towns created a staggered schedule to ensure that a town would never go longer than one year without representation. This agreement was adapted after 2006 to include two selectmen and two residents to create greater representation.

Did the Tri-Town Initiative Achieve Results?

There is not one way to answer this question. As with any effort to measure performance, there are multiple perspectives and multiple modes to measure results. The town managers believe the initiative was quite successful. Admittedly, it is not always data that is driving this perspective. According to one manager, an assessor's product is not like that of a police chief: the "police chief you can monitor on a regular basis"; with an assessor this is not necessarily the case. A different manager said, "An assessor's goal is different." He said the assessor's "history and professional reputation" speak quite loudly about his performance. Lastly, the third manager offered: "I know it worked based on my experience. The alternative would not have given me anywhere near the customer service that we're getting and I'd still be paying the same amount of money." As Selden and Sowa (2004) argue, perception is an equally important measure of performance as some of the more objective measures. Therefore the managers' perception of performance does lend some credence to their model achieving results. That being said, perception is not the only indicator.

The citizens were a major consideration in deciding to create the tri-town assessor position. According to the managers, the level of customer service has been significantly heightened. One manager said, "The assessor wants it all to work for the community." In the old system, property owners had limited time to talk to the private contractors about their property's assessed value. Due to this limited time frame, citizens were less likely to be satisfied with the process and more likely to file an appeal. This drove up costs for the three towns. In the new system the assessor is available every day to meet with citizens. The managers said that compromise between the assessor and property owners is more frequently utilized to solve disputes. The numbers of appeals have decreased, driving down additional legal fees.

It is also clear based upon data from the New Hampshire DRA that the collaborative arrangement is producing positive results. Each of the towns has experienced one certification—a process required by the state once every five years—since the ILA has taken place. Each town passed the certification, which requires that assessed values be within a range of 90 percent to 110 percent of sale price value. The managers noted that they are consistently coming within this range and that the assessment product is significantly better than products they had gotten in the past. One manager acknowledged that before the town had been revaluated in 2005, their waterfront property was assessed at 30 percent of market value. This meant that other properties in the town were subsidizing the waterfront properties. The manager said that in the past, if a specific strata or set of properties were "out of whack" they would not know what to do. With the new assessor position such disproportional ratios get taken care of in a systematic manner.

Achieving results in an ILA is not a given. As explained throughout this chapter, there are a number of obstacles and a number of building blocks. An ILA presents an opportunity to clarify goals, build consensus, and ensure accountability to citizens. Managers must be cognizant of service-specific problems as well as problems that arise from collaboration. While economies of scale are important to realize, they cannot be gained at the risk of reducing quality. The challenge for managers is to utilize ILAs in a manner that achieves both economies of scale and increased service quality. Performance measurement has complementary goals. It offers a mechanism in which to assess service quality and determine if economies of scale have created a more productive environment. The initial steps to establish a performance measurement system are similar to those needed to establish an ILA. Therefore, managers might consider utilizing performance measurement as a key tool in assessing the viability of an ILA.

KEY POINTS

- Local government organizations engaging in shared services or consolidation activities should ensure that needs are similar and that goals are aligned.
- The benefits of collaborative activity should be shared in an equitable and practical manner. Equitable does not always mean equal.
- All parties to an ILA should be cognizant of the costs of collaboration both before and after arrangements are made.
- Transparency, accountability, and political support are crucial components of the process.
- Parties to an ILA should work to create a flexible environment in terms of community, organization, and professional cultures.

NOTE

1. For the purpose of consistency and anonymity, I will refer to the two administrators as managers or public officials.

REFERENCES

Ammons, David N. 1996. *Performance Measurement of State and Local Government*. Public Policy Analysis, Management and Methodologies Seminar and Workshop Series Dissemination Paper No. 3. Washington, DC: Inter-American Development Bank.

Andrew, Simon. 2009. Recent developments in the study of interjurisdictional agreements: An overview and assessment. *State & Local Government Review* 41(2): 133–142.

Behn, Robert D. 2001. *Rethinking Democratic Accountability*. Washington, DC: Brookings Institution Press.

———. 2003. Why measure performance? Different purposes require different measures. *Public Administration Review* 63(5): 586–606.

Bernaiche, Normand, Jessie Levine, Donna Nashawaty, and Dennis Pavlicek. 2006. Tri-town assessing: An innovative intergovernmental agreement. *New Hampshire Town and City* (November/December).

Brown, Trevor, and Matthew Potoski. 2005. Transaction costs and contracting: The practitioner perspective. *Public Performance & Management Review* 28(3): 326–351.

Burns, Timothy, and Kathryn Yeaton. 2008. *Success Factors for Implementing Shared Services in Government.* Washington, DC: IBM Center for the Business of Government.

Chen, Yu-Che, and Kurt Thurmaier. 2009. Interlocal agreements as collaborations: An empirical investigation of impetuses, norms, and success. *American Review of Public Administration* 39(5): 536–552.

Feiock, Richard. 2009. Metropolitan governance and institutional collective action. *Urban Affairs Review* 44(3): 356–377.

Ho, Alfred Tat-Kei. 2004. *A Quick Guide to Citizen-Initiated Performance Assessment for Local Governments.* School of Public and Environmental Affairs, Indiana University–Purdue University Indianapolis.

Mehta, Shekhar, and Fred Giertz. 1996. Measuring the performance of the property tax assessment process. *National Tax Journal* 49(1): 73–85.

Morton, Lois, Yu-Che Chen, and Ricardo Morse. 2008. Small town civic structure and interlocal collaboration for public services. *City & Community* 7(1): 45–60.

The National Center for Public Performance (NCPP). N.d. *A Brief Guide for Performance Measurement in Local Government.* Newark, NJ: Rutgers University.

New York State, Office of the Comptroller. N.d. *Intermunicipal Cooperation and Consolidation: Exploring Opportunities for Savings and Improved Service Delivery*. New York: Division of Local Government and School Accountability.

Selden, Sally Coleman, and Jessica Sowa. 2004. Testing a multi-dimensional model of organizational performance: Prospects and problems. *Journal of Public Administration Research and Theory* 14(3): 395–416.

Sjoquist, David, and Mary Beth Walker. 1999. Economies of scale in property tax assessment. *National Tax Journal* 52(2): 207–220.

State of New Hampshire. 2013. *2012 Population Estimates of New Hampshire Cities and Towns.* Concord, NH, July. www.nh.gov/oep/data-center/documents/population-estimates-2012.pdf.

Town of Newbury, New Hampshire. 2007. Newbury and New London to share prestigious community partnership award: ICMA recognizes towns for intercommunity assessing program. Press release.

Towns of Newbury, New London, and Sunapee, New Hampshire. 2007. Intermunicipal Agreement for Assessing Services Between the Towns of Newbury, New London, and Sunapee. April 30.

Warner, Mildred 2011. Competition or cooperation in urban service delivery. *Annals of Public and Cooperative Economics* 82(4): 421–435.

Williamson, Oliver. 1981. The economics of organization: The transaction cost approach. *American Journal of Sociology* 87(3): 548–577.

Zeemering, Eric. 2012. The problem of democratic anchorage for interlocal agreements. *The American Review of Public Administration* 42(1): 87–103.

8

Toward Interlocal Collaboration

Lessons from a Failed Attempt to Create a Fire Authority

William D. Hatley, Richard C. Elling, and Jered B. Carr

Interlocal collaboration is not easy to achieve. If it were, it would be more common than it is and there would be fewer calls for more of it. But why is this so? What is it that makes interlocal collaboration so challenging? While existing research on the subject provides some insights, it is far from definitive. In this chapter we attempt to address these issues by focusing on a single effort to achieve interlocal collaboration. Specifically, we examine the efforts of five suburban communities in the Detroit metropolitan area to create a multicommunity authority to provide both fire and emergency medical services. Demographic, political, and fiscal similarities, combined with a past history of fruitful collaboration, suggested these communities were good candidates for interlocal collaboration. Nevertheless, despite several years of work the effort failed. Among the factors we identify as impediments were the opposition of affected fire unions, an ambivalent public, and state laws that, intentionally or not, hampered collaboration.

THE SETTING AND DATA SOURCES

As already noted, this study examines the efforts of five Detroit-area suburban communities to establish a multicommunity authority to provide fire and emergency medical services to the residents and businesses of these communities. One source of information relevant to the case was available documents and media reports.

A second more important resource was interviews with a number of those involved in the planning and development of the Five Community Fire Authority (FCFA).[1] The positions of the 20 participants initially interviewed are located in Appendix 8.1. These interviews consisted of a large number of both open-ended and close-ended questions and were conducted between August 2007 and April 2008. Individual interviews averaged between 60 and 90 minutes in length and were done face-to-face. In light of the collapse of the FCFA effort, we decided to re-interview as many of our previously interviewed respondents as possible. Sixteen of the 20 original interviewees agreed to speak with us. All five of the communities were represented in these interviews. This round of interviews was conducted between early April and August 2009. In the case of the 16 re-interviews, half were done face-to-face while the other eight were conducted by telephone or via e-mail. The two interview instruments we used are included in Appendices 8.2 and 8.3.

The five Detroit suburban communities that undertook to create the FCFA are geographically contiguous. All are inner-ring, mature suburbs with relatively small—and shrinking—populations. Information on these and other demographic and governmental characteristics of the communities is presented in Appendix 8.4.

WHY DID THE FIVE COMMUNITIES CONSIDER COLLABORATING?

The effort to create the FCFA began in 2006 when some 20 suburban communities in one part of the Detroit metropolitan area were invited to discuss the possible consolidation of their fire services. After several meetings, the number of interested communities was reduced to just five—a group that one city manager involved referred to as a "coalition of the willing." These five communities began serious discussions in early 2007.

At the outset there was reason to be hopeful about the prospects for the effort. This reflects the existence of certain conditions that the literature on interlocal collaboration suggests may increase the likelihood of such collaboration occurring.[2]

The literature generally agrees that successful collaboration is more likely when the units involved are similar to one another (Hatley 2010). The five communities involved in this effort were similar with regard to area, number of residents, and the demographic characteristics of their residents. Our interview data support the importance of such considerations. The mayor of one of the larger of the communities said it was "almost organic how we came together . . . we border one another . . . we have very similar populations, same demographics . . . [I]t was a natural sort of thing."

These communities had the same governmental-political structures—another factor that some scholars contend can facilitate collaboration. As shown in Appendix 8.4, all five had a mayor–council form of government. Each elected its city council members at-large. Each community also had a professional city manager.[3]

The fact that the communities had roughly comparable fire service needs, and that their fire services were similarly structured, also may have encouraged them to collaborate (see Table 8.1). The president of the fire union in one city observed that the fire departments in all five cities are structured the same way and all are full-time. A city manager asserted that "any community that has a volunteer or part-time department might not be a good partner. Then you're talking different wages, different personnel. . . ." There was strong agreement that having similar requirements for the type of training that firefighters needed, and the types of equipment normally required to fight fires, were important considerations in deciding with whom to partner.

Some writers emphasize that fiscal stress prompts interest in collaboration, presumably because collaboration offers the possibility of maintaining the quantity and/or quality of service at a lower cost. Although the collaborative effort began prior to the onset of the "Great Recession" in 2008, many local governments in Michigan were experiencing considerable fiscal stress earlier in the decade (Elling, Carr, and Glenn 2009). There was

Table 8.1

Comparison of Fire Services in Five Study Communities

	Community				
	A	B	C	D	E
General Fund Budget*	$10,145,000	$21,454,555	$20,615,192	$22,863,465	$23,352,647
Fire Dept. Budget*	$1,439,000	$3,266,526	$3,353,490	$3,456,590	$3,276,523
Fire Spending Per Capita*	$135.45	$113.87	$129.27	$127.79	$87.39
Fire Spending as % of General Fund Budget	14.2%	15.2%	16.3%	15.1%	14.0%
Equivalent Millage for Fire Services	2.10	2.87	3.42	5.26	4.28
Employment Status of Firefighters and EMS Personnel	Full-time, professional	Full-time, professional	Full-time, professional	Full-time, professional	Full-time, professional
Unionized	Yes	Yes	Yes	Yes	Yes

Sources: Individual city Web sites, fire department annual reports, and 2006 fire authority feasibility study.

*Data for FY 2009–10.

nearly universal agreement among those interviewed that a combination of decreasing revenues (at the time largely due to reductions in state aid) and increasing costs for firefighting equipment were stimulating interest in collaboration.

Governmental units that have worked together in the past may be more willing to do so in the future, and to be successful in doing so. The five communities focused on here were part of a larger group of suburban communities in this portion of the Detroit metropolitan area that joined a mutual aid agreement in the late 1960s to provide personnel backup to one another in the area of fire services as well as with respect to police services and antidrug activities. A decade later this led to the creation of the Suburban Community Conference (SCC) with a membership of some 20 local units of government.[4] It was the SCC that stimulated interest in a formalized fire authority in 2006 and facilitated some of the early work on the effort.

In short, there was reason to believe that this effort to create an independent fire authority that provided services across all of the communities had good prospects.

THE COLLABORATIVE EFFORT COMMENCES

The efforts of the five communities to form a multijurisdictional fire authority began as part of an initiative by the Suburban Community Conference to form an authority that would encompass all 20 of the communities that were members of the SCC. Aided by a grant from the state of Michigan, and with the support of the county Department of Homeland Security and Emergency Management, the SCC engaged a consulting firm to conduct a study of the feasibility of establishing such an authority.

The feasibility study was completed in late 2006 and it concluded that such a joint fire/EMS authority could be created under existing state law.[5] The report included a cost model and proposed articles of incorporation consistent with the provisions of state law. The study also recommended the transfer of assets and liabilities from each of the 20 individual communities to the authority. It recommended the independent funding of the authority via a property tax millage. In essence, the authority would operate as a special district. The study's cost model indicated the potential for long-term savings of 20 percent for each community while providing higher levels of service and achieving compliance with National Fire Protection Association service standards. At the time, many of the fire professionals we interviewed said their departments were not compliant with those standards.

Shortly after the consulting study was completed it became clear that attempting to create a fire authority to replace the fire and EMS operations of 20 municipalities was going to be impossible.[6] Hence, in early 2007, five of these communities decided to enter into discussions to create a fire authority to replace their individual fire and EMS operations. Representatives of the five communities—to include city managers, elected officials, and representatives of both management and labor from the respective fire departments—began to meet regularly.

There was not a single specifically designated convener for these meetings. Instead, the convener tended to vary depending on the focus of individual meetings. Nonetheless, two city managers were more regularly engaged, and one or the other generally chaired the meetings, and acted as policy entrepreneurs moving the project along. Those we interviewed indicated that these individuals were viewed as being critical to the effort.

Since the effort to create the FCFA was largely unsuccessful, it might be asked if those involved were sincere in their pursuit of this goal. Our best judgment is that, at least initially, most of the participants were actively and genuinely engaged in the effort and wanted it to succeed. The one exception might have been the representative of one of the community fire departments whose members were less enthusiastic about the effort than were their colleagues in the other four departments. But reflecting the more common position, the leaders of two fire departments told us that they no longer had a choice but to embrace such an effort since they would be unable to provide adequate fire and EMS services for their citizens in the face of rising costs and shrinking revenues.

Even though the effort did not succeed in consolidating the five city fire departments into a multijurisdictional authority, it did achieve some of its goals. Both management and labor from the five fire departments developed a detailed presentation as to how the authority could be developed. One fire official developed a computer simulation that allowed participants in the discussions to see how personnel and equipment could be best utilized across the area of the authority given various types of emergencies. The working group had also drafted a proposed organizational structure for the authority and there had been discussion on who would head the authority. More tangibly, all five communities entered into a joint purchasing agreement for supplies and various types of operational equipment other than vehicles. And three of the five agreed to establish a joint dispatching center.

THE EFFORT COLLAPSES

At the first meeting of the FCFA working group in early 2008 it was evident that the effort was stalled, at best, and dead, at worst. The newly elected mayor of Community E attended this first meeting after the election. He went so far as to observe that "within a matter of twenty minutes, eighteen months of work went right out the door." While this was too pessimistic a view in our judgment, the momentum to develop an authority that had existed earlier was largely gone.

The proximate cause of this change was the results of the municipal elections that were held in the five communities the previous November. Four of the communities (A, B, D, and E) elected new mayors. The mayors of Communities A and D who were supportive of the FCFA effort lost their bids for reelection and were replaced by mayors who were considerably less supportive. So did several councilpersons who had endorsed the effort. The new mayor in Community E—who replaced an incumbent who had been supportive of the collaborative effort but chose not to seek reelection—was a former council member who was very familiar with the collaborative effort.

The majority of those interviewed in 2009 believed changes in mayoral leadership associated with the November 2007 municipal elections significantly changed the political dynamics. The newly elected mayor of Community E—who was a supporter of the FCFA concept—believed that his counterparts in three other communities were not up to speed on efforts to form the authority or were actually hostile to the idea. The city manager of his community—who also felt that the election results were a major factor in the collapse of the FCFA effort—stated that "from public statements, it appears that was the case in [Community D] and [Community A] as those new mayors stated that they did not wish to continue." The fire chief in Community E observed that "absolutely the election had a very strong impact in [Community D] and [Community B]. In my opinion there was a real serious change in the wind right after the election."

Many of our interviewees pointed to the efforts of firefighter unions in the various communities—and their opposition to the collaborative effort—as a key factor in the political changes that occurred. The newly elected mayor of Community E told us that "the unions got very active in that election; they had a lot of influence in the process." The mayor of Community D, a supporter of the FCFA who was defeated for reelection, told us that "the fire union . . . worked to defeat two of the mayors and were successful." Fire department officials generally supported these assessments. The fire chief in Community D asserted:

> Yes, in some sense, I think the political views changed . . . [T]he new politicians expressed very pro-union sentiments during their election campaigns. This is a hard working union town and I think that influence is going to be felt.

The 2007 municipal elections may have administered the coup de grace to the effort to establish the FCFA, but they were not the fundamental cause of the failure. The working group's inability prior to November 2007 to address two key issues—financing arrangements and a new labor agreement—was a result of more basic causes. In this section of the chapter we explore these more basic causes.

Differing Expectations for Cost Savings

Especially in times of fiscal stress, and for elected officials in particular, the promise that interlocal collaboration can reduce operating costs—while hopefully also maintaining the quality and quantity of services provided—is a major consideration. Interlocal collaboration can reduce costs in various ways. But when such collaboration also threatens employment levels, then the political dynamics change dramatically. This is most obviously so for rank-and-file employees and any unions that represent them. This reality was clearly evident from the data in our study. Table 8.2 indicates that elected officials were much more likely than either city managers or fire personnel to consider achieving short-run cost savings (three to five years) to be an important justification for collaborating. Interestingly, there was little difference in expectations across the various respondents insofar as longer-term cost savings were concerned.

Another factor that limited the working group's ability to reach agreement on employee wages and benefits was disagreement as to implications of several state laws. One of the state statutes that could provide the legal basis for the proposed FCFA—the Michigan Urban Cooperation Act—could be read as requiring that rank-and-file employees of the new authority would have to receive pay and benefits *equal* to those currently being provided by the community with the *highest level* of compensation. This provision would have increased compensation for personnel in four of the five city fire departments affected by the creation of the FCFA. With labor costs constituting roughly 75 percent of the total costs of fire and emergency medical services, this provision would make any short term-decrease in operating costs unlikely (for more on this issue, see Hatley and Carr 2011).

There was a second Michigan statute that could be used to form the authority. This was Michigan's Public Act 57 of 1988—also known as the Emergency Services Act. One part of this act provided that the collective bargaining agreements currently in force in communities seeking to form a new authority would remain in force until their expiration. While less restrictive than the provision in the Urban Cooperation Act, this provision also would have the effect of making short-term savings less likely or significant.

Public Opinion and a Feared Loss of Local Control

The nature of fire and emergency medical services, like police services, are important to most residents. Hence, changing how those services will be produced requires a generally supportive citizenry. It is not clear that this was so in the five communities seeking to establish the FCFA. When asked prior to the 2007 election to characterize public opinion in their communities on the possible creation of the FCFA, most of our informants indicated that citizens were either uninformed or generally opposed to efforts to collaborate with neighboring jurisdictions. To be sure, some respondents believed that public opinion

Table 8.2

Importance of Reasons for Pursuing Collaboration

	Mayors (N = 3)	City Council Members (N = 4)	City Managers (N = 3)	Fire Chiefs (N = 5)	Firefighters (N = 5)
Our city will save money in the short run (3–5 years)	6.50*	7.00	3.67	2.80	3.80
Our city will save money in the long run (over 5 years)	9.00	9.00	7.67	7.80	8.80
Our residents see improvements in the quality of services compared to what we have provided previously	8.00	7.00	8.33	7.40	8.00

*On a 10-point scale where 1 = "not important at all" and 10 = "critically important."

became more positive as citizens learned more about the potential benefits of creating the FCFA. But one mayor warned that "political leaders need to do a better job of educating the public about what is going on."

One factor that shapes public opinion is a fear that consolidation may decrease how much control residents have over the service in question. It has been argued that loss of local control over fire services is an obstacle to collaboration (Bickers 2005). Ferris (1986) argued that the fear of losing local control over service production is strong and therefore the net gains of turning to other sources must be substantial (see also Morgan and Hirlinger 1991).

Several of the questions we asked in our interviews explored this issue. Elected officials—whether mayors or council members—were less likely than were fire professionals to agree that residents of their communities viewed direct provision as the "default option for most public services" (see Table 8.3). City managers tended to have views that fell between those of the first two groups of respondents. Respondents were also asked whether they agreed that residents of their community placed more value on retaining control over public services than on reducing service costs. Elected officials were less likely than were fire professionals to agree that this was so, with city managers falling in the middle (see Table 8.3).

Asked a similar question with respect to the trade-off between local control and the improvement of service quality, fire professionals were substantially more likely to believe that desires for local control trumped enhanced service quality than were elected officials, with the views of city managers being similar to those of the fire professionals interviewed (see Table 8.3).

Reflecting the views of fire department respondents, the fire chief of Community C remarked: "[O]ur city has a long history of being self-sufficient. . . . [W]e have our own hospital, our own water, power, and cable and have had them for a long time. . . . [T]his [collaboration] is going to be hard for us to sell to citizens because of that sense of identity, separate identity." In contrast, a council member in Community E believed

Table 8.3

Respondents' Views on How Citizens Felt About Direct Service Provision and Local Control of Service Provision

	Mean Agreement Score (1 = Strongly Disagree; 10 = Strongly Agree)					
Question	All Respondents (N = 20)	Mayors (N = 4)	Council Members (N = 3)	City Managers (N = 3)	Fire Chiefs (N = 5)	Fire-fighters (N = 5)
Residents support direct provision as the default option for most public services	6.72	5.00	6.00	7.00	7.80	7.80
Residents place more value on protecting community's control over public services than on lower costs	6.91	5.33	5.00	6.00	6.40	7.20
Residents place more value on protecting community's control over public services than on improving service effectiveness	5.72	3.67	4.67	6.67	6.40	6.80

that "as long as it saves money and provides a good service I think people are favorable toward this ideal."

The results of the 2007 municipal elections suggest that the views of fire professionals (and perhaps of the city managers) may have been more accurate and that many voters had doubts about the desirability of creating the FCFA.[7] Interviewed prior to the collapse of the effort, the then-mayor of Community D boldly told us that "even without it [considerable public support] I would still pursue it . . . [If] they're against it maybe I haven't explained it well enough. . . . They can always vote me out of office, but I'm not going to change my standards for political reasons." Bravely stated, but this mayor was defeated when he ran for reelection in 2007 and was replaced by a candidate who was opposed to creating the FCFA!

A Lack of Trust Among Participants

While there was a past history of collaboration among the five communities, any trust generated by this past collaboration does not appear to have been sufficient to sustain as radical a change as was represented by the creation of the FCFA. While a certain level of distrust existed between the individual communities involved in the effort, the lack of trust was particularly acute between elected officials and—to a lesser extent—administrative officials, on the one hand, and rank-and-file fire/EMS personnel and the unions that represented them, on the other.

The lack of trust between rank-and-file employees and their unions, and between elected and administrative participants, was especially apparent when it came to negotiating an agreement regarding terms of employment in the new authority. This was one of the two major issues—the other being how to fund the authority—that was not resolved prior to the 2007 municipal elections. At one point in the discussions it was suggested that representatives of the fire unions provide a draft document on labor issues. This they declined to do. A fire captain in Community C stated that "even the union couldn't agree on the labor agreement . . . [T]hat was a mistake, the union not being able to agree on a draft of how we would handle all of these issues." The fire chief in Community A observed that "the unions were afraid because they thought that if they drafted the labor agreement, that would cap them [pay and benefits] and they couldn't ask for more; they wanted the city to write it." Finally the representative of the fire union from Community E stated:

> [W]e should have had a master agreement to start with. We [the unions] were given the authority to draft it ourselves and not doing that was a mistake I think. . . . It's hard when you're used to traditional [collective] bargaining methods. It's tough to show all of your cards and put everything on the table.

There is an important lesson here. Early on, participants in the effort agreed that no fire personnel would lose their jobs as a consequence of the creation of the FCFA. This was a foolish thing to do in light of high levels of unionization among fire service personnel, given differences of opinion on the likelihood of short-term cost savings and disagreement over the implications of relevant state laws for employee compensation. Much time and effort would have been saved by participants being more candid about the fact that cost savings under the authority would at least partially be achieved by reducing the number of personnel needed to provide fire and emergency medical services as compared to having them provided separately.

CONCLUSION

In this chapter we have explored the dynamics of an effort to create a multicommunity authority to provide fire services in suburban Detroit. Although the effort had a number of things going for it, after several years of discussion it collapsed. Hindsight is always 20/20, and in retrospect it was possible to discern a number of causes for the lack of success. These included the power of municipal unions in grassroots elections; citizen concern over various supposed adverse impacts of collaboration on current fire and EMS employees in particular communities; state legislation that—intentionally or not—made collaboration more difficult; a desire on the part of many citizens for local control; and continued distrust among some of the participants in the project.

That having been said, nothing is forever. The interviews we conducted after the collapse of the effort to create the Five Community Fire Authority revealed considerable sentiment that it was only a matter of time before something like it was created. A majority of those interviewed felt, however, that it will take more effort by state government for this to happen, including changing some laws relating to compensation levels for employees of newly created authorities, which many felt stood in the way of concluding an agreement. A number of respondents also suggested that it would be helpful if state government, the Michigan Municipal League, and the state firefighters' union could develop a model agreement that might serve as a template for communities contemplating the creation of a multijurisdiction authority.

Finally, it may have been—as a number our respondents believed—that things were just not "bad enough" for a multicommunity fire authority to make sense. If so, these respondents were prescient.

The initial effort to create a FCFA collapsed just as the Great Recession was gathering steam. Within a few years, two of the three domestic automobile companies had been radically restructured and downsized as part of the federal government's managed bankruptcies and bailouts. By 2009, the unemployment rate in the Detroit metropolitan region was 15.1 percent, the highest rate among the 50 largest metropolitan areas. The rate did not drop below 10 percent until early in 2012. The region also had one the highest rates of home foreclosure in the period from 2009 to 2012. Given these economic conditions, property valuations and local government property tax revenues plummeted.

The impact of these developments on the five communities that had tried to form the FCFA was significant. All five have lost a number of firefighters due to budget cuts. Other firefighters had voluntarily left some of the communities for other fire departments due to the fiscal stress that the five study communities were experiencing.

As of early 2013, one of these communities (Community D) had fiscal difficulties so severe that a state-appointed emergency manager had taken control. The state law relating to such a state takeover of a unit of local government had been revised in 2012, giving such emergency managers almost unlimited powers to address fiscal imbalances, including ceasing to bargain with existing employee unions and being able to unilaterally modify existing collective bargaining agreements. The irony is that the firefighters of Community D, and their union, were among those who were less enthusiastic about the proposed FCFA and worked hard to prevent its creation. Now they face a situation in which serious reductions in the number of firefighters and/or significant cuts in pay and benefits are quite likely.

In early 2013, the smallest of the five communities involved in the effort to create the FCFA (Community A) agreed to have another neighboring community—one that was not part of the effort to create the FCFA—absorb its fire staff. This much more populous community had a voter-approved minimum staffing level for firefighters in place, but it had no interest in entering into a multicommunity fire authority. Instead, it had determined that one way to cope with its costly minimum staffing requirement was to proceed to sell fire services to surrounding communities. This larger jurisdiction was also in discussions with Community D about a similar arrangement. Two other suburban communities in the same county as the five that had sought to create the FCFA had agreed to a fire authority that would begin operating in 2015.

Various changes have also occurred that address the concerns held by participants in the FCFA effort about state laws discouraging collaboration. Significant changes were made in two state laws to make such collaboration easier or more likely. One important change involved the requirement that when communities formed an authority, the compensation levels for all of the fire staff in the new authority had to equal that of the best-paying jurisdiction.[8] Finally, the state firefighters' union is in the process of drafting a model labor agreement to be used by communities considering the formation of a fire authority—the lack of which had been cited by a number of our respondents as making the establishment of the FCFA more difficult. In fact, it is a member of the firefighters' union in Community E who is chairing the committee working on the development of such a model agreement.

In short, the earlier effort to create an FCFA may just have been ahead of its time both economically and politically. Recent developments suggest the accuracy of the view of a city manager we interviewed in 2009: "the crisis of the economy is very real and this is the end of the present way of funding municipal services as we know them."

KEY POINTS

- Insufficient initial agreement or understanding about the expected benefits and costs of collaboration damaged this effort when they were subsequently revealed.
- State-level rules can encourage or hinder collaboration; a thorough understanding of how they influence collaborative efforts is necessary.
- The existence of statewide model agreements relative to labor and funding issues would be beneficial in this type of collaborative effort.
- The feared loss of local control over public service provision appears to be an important factor to some voters, therefore the parties and the public should be educated on the costs and benefits of collaboration before it is undertaken.
- Lack of trust between the parties in a collaborative effort can outweigh community characteristics that have long been considered to be incentives to collaboration.
- Even significant fiscal stress might not be sufficient to facilitate collaboration unless other important factors are properly addressed.
- In many jurisdictions, unionization levels are high in the public services, and that fact must be taken into consideration in building support for a collaborative effort.

NOTES

1. This is not the actual name of the proposed authority. Although only one of the officials we interviewed requested anonymity, we decided not to identify any of them by name. We have also not provided the specific names of the communities involved. The true names of other organizations involved in the collaborative effort have also been changed.

2. Since Chapters 1, 2, and 3 of this volume review the research on the conditions thought to facilitate interlocal collaboration, that literature is not cited here.

3. In each of the communities, the city manager is appointed by the city council and serves

at its pleasure. Despite the strong conventional wisdom suggesting that the presence of a city manager facilitates collaboration, empirical research on the question does not support this contention (Carr 2013). Those we interviewed in our study were divided on this point (Hatley and Carr 2012).

4. In keeping with our practice in this study, the name of this organization is fictitious.

5. Specifically, the Michigan Public Act 57 of 1988, also known as the Emergency Services Act.

6. One reason for this conclusion was that some of these communities had full-time "professional" fire departments while a number of others had volunteer forces.

7. While this may have been so in these five communities, two studies among Michigan citizens on how to cope with local government fiscal stress conducted at roughly the same time suggest a different conclusion. Random samples of Michiganders were asked specifically about service delivery options for fire services (as well as four other services). The 2007 survey (Elling, Carr, and Glenn 2009) found that slightly more than two-thirds of those surveyed expressed support for consolidating the production/provision of fire services with a neighboring local government. By 2010, support for this option had increased to more than 70 percent (Elling, Krawczyk, and Carr 2011).

8. But this change may be a double-edged sword. While it pleased management, it would probably cause at least the best-paid firefighters in any community considering joining a multijurisdiction authority to be less amenable to creating one.

REFERENCES

Bickers, Kenneth N. 2005. The politics of interlocal cooperation: A theory and a test. Paper presented at the Creating Collaborative Communities Conference. Detroit: Wayne State University.

Carr, Jered B. 2013. Form of government and policy choices: Lessons from the empirical literature. Working Paper. Kansas City: L.P. Cookingham Institute of Urban Affairs, University of Missouri–Kansas City.

Elling, Richard C., Jered B. Carr, and Mark Glenn. 2009. Meeting the challenge of local government fiscal stress: The views of Michigan citizens. Paper presented at the 2009 Annual Meeting of the Southern Political Science Association. New Orleans, LA, January 7–10.

Elling, Richard C., Kelly Krawczyk, and Jered B. Carr. 2011. Confronting local government fiscal stress: Citizen attitudes across time. Paper presented at the 2011 Annual Meeting of the Midwest Political Science Association. Chicago, March 31–April 3.

Ferris, James. 1986. The decision to contract out: An empirical analysis. *Urban Affairs Quarterly* 22: 289–311.

Hatley, William. 2010. The art of collaboration: Interlocal collaboration in the provision of fire services in the Detroit area. Unpublished PhD dissertation. Wayne State University.

Hatley, William, and Jered B. Carr. 2011. State regulation and functional consolidation in Michigan: The case of the Downriver Fire Authority. Paper presented at the 2011 Annual Conference of the American Society for Public Administration. Baltimore, March 14.

———. 2012. Services collaboration through multijurisdictional organizations: Obstacles and opportunities in times of fiscal stress. Paper presented at 2012 Annual Conference of the American Society for Public Administration. Las Vegas, March 3.

Morgan, David R., and Michael W. Hirlinger. 1991. Intergovernmental service contracts: A multivariate explanation. *Urban Affairs Quarterly* 27(1): 128–144.

Southeast Michigan Council of Governments. 2012. Community Profiles. Retrieved from: www.semcog.org.

United States Bureau of Census. 2010. *Demographic profile*. Retrieved from: www.census.gov.

———. 2000. *Demographic profile*. Retrieved from: www.census.gov.

APPENDIX 8.1. Participants Interviewed for the FCFA Research Project

Role/Position of Participants Interviewed	Number of Interviews*
Mayors	3 (4)
City Council Members	4 (1)
City Managers	3 (2)
Fire Chiefs	5 (5)
Firefighting Personnel	5 (4)
Total	20 (16)

*Figures in parentheses are those re-interviewed subsequent to the collapse of the collaborative effort.

APPENDIX 8.2. Instrument Used in Interviewing 20 Participants Involved in the Effort to Create the FCFA

Note: The actual name of collaborative effort has been changed consistent with the practice in the chapter.

Today's date: ____________________

Place interview took place: ____

Time of the interview: ____

Interviewer's name: ____

Interviewee's name: ____

Organization's name: ____

A. Respondent Professional Experience

A1. I want to begin with some questions about your professional experience.

a. How long have you been with the city? Do you also reside in the city?
b. What is your current position? How long have you been in it?
c. Have you had other positions in this organization?
d. Have you ever worked for any of the other cities participating in the Authority?
e. Do you have any previous experience as an elected official (or as an administrator) in this or another local government?

B. Factors Stimulating Interlocal Cooperation

Next, I want to ask you a few questions about the factors that led to this current effort to cooperate on fire services across these several cities. Initially, I would like to focus on the stimulus for cooperating on fire services, not on cooperating in terms of a fire authority. The fire authority is a specific approach to collaboration and I will ask you about the authority in the next section. At this point, I am interested in understanding the factors that simulated your city's interest in cooperating across jurisdictional lines on fire services.

B1. Please turn to Scale A on the back of the instructions I provided you. Use them to indicate the extent to which you agree with the following set of statements about how the organizational and political culture in your city affects the likelihood of these types of cross-border efforts emerging.

On a scale of 1–10, how much do you agree these statements generally describe your organization and/or community

a. My organization is usually receptive to doing things in new ways.
b. My organization usually approaches problems proactively.
c. My organization is usually open to possibilities for collaborating on services with other local governments. (Here, we refer to governments other than the county.)
d. Our residents demand that direct provision be the default option for most basic public services.
e. Our residents demand that we consider what's good for [communities in the Authority's response territory] when we make decisions about providing important public services.
f. Our residents tend to be suspicious of the motivations of elected officials from the neighboring jurisdictions.
g. Our residents do not care about how services are delivered because they focus only on the quality and cost of these services.
h. Our residents would rather we contract with other local governments than with private or nonprofit organizations for most services.
i. Our residents want us to let the county provide services whenever possible.
j. Our residents place more value on protecting our city's control over public services than on lowering costs.
k. Our residents place more value on protecting our city's control over public services than on improving service effectiveness across the [communities in the Authority's response territory].
l. Our residents see themselves as highly interdependent with the local governments that surround this community.
m. There is a significant constituency in my community for seeking regional solutions to our problems.

B2. In your view, what are the factors that led to this effort? (Depending on the answer, follow up with the following prompts):

a. Were there any specific events that directly encouraged your city's participation in this effort? If yes, explain.
b. Is there a person in your city that has stood out as an entrepreneur/leader in this effort? If yes, who? What are some examples of the activities this person undertook? Why do you think this person took on this role? What motivated his or her efforts in this regard?
c. In your view, has a person from another city been instrumental to this effort going forward? If yes, who? What are some examples of the activities this person undertook? What do you see as his or her motivations for this leadership role?
d. Are there any third parties whose involvement was instrumental to this collaboration moving forward? If yes, who? How so? Can you offer some examples of how they helped? Do you have any thoughts about their motivations for involvement in this effort?

B3. This effort involves collaboration on fire services. Does the fact that it involves fire services make it more or less easy to do this? Explain.

C. Perceptions of the Terms of Collaboration

Now, I have a few questions about your view of the costs and benefits of cooperating on fire services. These include an identification of the benefits anticipated to flow from this collaboration and your expectations about how these benefits will be distributed among the cities participating in this collaboration. We are also interested in the expected costs, if any, of this collaboration and how the fire authority is expected to affect the costs and benefits of participating in this project.

C1. Turning to Scale B on the back of the instructions I provided you, please indicate your agreement with the following statement about the importance of these specific factors to your support of this effort to cooperate on fire services.

a. Our city will save money in the short run (3–5 years).
b. Our city will save money in the long run (over 5 years).
c. Our residents see improvements in the quality of the service over what we have provided previously.
d. Cost savings are distributed equally among the participating communities.
e. None of our fire department staff will lose their jobs due to this collaboration.
f. Participation in the authority gives our community access to existing facilities and equipment currently unavailable to us because of their location in another jurisdiction.
h. Participation in the authority gives our community access to the financial resources needed to construct facilities or purchase equipment that we cannot afford by ourselves.
i. The authority will distribute future nonlocal (state and federal) resources among the [communities in the Authority's response territory] in a more rational way than is now the case.
j. Creation of this authority results in equal spending on fire protection among the participating jurisdictions.

C2. Are there benefits I have NOT mentioned that you hope will result from this collaboration?

C3. Previously, we discussed the perceptions of your city's residents about the existence of interdependencies among the [communities in the Authority's response territory]. I would like you to elaborate further on this question of interdependence.

a. Do you agree these interdependencies exist among the [communities in the Authority's response territory]?
b. If so, what is the nature of this interdependence?

C4. Turning to the specific issue of the fire authority as the mechanism for this collaborative effort, I have several questions about your views of and expectations for the authority.

a. Is the use of a fire authority important to your support for this effort? Why or why not? How confident are you that your city will be better off by participating in this authority?
b. Are you confident that your community will retain sufficient control over the quality of services provided to your residents? If so, why?
c. In your mind, how do the potential gains of the fire authority outweigh the loss of complete control over this service?
d. How confident are you that the elected officials of your community will be able to exert meaningful influence over the managers of the fire authority?
e. If your residents become dissatisfied with this arrangement, can it be easily altered? Can your community easily withdraw from the authority?
f. How will the costs of the fire authority be allocated among the participating communities?

D. Perceptions of Partners (and Potential Partners) in the Collaboration

Next, we are interested in your perceptions of the partners in this collaboration. We are especially interested in understanding the levels of trust that existed among the participating communities prior to this collaboration and how confident you are that these other communities will meet their obligations to the others.

D1. Turning again to Scale B, how important are the following characteristics in a potential local government partner for ANY significant effort to collaborate on public services, and not just fire services? These can be thought of as general principles of collaboration. They should be:

a. communities we do not directly compete with for residents and development.
b. similar to our community in terms of wealth and racial composition.
c. similar to our community in terms of governmental structure (i.e., either both council-manager or both mayor-council systems).

d. similar to our community in terms of powers (i.e., both cities or both townships).
e. able to provide similar levels of resources to the effort.
f. seeking the same benefits from this collaboration as we are.
g. communities that have successfully collaborated with us in the past.

D2. A general concern about intergovernmental collaborations on public services involves the level of trust among the participating governments. We are interested in understanding how trust is developed, maintained, and lost. First, using Scale B, please answer the following questions about trust in your collaboration partners.

a. I must be able to trust the political leadership in the other communities.
b. In your opinion, how important to your community is the reputation of your collaboration partners for trustworthiness and cooperation?
c. Do you think your community has a generally trusting orientation toward other communities?
d. In your opinion, has the level of trust between the participants gone up, down or stayed about the same since this collaboration effort began?
e. Do you trust your partners in this effort? All of them?
f. How do you define trust?
g. How can the required trust be built?
h. How can this trust be undermined?

D3. I am interested in understanding how the participants in this effort were decided on.

a. How were the participants decided on? Is this the final group or do you envision others will be added in the future?
b. Are there any nonparticipating communities you wish were involved? If yes, why do you think they are not participating at this time?
c. What makes the current participants good partners for your community on this service?
d. Can you think of some local jurisdictions that would NOT be good partners for your community? If so, why?
e. How are your perceptions about these actual and potential partners affected by past interactions? Please explain with an example or two.

D4. Does your city already cooperate on any of the services that will be provided through the fire authority? If yes, could you talk about the specific services, which of the [communities in the Authority's response territory] are involved, and the nature of the cooperative arrangement with the city. (Some examples are an interlocal services contract, mutual aid, etc.)

D5. What has been the public reaction in your community to this effort?

E. Differences in Roles Played by Elected Officials and Public Managers

Next, we are interested in understanding the roles played by the elected officials and public managers in this effort. A common perception by researchers is that elected officials play a secondary role in interlocal arrangements. Elected officials are often described as having jurisdictional-based interests, whereas managers are said to be more likely to embrace solutions that involve intergovernmental cooperation.

E1. I would like to ask you a few questions about any institution(s) or network(s) either formal or informal that helped bring about this collaboration effort. (Interviewer: note whether interviewee is an appointed administrative person or an elected official.)

a. Do you talk with officials from other local governments on a regular basis? If so, how often in a typical year?
b. What form do these contacts take? (Choose all that apply.)

   Political meetings:
   (1) SEMCOG (Southeast Michigan Council of Governments)
   (2) MML functions (Michigan Municipal League)
   (3) SCC (Suburban Community Conference)
   (4) MSA
   (5) Regular meetings of city managers
   (6) Other

c. Was any particular institution (hierarchy?) used in bringing about the start-up of this collaboration? If yes, what was that institution?
d. How necessary was any institution to the emergence of this collaboration?
e. How much time would you estimate you spend monthly on this collaboration effort?
f. How much time would you estimate you spend monthly meeting with your counterparts in surrounding communities?
g. In regards to working on this collaborative effort, how important do you think your knowledge, expertise and shared beliefs with your counterparts is? Why?
h. How difficult will it be/has it been to sell this collaboration to the political leaders of your community? How did you/will you do that?
i. Is there any way these issues could have been dealt with solely within your jurisdiction? If yes, how?

E2. Do you belong to any professional organizations or local networking group that have been important to this effort?

E3. Have you relied on your professional network within the participating communities in the development of this proposed fire authority? If yes, how? (Have we answered this with the above questions or do we still need something more?)

E4. Is it important to have a political constituency for cooperation? Do administrators play a role in creating one?

F. Final Questions

- In your view, what is the most difficult aspect of pursuing this effort?
- As you look forward, what are your three biggest concerns about the future of this effort?
- Are there any topics I have not covered that you would like to talk about?

APPENDIX 8.3. Instrument Used in Interviewing 16 Participants Involved in the Effort to Create the FCFA Following the Collapse of the Effort

Note: The actual name of the collaborative effort have been changed consistent with the practice in the chapter.

Today's date: ____________________

Interviewer's name: Bill Hatley

Interviewee's name: ____

Organization's name: ____

Hello, my name is Bill Hatley. I'm working on a project examining the proposed FCFA [fictitious name]. You will recall that I interviewed you previously and we discussed various factors and issues surrounding the effort to establish the FCFA. Your participation in that phase of our investigation helped us to better understand interlocal cooperation in general and the FCFA effort in particular.

We are currently examining the attitudes and insights of public managers and local elected officials as to the current state of the FCFA collaborative effort. We are particularly interested in your thoughts as to why the FCFA effort appears to be suspended and what may have happened that caused that.

We are interviewing several officials from each of the jurisdictions that previously participated in our study. Thank you for your willingness to participate again in this research project. Your participation is very much appreciated.

Question 1: What do you believe is the current state of the effort to implement the FCFA? Is the planning group still meeting? When was the last meeting held? Is the concept still being discussed formally or informally? If yes, how?

Question 2: If the FCFA effort has been discontinued, what do you believe are the main reasons why this has occurred? Were there any specific events that directly caused your city to stop participating in this effort?

Question 3: Did the local elections of 2008 have any impact on your city's decision to continue or discontinue the FCFA effort? For example, did the election of a new Mayor in three of the five cities make any difference to your participation?

Question 4: When we conducted the last interviews for this research, the planning group had not yet drafted a proposed labor agreement nor had it drafted a proposed method for funding the FCFA. What importance, if any, do you attach to those two factors?

Question 5: Do you believe that anything can be done to re-start the FCFA collaboration? If so, what specifically?

Question 6: Our previous research indicated that all of the participating cities were experiencing considerable fiscal stress and had hoped to alleviate some of that stress through the FCFA effort. Has that fiscal stress been eliminated in some other way? If yes, please explain how.

Question 7: Looking back on your effort to establish the FCFA, what were the three biggest obstacles to your achieving your goals? What in your opinion are the biggest mistakes that were made in this effort to form the DFA?

APPENDIX 8.4. Selected Demographic and Governmental Characteristics of Five Detroit Suburban Communities Seeking to Create a Joint Fire Authority

	Community				
	A	B	C	D	E
2000 population[1]	10,735	30,136	28,006	29,070	40,008
2010 population[2]	10,715	30,047	25,833	28,210	38,144
Total acres in community[3]	1,740	4,400	3,316	4,486	3,744
Percent minority residents[1]	14%	6%	4%	4%	8%
Percent residents below poverty level[1]	11.4%	4.8%	6.2%	3.2%	7.7%
Type of government[3]	Mayor-Council	Mayor-Council	Mayor-Council	Mayor-Council	Mayor-Council
City manager present[3]	Yes	Yes	Yes	Yes	Yes

[1]2000 U.S. Census.
[2]2010 U.S. Census.
[3]Southeast Michigan Council of Governments, Community Profiles, 2012.

9

Mapping the Shared Services Landscape

Ricardo S. Morse and Charles R. Abernathy

Shared service arrangements, also referred to as interlocal cooperation, service-sharing, and joint public service, are an increasingly heralded metastrategy for improving the efficiency and effectiveness of local government service delivery. As evidenced by this volume and other research that has come before, [1] shared services is widely viewed as an important innovation in the way local governments provide public services and otherwise create public value. With shrinking resources and ever-expanding demand for service, local governments must figure out how to do more (or at least the same) with less. Furthermore, as states face their own fiscal crises, they are increasingly looking to boost efficiencies in local service delivery as a way to lessen the burden of reduced state support. Thus we see states using both carrots and sticks to incentivize shared services.[2]

But when we speak of shared services we are not referring to any single service delivery arrangement in particular. Rather, shared services is more of a catchall term to describe a suite of partnership strategies that vary in the *degree of functional service consolidation and shared governance involved.* Handshake agreements to share information, staff, or equipment involve much less real change than a merger of departments from two separate entities. It is important, therefore, to be specific about what kinds of shared service arrangements are in play, and to be open about the administrative and political risks and rewards in discussions about alternatives. This chapter outlines and defines the various shared service strategies and organizes them into a typology or map, considering in particular the degree of consolidation (which also, for the most part, represents the political difficulty involved), as well as the extent of shared governance, the later point being an element missing from other continua-oriented typologies.

EXAMINING THE SHARED SERVICES LANDSCAPE

For the purposes of this chapter, we include in the suite of shared service opportunities forms of collaboration that may include nongovernmental organizations as well as individuals or groups of citizens. Shared services refers primarily to intergovernmental cooperative arrangements, which is why it is (or should be) distinguished from privatization, as well as political consolidation (e.g., city–county consolidation). However, there are many cases where shared services involve nongovernmental actors and/or citizens.

The following shared service strategies represent common forms, though certainly the list is not exhaustive. Several examples are used from McDowell County,[3] North Carolina, the organization managed by one of the authors (Abernathy). These examples are meant to be illustrative but also demonstrate how common shared services are, not just in metropolitan areas, but also very much so in rural jurisdictions across the United States that leverage shared services to create public value in a seriously resource-constrained environment.

Co-production

Co-production has a long history in public administration as a mechanism through which public services are jointly produced by a government agency and citizens, groups, or organizations in the community, with the intent of improving service quality and/or reducing the (public) costs of providing the service. Thomas explains that co-production refers to the public and government partnering in the production of public services (2012, 85). This approach is often used where the service is difficult to provide without the co-producers. Recycling is a great example of this need because a recycling program cannot be effective without a critical mass of citizens and organizations participating. Other common examples of co-production include athletic programs that utilize volunteer coaches as well as fire and emergency medical services (EMS) and public libraries that often utilize volunteer labor.

Co-production is frequently part of more complex partnership arrangements, such as a volunteer fire district receiving support from multiple local government entities (a county and municipality, for example). A county basketball league might be co-produced by a county recreation department in concert with municipal recreation departments, as well as citizen volunteers. At its core, though, co-production is about nongovernmental actors voluntarily contributing (labor or other resources) toward the production of a public service. A good example from McDowell County, North Carolina, is a program that provides transportation services for veterans to the Veterans Administration (VA) Hospital in Asheville. The local American Legion provides the driver, the county donates the vehicle, and the program is administered by a local nonprofit.

Grants or Other Types of Subsidies

Grants or other types of subsidies involve local government contributions to the provision of a service for its community through some form of contribution (e.g., in-kind donations) to a service provider, which could be another local government, nonprofit, or for-profit organization. Examples include local government grants to nonprofit agencies and municipal contributions to a county-wide economic development agency. It is important to note that grants and subsidies of this sort are different from contracting, where a local government pays a contractor (private, nonprofit, or otherwise) to produce a service on its behalf. What we are talking about here are contributions toward the provision of some public good or service by another entity, but not as part of a contractual arrangement. Grants and other contributions to nongovernmental public service organizations can be a source of real competition and perhaps even conflict for resources among county and city decision makers.

Local governments commonly make annual allocations to nongovernmental organizations in order to support some public purpose being provided. In McDowell County, the Chamber of Commerce and local community college operate community leadership development programs (called LINK and Junior LINK) that are seen as a benefit to the community. The county helps support the cost of the program with an annual allocation. Duke Energy and the City of Marion also make an annual allocation to support the program. There are many other community organizations that the county supports with grants, such as a homeless shelter, the local arts council, a museum, a battered women's shelter, and a community wellness organization.

Resource Sharing

Resource sharing involves the sharing of information, personnel, equipment, and other types of assets, between local governments and/or between a local government and other community organizations. Examples include two municipalities sharing equipment or local law enforcement sharing personnel in certain situations.[4] Resource sharing is very common and most often is informal and based on norms of reciprocity; however, it may also be formalized through interlocal agreements of various kinds (Thurmaier and Wood 2003; Chen and Thurmaier 2009; Andrew 2009).

Mutual aid agreements, for example, are very common, particularly in public safety and public works. They are often formalized in written agreements between jurisdictions; however, they too can be informal. There has been considerable interest in mutual aid agreements as they relate to disaster preparedness in the post-9/11 era (Cohn 2005).

A good example of resource sharing in McDowell County, outside of mutual aid, involves the construction of trails and greenways. Many local governments across the United States are building greenways, and substantial interest exists on the topic of community wellness. McDowell County has a fragmented system of trails that includes two trails connecting to neighboring Buncombe County. The two municipalities within McDowell County and the county itself, along with the nonprofit McDowell Trails Association (MTA), cooperate on the maintenance of the trails that have been built. The trails are in all three jurisdictions and the logic of cooperation and resource sharing in the maintenance of the trails is straightforward.

Cooperative Purchasing Arrangements

Cooperative purchasing arrangements involve two or (often many) more organizations purchasing materials and equipment together in order to save money (Hondale 1984). Cost savings can occur through obtaining volume discounts not available to a smaller, single purchaser, reducing administrative costs of purchasing and expanding purchasing expertise. Joint purchasing can be organized with a lead agency as purchaser, through a third-party contracted program, or through a regional council program. Many state governments also have cooperative purchasing programs for local governments and state agencies. The General Services Administration (GSA) has a cooperative purchasing program available to state and local governments.

Service Contracts

Service contracts are a very common tool for local service provision. Local government contracts with outside entities, whether public or private, for the provision of a public service or support services for the local government organization, are widespread cross most local government functions (Warner and Hefetz 2009). Examples include municipalities contracting with for-profit firms for solid waste collection, counties with nonprofits for social service programs, or municipalities with counties for tax collection. The tax collection area is a very common example of service contracts between counties and cities. The State of North Carolina already mandates that counties collect motor vehicle personal property taxes for cities. Many municipalities also contract with counties for the collection of real property taxes as well.

Service contracting has perhaps received the most attention in the scholarly literature as a principal service delivery alternative. Warner and Hefetz have studied local government service contracting for many years, examining various factors that influence the contracting decision, such as service and management characteristics (Warner and Hefetz 2012; Hefetz and Warner 2012). Service contracting, whether in the form of intergovernmental service contracts or nongovernmental contracts, is one of the primary "tools" (Salamon 2002) of government associated with New Public Management and a public choice perspective on local governance in general (Hefetz and Warner 2012).

Joint Operations

Joint operations are found where a local government and one or more other organizations jointly produce a public service through a partnership arrangement. These are true collaborations, where the partners work together to plan for and deliver a public service. Joint operations are differentiated from co-production in that responsibility and accountability are shared in a partnership, whereas co-production is more about the public's role in assisting the local government in service delivery. With joint operations or partnerships, equal partners work together to co-create something. In co-productions the partners are not equal in the same sense.

Examples of joint operations include recreation programs provided through collaboration between local governments and/or nongovernmental organizations. Soccer leagues often involve collaboration between local governments, a nonprofit soccer league, and local businesses (sponsors). The McDowell High School swim team collaborates with the YMCA for use of a covered pool in the winter, with the county recreation department for use of the outdoor pool, and with a summer swim team called the McDowell Mariners.

McDowell County has a joint operation with the State Department of Corrections (North Carolina) where inmate labor from the local minimum-security prison is used to staff the county recycling operation. The state recognizes the positive impact on the inmates who are nearing the completion of their term.[5] The inmates enjoy the freedom afforded by getting outside the prison and the benefit of learning to operate the equipment.

Another unique partnership with the county prison involves staffing a poultry-processing facility for small farmers with inmate labor. This unique enterprise of the county provides U.S. Department of Agriculture (USDA) inspected organic poultry processing for local farmers in a cost-sustainable manner. Inmates who opt into the program earn minimum wage but also learn valuable work skills such as teamwork, showing up on time, and the importance of quality work performance. The inmates are often able to secure employment in a larger poultry-processing facility located in an adjacent county after 1their release.

It is our observation that there is probably much more creativity in the realm of joint operations taking place than is recognized. The competition for scarce resources combined with public demand for services can be a compelling force for creativity and innovation. Joint, or collaborative, operations represent a safe middle ground for managers and elected officials to enjoy greater efficiencies or effectiveness in service delivery through partnerships, while maintaining organizational autonomy. These forms of service sharing are harder to "see" in terms of research though, which may explain why so much attention is given to interlocal agreements and service contracts—which are more easily measured—while less is given to the variety of creative joint-operations arrangements that are less easily captured in terms of large-*N* research studies.

Joint Facilities and Co-location

Joint facilities (or assets) and co-location involve two or more organizations sharing a common facility or other asset. Public buildings shared between a municipality and county, or shared water treatment plants, are examples of joint facilities. It is not uncommon to see a county and one or more municipalities co-locating inspection and zoning services. On a smaller scale, organizations can share other capital assets, such as two or more entities jointly purchasing an expensive piece of equipment (e.g., a backhoe)—or alternatively, one entity purchasing it on behalf of two or more entities—and then establishing agreements (formal or informal) on how it will be shared.

A great deal of contracting out of jail space across jurisdictions occurs in North Carolina. McDowell County contracts out space to the federal government and other local governments. The county also purposely overbuilt a new senior center to include an area that is leased to the hospital and also an area that is leased to a dialysis clinic.

Another example of a joint facility involves multiple jurisdictions sharing emergency radio towers and other communications infrastructure, which is the case in McDowell County and common elsewhere. McDowell County also co-located its building inspection offices with the offices of the district (regional, three-county) health department. The health department inspects septic system installations and well construction. Prior to the co-location move, contractors and citizens were traveling back and forth between the two departments to obtain necessary construction permits. Thus, co-location is not only a resource-saving strategy, it can also explicitly be used to improve customer service and overall program effectiveness. Russ Linden (2010) cites co-location as a growing trend in the public service sector and notes that financial savings are not the most important payoff. Rather, he says:

> The biggest benefits for employees are the trust, shared information, creative ideas, and energy that are produced. For clients, other stakeholders, and our communities, the payoffs include faster service, easier access to information, and one-stop operations (no need to shop around for the right service provider). (217)

Co-location can also engender greater collaboration because of the social capital that can be developed due to staff being in the same space. At the same time, it can provide a higher level of service to citizens.

Transfer of Functions

Transfer of functions occurs when one entity permanently transfers responsibility for providing a public service to another entity. This strategy represents perhaps the purest form of service consolidation, as one entity simply takes over service provision and production for another. An example is a municipality turning over water and wastewater service to a neighboring provider. Such transfers can be thought of as achieving a functional consolidation of that particular service across two or more jurisdictions.

In Raleigh, North Carolina, a de facto regional water utility has been established through the divestiture of six smaller utilities in neighboring municipalities to the Raleigh Public Works Department. The City of Raleigh thus operates a water utility for its residents plus the residents of six other municipalities (City of Raleigh 2013). Residents of Wake Forest and Garner, for example, receive water, and water bills, from the City of Raleigh. The smaller municipalities divested their assets to the City of Raleigh Public Utilities Department under terms spelled out in interlocal agreements between the municipalities and the City of Raleigh. In other words, the municipalities of Garner, Wake Forest, Rolesville, Knightdale, Wendell, and Zebulon *transferred the function* of water provision to the City of Raleigh.

Merged Departments

Merged departments are another form of true service consolidation, though this often involves more collaboration than transfer of functions arrangements. A unit merger occurs when two or more departments combine into one that is shared by all partners (though usually operating administratively under one of them). The terms of the merger agreement are spelled out formally, usually through memoranda of understanding (MOUs). Examples include joint 911 dispatch facilities and shared purchasing departments.

Geographic information systems (GIS) and technology are commonly seen merged or consolidated in this way in small counties. An information technology (IT) department in a low-population county might consist of a single employee shared across multiple jurisdictions. In a larger county, the function could still be shared, but would likely be part of a true IT department and be an example of a merged department. Grant writing is another function often merged or consolidated across jurisdictions.

Merged, cross-jurisdictional emergency (911) dispatch centers are clearly a good example of merged departments/functions. McDowell County merged three dispatch offices across two jurisdictions into one in 2012. The new entity, operated by the county and located in a municipal building, is more cost effective and provides more responsive service since the calls are not transferred from one agency to another, a situation that previously could have resulted in lost or delayed calls for emergency services.

Merged building inspection offices are another example. Merger of services is often a logical option and occurs where the type of service is very similar to that offered by another agency—in other words, where there truly is a high degree of duplication. Thus, there is great potential for merged departments in many other areas, such as building and health inspection, but proposals often meet resistance because of the diverse nature of environmental inspection, or more generally due to political issues.

New Joint Entities

New joint entities are similar to merged departments, except instead of merging into an administrative unit that is part of one of the partnering organizations, two or more organizations create a new, separate entity for the purpose of managing and governing a shared asset and/or service. Authorities and special districts have long been a popular cross-jurisdictional service delivery option in the United States. The U.S. Census of Governments reported 31,555 special districts nationwide in 1992, and 37,203 in 2012, an 18 percent increase over the last two decades (U.S. Census Bureau 2012). Examples of special districts or authorities include water and airport authorities.

Authorities are a natural outcome where entities or users, such as fire protection personnel, do not want a service to be transferred and thus relinquish control to another unit of government. Service or tax districts serve a similar purpose. McDowell County formed a new fire tax district in order to provide fire service to a number of property owners that the county could not easily serve. There are, in fact, two of these new fire districts, one created jointly with Mitchell County (to the north) and another with Burke County (to the east). The growth in the number and use of regional authorities is evidence of this shared service arrangement being important. Nonprofit organizations are also often created as joint entities across jurisdictions. Economic development commissions are a good example of cross-jurisdictional nonprofit entities.

As mentioned, this list is not exhaustive, but we do feel it is inclusive of the main categories of shared service alternatives available to local governments. It is important, though, to view these strategies as broad categories rather than discrete alternatives. In practice, shared services arrangements are all rather unique due to the circumstances surrounding their creation.

Frequently, different types of shared service strategies are combined, such as the creation of a façade restoration grant program in the City of Marion (county seat of McDowell County). The goal of the program is to renovate and restore the historic downtown area. The City of Marion, McDowell County, the Marion Business Association, and the McDowell Economic Development Association entered into an agreement to jointly fund the program that pays 50 percent of the cost for façade renovations, awnings, window replacements, painting, and so forth. The entities each contribute an equal amount, which is administered by a committee that reviews and approves the applications. The owner of the building or the business located in the building pays the remaining 50 percent. A program like this touches upon several of the categories discussed above, including co-production, joint operations, and grant giving. So while this outline of the shared services landscape can serve as a general guide or catalog of options for local government practitioners and elected boards to consider, it is important for practitioners to remember that these are not discrete choices but more of a menu from which to select components that work together to meet the needs of the partnering entities.

In exploring possibilities for shared services, the menu of options is helpful but incomplete. Potential partners need to have a framework from which to analyze and make sense of the different alternatives. They need a map to help them understand the landscape better. With this in mind, we now turn to an approach to mapping the different alternatives along two critical dimensions that decision makers must consider when exploring service delivery alternatives. The choice to create or enter into a shared service arrangement usually involves political as well as administrative considerations. Local officials need to explore options with eyes wide open and seek to select an alternative that improves efficiency and/or effectiveness but is also consistent with community and organizational values and goals. The discussion of a two-dimensional typology seeks to equip decision makers with a framework for analyzing alternatives.

CREATING A TWO-DIMENSIONAL TYPOLOGY: DEGREES OF CONSOLIDATION AND SHARED GOVERNANCE

Discussions of shared services or intergovernmental cooperation in the literature often involve an implicit, if not explicit, notion of a spectrum or continuum of alternative arrangements (e.g., Rugginni 2006; Holdsworth 2007; Sullivan and Skelcher 2002; Walker 1987) with the left-right poles representing simple-to-complex or easier-to-harder, or even more-common to less-common. But the most important observation of the spectrum typology is that *shared service arrangements vary greatly in their degree of actual service integration or consolidation*. The simple continuum presented in Abernathy (2009), representative of other continua in the literature, explicitly states it in terms of service delivery fragmentation versus consolidation, or decentralization and centralization (see Figure 9.1).

This and other continua are helpful but incomplete. We next discuss the utility of the degree of service consolidation dimension, and then turn to what we feel is another important dimension to add, which is the extent to which governance is shared.

Service Consolidation Dimension

Many different service production models have proliferated over the years, and many of these offer innovative alternatives to the service provider being the sole producer, thus falling under the category of shared services. A key way to differentiate the alternatives

Figure 9.1 **Continuum of Local Government Service Delivery Alternatives**

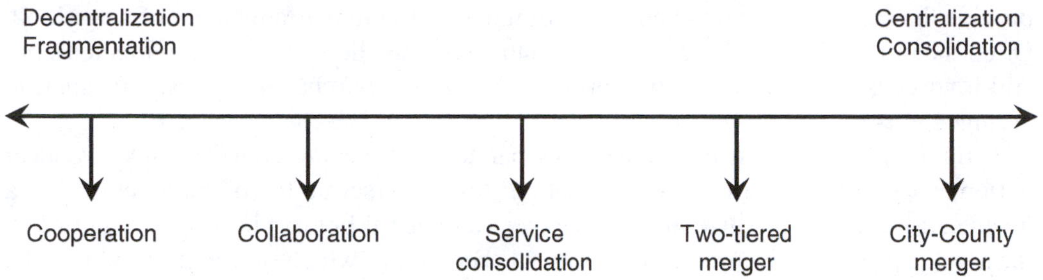

Source: Abernathy 2009, 11.

is the degree to which they integrate, consolidate, or centralize service production, as well as the locus of service provision, across a given service delivery area. Thus, more informal agreements that are more or less cooperative, like information sharing or mutual aid agreements, fall on the less consolidated, more decentralized end of the spectrum. On the other hand, merged departments, or the creation of new regional entities, represent centralized or consolidated service production in a single unit, and in some cases, such as transfer-of-functions arrangements, these arrangements centralize even the locus of service provision.

Thinking about service delivery alternatives in this way—fragmented versus consolidated, decentralized versus centralized—is based on the important distinction between local service *provision* and *production*. A central argument in Ostrom and Ostrom's (1971, 1999) delineation of public choice theory, applied to local public economies, is that local governments are organized as what the authors call "collective consumption units," where collective action is undertaken to procure public goods and services. In other words, local governments are set up to be *providers* of public goods and services. They take on the responsibility to *provide* certain public goods or services. But being a service provider does not mean the local government is the best *producer* of a given public good or service. In the ideal public choice model, the service provider (local government unit) seeks out the most efficient production mechanism for a given service. This might be a private contractor, another local government, or some other arrangement (Salamon 2002).

What we mean by level of consolidation or centralization, therefore, can be illustrated by a generic example. Suppose there are three local government entities: A, B, and C. Each *provides* service X and also currently *produces* that service. In examining various service-sharing alternatives, we might think about the degree to which service *production* (under each alternative) is centralized or consolidated. If a given alternative means that one of the three entities will now *produce* the service on behalf of all three, then it is *more consolidated*. If the alternative is such that A, B, and C are still *producers*, but are working together in a more integrated fashion, then it is *less consolidated* than the single-producer alternative and yet, still more consolidated than the status quo where A, B, and C each produce the service independent of one another.

Service X could be library services. The three entities could consolidate production of library services by merging to form a regional library or having one of the entities provide the service to the other entities through a contractual arrangement of some kind. Or on the other hand, production could remain less consolidated (more fragmented), but still involve service sharing in the form of cooperative purchasing or resource-sharing arrangements.

In thinking of provision and production separately, we see that even the single-producer options vary in their degree of consolidation. An entity set up to collect revenues for a given service and to produce that service (e.g., a regional library) becomes more or less the service provider *and* producer. A contract scenario, in which one entity produces the service for itself and other entities, however, means that entities A, B, and C are retaining the responsibility to provide the service, and to raise the revenues for that service separately; only the service production aspect has been consolidated. Contracting in this scenario is less consolidated than setting up a separate entity that becomes the service provider.

Why is it important to think in terms of consolidation? The primary reason is that the *degree of consolidation* likely carries with it an equal degree of political (and likely administrative) difficulty—and risk—as far as establishing it and carrying it out. Engaging stakeholders in co-production can improve service delivery with virtually no increase in centralization/consolidation, and little to no difficulty in terms of political turf or administrative complexity. On the other hand, divesting assets into a regional authority can be a significant challenge due to the political environment, administrative inertia, and the legal complexities of establishing a new government organization. Such a move is riskier too as it is a decision that is often very difficult to "undo."

These considerations are very important, and naturally do entail more or fewer degrees of complexity, as well as political and administrative difficulty. It is important to note, however, that the spectrum should not be interpreted normatively. More consolidated or centralized does not mean "better" or "more efficient" service delivery. Every situation is different, and a complex combination of transaction costs (Feiock 2007; Carr, LeRoux, and Shrestha 2009), local context and culture (Visser 2002; Morton, Chen, and Morse 2008), and other variables (Andrew 2009) will indicate what is best for a given mix of local government service providers.

But the degree of service consolidation is not the only relevant variable for classifying shared services alternatives. While there are likely many other relevant variables on which to distinguish different shared services alternatives, one that stands out is the degree of *shared governance*. Some shared service arrangements involve a high degree of shared governance across service providers, while others retain more autonomy.

For example, a joint city–county library likely involves a high degree of shared governance over library services, whereas a transfer-of-functions scenario (in which the municipalities transfer library service provision responsibility over to the county through an agreement to contribute to the enterprise financially) involves relative autonomy in governance by the service provider. The jurisdictions may or may not have interlocal agreements spelling out some specifics on how the service will be provided to their residents, but it would be a stretch to view such arrangements as shared governance.

In other transfer-of-function cases, the service producer may have an advisory board made up of representatives from the entities it produces the service for, representing a higher degree of shared governance than interlocal agreements. The important take-away here is that *the same shared services strategy* (transfer-of-functions or service contracting arrangements, for example) *could have very different governance mechanisms in place*, from more autonomous to more shared, depending on the desires of the partners for shared governance. We turn now to the governance dimension of the shared services map.

Governance Dimension

The verb "govern" comes from the Latin *gubernare*, which means to steer, as in steering a ship. In the public administration literature, governance is usually referred to in a very broad sense to mean the "steering" of communities, regions, states, and nations. The New Public Management movement used the idea of governance as steering to underscore the provide/produce distinction noted above. A public organization might "steer" in terms of taking responsibility for providing certain public goods and services, but that does not mean it must "row" in the sense of being the sole producer of the good or service (Osborne and Gaebler 1992).

More contemporary discussions of governance broaden the focus of governance from primarily the province of governments to a broader range of societal institutions that have a hand in "steering society" (Osborne 2010). However, in thinking about the governance dimension of shared service arrangements, we concur with Sullivan and Skelcher (2002) that a more narrow definition, drawn from the idea of corporate governance, makes the most sense. This approach keeps the focus on the steering or direction of an enterprise. Here, governance involves the interaction of the policymaking body with management and staff, and often with stakeholders as well, to make decisions and to carry out the activities of governing, or running, a given enterprise.

Among practitioners, governance implies a professional function with responsiveness to the policymaking entity. Governance typically addresses large questions, including the development of an agency or departmental mission and the establishment of goals and objectives. These questions also encompass issues such as hiring processes, the development and implementation of operation procedures, procurement, and training.

Hodges et al. (1996, 7) refer to corporate governance as "the procedures associated with the decision-making, performance and control of organizations, with providing structures to give overall direction to the organization and to satisfy reasonable expectation of accountability to those outside it." Thus while governance suggests the policymaking sphere only—the "principal" part of principal–agent theory—this definition reminds us that "to manage is to govern" (Feldman and Khademian 2003). *So the question, therefore, is: To what extent does a given shared service arrangement establish governance procedures for the given service in a shared or joint manner, versus retaining governing autonomy?*

We see a continuum of governance arrangements ranging from those that leave the governance of service production largely autonomous (governance is still in the control of the entity producing the service) to largely shared (governance is the purview of the different partners, together). The degree of shared governance does not necessarily follow the degree of integration or consolidation either. Thus, governance represents a second dimension worth adding to the more standard degree of integration or consolidation dimension.

Various forms of shared governance are discussed in the literature (see Sullivan and Skelcher 2002, for example), with some forms being more "shared" in terms of authority, control, and power than others. For example, a regional authority governed by a board made up of representatives from partnering entities represents a high degree of shared governance. On the other hand, a single local government entity may be a regional service provider/producer (such as Raleigh's water utility) and utilize an informal advisory committee made up of representatives from other jurisdictions it services. This is a form of shared governance, but clearly not as extensive as would be with an authority.

Shared service arrangements inevitably involve a paradoxical process of creating two goals that essentially work against each other—sharing power and authority, at least to some degree, while still retaining control. Abernathy's two in-depth case studies of service merger through the creation of authorities illustrate the complexity of the governance dimension (2009). Both cases resulted in the creation of authorities where authority was removed from all of the affected agencies and transferred to a newly created legal entity. In Jackson County, North Carolina, the merger of a water system into a regional water authority grew out of a joint recognition that "something substantial" had to be done (2009, 157). A crisis existed on the part of several of the towns. The new authority involved three towns and county.

The other case involved the merger of a 911 dispatch system in San Juan County, New Mexico. The process of negotiation often means that one entity is more desirous of the merger than the other. Shared governance on a somewhat equal footing may be more likely when the entities are equal in the desire to consolidate. The question becomes whether the negotiation process is voluntary and made up of common interests or whether the issue is of greater significance to one of the parties. A crisis on the part of one of the entities may make it less likely that governance will be shared equally, as one entity may have an advantage.

Because governance arrangements can vary from more autonomous (or distributed) to more shared, and shared service arrangements can vary structurally from more decentralized to more centralized or consolidated, we think it is useful to "map" shared service alternatives in terms of a field created by the two dimensions, as represented in Figure 9.2. We have mapped the common shared service alternatives discussed above on this field to give a general sense of how different arrangements typically represent certain combinations of shared governance and service consolidation, noting, however, that in practice specific arrangements are unique and will take their own unique space on the map.

What is immediately evident when sorting shared service strategies onto this two-dimensional field is, first, the simple notion of "easy" to "hard" has to be questioned. There is no left–right progression in that sense anymore. "Easy" or "hard" is probably much more a result of local political, economic, and administrative dynamics than any given place on the map. One might assume that less consolidated options that retain governing

Figure 9.2 **Typology of Shared Services Arrangements**

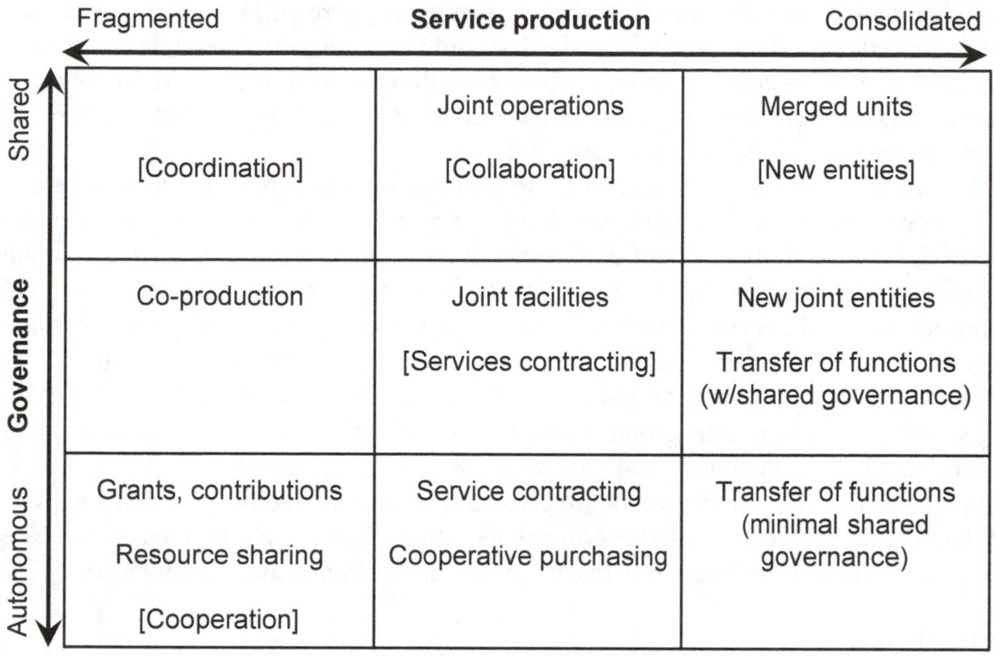

Governance \ Service production	Fragmented		Consolidated
Shared	[Coordination]	Joint operations [Collaboration]	Merged units [New entities]
	Co-production	Joint facilities [Services contracting]	New joint entities Transfer of functions (w/shared governance)
Autonomous	Grants, contributions Resource sharing [Cooperation]	Service contracting Cooperative purchasing	Transfer of functions (minimal shared governance)

autonomy, like resource sharing, would be widespread because they must be "easier," but that is not always the case. Local politics may prevent neighboring jurisdictions from working together no matter how much sense it makes or how little risk it entails.

The most important value for a concept map like this is not in examining alternatives in the abstract, however. Rather, the value is more for practitioners exploring shared service alternatives, reminding them to think carefully and talk openly about interests along each dimension. What level of consolidation makes sense? Could economies of scale be achieved through more centralization? What degree of consolidation makes sense given the financials, political dynamics, and other local considerations? Then, with a grasp on what makes sense from a production standpoint, the consideration turns to asking what degree of shared governance is appropriate.[6] Here, the issue of responsibility for and control over service provision comes into play. Parties may agree that consolidating service production makes sense. But in considering the governance dimension, the question turns to how important it is for the separate parties to maintain a hand in governance, or in other words, maintain accountability for and control over service provision. If it is very important, then shared governance options make more sense. If it is less important, then more autonomous governance options make sense.

In some cases, the nature of the production strategy may dictate the degree of shared governance. For example, if the best alternative is to collaborate, to jointly produce a service (maintaining separate production units but joining those units in the production of a particular service), naturally the governance of such an entity will need to be highly collaborative. But if the best alternative is to consolidate multiple production units into one, then the question of how much shared governance there will be of the new consolidated unit comes to fore. A scenario like that could give the new consolidated unit relative autonomy (especially if the unit is housed within the overall organization of one of the partners). On the other hand, the partners could strongly desire a shared governance arrangement in the context of the new single unit.

The map also serves to organize broad terms often used in conversations about shared services or local government collaboration (see Figure 9.2). Setting up new joint entities seems to be high in its levels of consolidation and shared governance, whereas transfer of functions is a case where consolidation is high but governance remains mostly autonomous (in the service producer). Various types of coordination represent shared governance without much consolidation, whereas forms of cooperation, like mutual aid, retain autonomous governance and decentralized service production. Service contracting seems to strike a middle ground along both dimensions. Service production is more consolidated in the contractor, and governance is somewhat shared through the contracting process. Finally, what the literature calls "collaboration" seems to be at the high end of shared governance (indeed, the term collaboration is almost synonymous with shared governance) and somewhere in-between on the service consolidation dimension.

CONCLUSION

We present this typology as a way to organize or map the landscape of shared service options. While it is not a decision tool, it can aid decision makers in the process of carefully considering alternatives and the implications of those alternatives for the organization. If, for example, leaders of an organization know up front that having a high degree of shared governance is a priority, then they can limit the range of alternatives to those that logically lend themselves to shared governance. If another organization knows up front that its ultimate goal is consolidated service production, then that narrows the scope of alternatives and zeroes the discussion in on the question of what, then, is the appropriate level of shared governance.

We believe that adding the governance dimension represents a critical recognition of the primary obstacles facing shared service possibilities, namely, turf and trust. The governance question addresses these issues up front. Governance addresses who is in control, who is accountable, who takes on risks and rewards, and so on. All too often, discussion of shared services skirts these issues, focusing only on the more structural considerations represented in the integration/consolidation dimension. Adding governance completes the picture, or at least fills it out in more detail.

This two-dimensional typology also points to several research questions in need of further investigation. First, there is the question of innovation and creativity in the realm of shared services. It does appear that very creative things occur when organizations work across boundaries and collaborate. How might more innovation and creativity be incentivized? Another question concerns citizen engagement in the creation of shared services.

Many of the shared service alternatives discussed in this chapter, such as volunteers for fire services, recreation, and libraries, involve direct citizen action. How might citizen engagement be more fully incorporated into the shared services conversation?

Abernathy (2009), Zeemering and Delabbio (2013) and others recommend up-front goal setting, evaluation, and measurement in more complex arrangements. The typology seeks to enable more careful or measured consideration of alternatives. What it does not do, however, is capture the potential transaction costs of adopting various shared service alternatives, and we know that transaction costs factor in heavily to the decision-making equation (Feiock 2007; Carr, LeRoux, and Shrestha 2009). Perhaps a potential future project could be the development of a model that would assess and measure transaction costs up front as well as after the new service delivery arrangement is put in place.

Shared service strategies represent an important innovation in local government service delivery. While much attention has been placed on the specific strategy of contracting out, we know that the universe of alternatives is vast, going well beyond contracting (Agranoff 2012). A typology or map for shared services, such as the one offered in this chapter, helps illustrate the variety and richness of options available. While a typology cannot overcome the many barriers to shared services that exist, it can serve as a guide to productive conversations that address the two most important dimensions—service integration/consolidation and governance—head on. We hope it might also provide a useful heuristic for research as well, for the importance of shared services to local government service delivery in the coming years will only increase.

KEY POINTS

- The term "shared services" represents a wide variety of alternative service delivery strategies, from relatively simple resource-sharing arrangements to the creation of new organizations with complex governance structures.
- The logic of shared services is based upon understanding service provision and production as two separate issues. Local governments that choose to provide a given service should seek the best production mechanism, which may involve service sharing with other jurisdictions or organizations.
- Service sharing options vary in their degree of service consolidation and shared governance. These two dimensions are critical features of any shared service scenario.
- Analysis of potential shared service options should include careful consideration of what degree of service consolidation is optimal and then what degree of shared governance is deemed most appropriate by the partnering entities.

NOTES

1. Academic research on shared services and related topics is extensive, particularly over the past decade (see, for example, Abernathy 2012; Andrew 2009; Kwon and Feiock 2010; Bae and Feiock 2012; Carr, LeRoux, and Shrestha, 2009; Chen and Thurmaier 2009; Feiock 2007; Hawkins 2009; LeRoux, Brandenburger, and Pandey 2010; LeRoux and Carr 2007; Thurmaier and Wood 2003; Warner and Hefetz 2009; and Zeemering 2008, 2009, and 2012). There are also many relevant practitioner-oriented

publications on the topic that are worthy of note, including Holdsworth (2007), Ruggini (2006), and Zeemering and Delabbio (2013). The global consulting firm Accenture (www.accenture.com/shared-services) has also produced a lot of materials related to shared services in the public sector.

2. In late 2012, for example, the New Jersey Senate passed a bill to set up a state commission to "determine whether taxpayer dollars can be cut through sharing services with other local or county governments, or internally among departments. The decision to share services would be put out to voters in a referendum in all involved municipalities. If the towns fail to take shared service opportunities, their state aid could be in jeopardy" (Romalino 2012).

3. McDowell County is a rural county in western North Carolina with a population of approximately 45,000. Nearly a third of the county is in the Pisgah National Forest.

4. One of the authors (Morse) produced a video case study of two municipalities that have developed a culture of collaboration and resource sharing. See Morse (2011) for the URL.

5. See North Carolina Department of Public Safety (2012) for more information on North Carolina's efforts to provide work opportunities for inmates.

6. Abernathy's study of service consolidation (2009) highlights the need for systematic evaluation up front, using benchmarking, performance measurement, and demand analysis to set performance goals and to determine the logic of shared services and of using a more complex arrangement. This helps during the process of consolidation because the efficiencies are often negotiated away or compromised.

REFERENCES

Abernathy, Charles R. 2009. Service delivery consolidation, governance and the enhancement of local government capacity: Creating a service consolidation model. PhD dissertation, University of Tennessee. http://trace.tennessee.edu/utk_graddiss/5/.

———. 2012. The consolidation of local government services: The incidence and practice of service delivery consolidation in North Carolina. *Public Administration Quarterly* 36(1): 42–83.

Agranoff, Robert. 2012. *Collaborating to Manage: A Primer for the Public Sector*. Washington, DC: Georgetown University Press.

Andrew, Simon A. 2009. Recent developments in the study of interjurisdictional agreements: An overview and assessment. *State & Local Government Review* 41(2): 133–142.

Bae, Jungah, and Richard C. Feiock. 2012. Managing multiplexity: Coordinating multiple services at a regional level. *State & Local Government Review* 44(2): 162–168.

Carr, Jered B., Kelly LeRoux, and Manoj Shrestha. 2009. Institutional ties, transaction costs, and external service production. *Urban Affairs Review* 44(3): 403–427.

Chen, Yu-Che, and Kurt Thurmaier. 2009. Interlocal agreements as collaborations: An empirical investigation of impetuses, norms, and success. *American Review of Public Administration* 39(5): 536–552.

City of Raleigh, North Carolina. 2013. Public Utilities Department. www.raleighnc.gov/services/content/Departments/Articles/PublicUtilities.html (accessed May 28, 2013).

Cohn, Alan D. 2005. Mutual aid: Intergovernmental agreements for emergency preparedness and response. *The Urban Lawyer* 37(1): 1–51.

Feiock, Richard C. 2007. Rational choice and regional governance. *Journal of Urban Affairs* 29(1): 47–63.

Feldman, Martha S., and Anne M. Khademian. 2003. To manage is to govern. *Public Administration Review* 62(5): 541–554.

Hawkins, Christopher V. 2009. Prospects for and barriers to local government joint ventures. *State & Local Government Review* 21(2): 108–119.

Hefetz, Amir, and Mildred E. Warner. 2012. Contracting or public delivery? The importance of service, market, and management characteristics. *Journal of Public Administration Research and Theory* 22(2): 289–317.

Hodges, Ron, Mike Wright, and Kevin Keasey. 1996. Corporate governance in the public services: Concepts and issues. *Public Money & Management* 16(2): 7–13.

Holdsworth, William A. 2007. Symbiosis. Symmetry. Synergy: The case for interlocal cooperation. *Government Finance Review* 23(1): 40–46.

Honadle, Beth Walter. 1984. Alternative service delivery strategies and improvement of local government productivity. *Public Productivity Review* 8(4): 301–313.

Kwon, Sung-Wook, and Richard C. Feiock. 2010. Overcoming the barriers to cooperation: Intergovernmental service agreements. *Public Administration Review* 70(6): 876–884.

LeRoux, Kelly, Paul W. Brandenburger, and Sanjay K. Pandey. 2010. Interlocal service cooperation in US cities: A social network explanation. *Public Administration Review* 70(2): 268–278.

LeRoux, Kelly, and Jered B. Carr. 2007. Explaining local government cooperation on public works: Evidence from Michigan. *Public Works Management & Policy* 12(1): 344–358.

Linden, Russell M. 2010. *Leading Across Boundaries: Creating Collaborative Agencies in a Networked World.* San Francisco, CA: Jossey-Bass.

Morse, Richard. 2011. Wilkesboro/North Wilkesboro: Creating a Culture of Collaboration (Video). YouTube, June 7. Chapel Hill: UNC School of Government and Nightlight Productions. http://youtu.be/rByyuKATZ6o (accessed May 28, 2013).

Morton, Lois W., Yu-Che Chen, and Ricardo S. Morse. 2008. Small town civic structure and interlocal collaboration for public services. *City & Community* 7(1): 45–60.

North Carolina Department of Public Safety. 2012. North Carolina Prison Inmates at Work. www.doc.state.nc.us/work/workover.htm (accessed May 28, 2013).

Osborne, David, and Ted Gaebler. 1992. *Reinventing Government: How the Entrepreneurial Spirit Is Transforming Government.* Reading, MA: Addison-Wesley.

Osborne, Stephen P., ed. 2010. *The New Public Governance? Emerging Perspectives on the Theory and Practice of Public Governance*. New York: Routledge.

Ostrom, Vincent, and Elinor Ostrom. 1971. Public choice: A different approach to the study of public administration. *Public Administration Review* 31(2): 203–216.

———. 1999. Public goods and public choices. In *Polycentricity and Local Public Economies: Readings from the Workshop in Political Theory and Policy Analysis,* ed. Michael McGinnis, 75–105. Ann Arbor: University of Michigan Press.

Romalino, Carly Q. 2012. Sweeney: Shared service bill about "reducing the cost of government." *South Jersey Times* (Woodbury, NJ), November 26.

Ruggini, John. 2006. Making local government more workable through shared services. *Government Finance Review* 22(1): 30–35.

Salamon, Lester M., ed. 2002. *The Tools of Government: A Guide to the New Governance*. New York: Oxford University Press.

Sullivan, Helen, and Chris Skelcher. 2002. *Working Across Boundaries: Collaboration in Public Services*. Basingstoke, UK: Palgrave.

Thomas, John Clayton. 2012. *Citizen, Customer, Partner: Engaging the Public in Public Management.* Armonk, NY: M.E. Sharpe.

Thurmaier, Kurt, and Curtis Wood. 2003. Interlocal agreements as overlapping social networks: Picket-fence regionalism in metropolitan Kansas City. *Public Administration Review* 62(5): 585–598.

U.S. Census Bureau. 2012. *2012 Census of Governments*. Washington, DC. www.census.gov/govs/cog2012/ (accessed May 28, 2013).

Visser, James A. 2002. Understanding local government cooperation in urban regions: Toward a cultural model of interlocal relations. *American Review of Public Administration* 32(1): 40–65.

Walker, David B. 1987. Snow White and the 17 dwarfs: From metro cooperation to governance. *National Civic Review* 76(1): 14–28.

Warner, Mildred E., and Amir Hefetz. 2009. Cooperative competition: Alternative service delivery, 2002–2007. In *The Municipal Year Book 2009*, 11–20. Washington, DC: ICMA Press.

———. 2012. Insourcing and outsourcing. *Journal of the American Planning Association* 78(3): 313–327.

Zeemering, Eric S. 2008. Governing interlocal cooperation: City council interests and the implications for public management. *Public Administration Review* 68(4): 731–741.

———. 2009. California county administrators as sellers and brokers of interlocal cooperation. *State & Local Government Review* 41(3): 166–181.

———. 2012. The problem of democratic anchorage for interlocal agreements. *The American Review of Public Administration* 42(1): 87–103.

Zeemering, Eric, and Daryl Delabbio. 2013. *A County Manager's Guide to Shared Services in Local Government*. Washington, DC: The IBM Center for the Business of Government.

10

Alternative Service Delivery Arrangements

Creativity and Innovation in Local Government

Suzanne Leland and Reid A. Wodicka

With the onset of the Great Recession, many municipal governments find themselves searching for creative ways to save money and improve service provision. Consolidation of governing bodies or even functional consolidation of two particular services, while desirable for some, are often too controversial to enact. So what are some other alternatives for local governments? Interlocal government agreements—arrangements that allow for cross-jurisdictional provision of local public goods—are common ways that governments are able to share services and achieve similar efficiencies. Larger units of governments such as state and regional councils and even large counties may act as facilitators of such agreements by offering some innovative options. The purpose of this chapter is to identify the innovative practices that have allowed local governments to share services across traditionally well-defined jurisdictional lines to ensure that services are provided in a high-quality and efficient manner. In the pages ahead, we will outline ways in which local governments have shared both operational resources and administrative arrangements that are commonly needed in every locality. Further, we will discuss policy actions that provide an opportunity for these innovative service delivery options to exist.

One example of a policy action designed to encourage towns, cities, and counties to cooperate with one another is found in the State of New York. The State of New York is encouraging interlocal cooperation by providing monetary incentives in the form of state grants. Local governments may receive such grants for collaboration. Other states, such as Illinois and New Jersey, provide other means of support, such as voluntary participation in state purchasing consortiums. Regional councils have also taken action to promote sharing of services (Leland and Whisman 2011). In some cases, a municipal government might go it alone and try to overcome the collective action problem without the involvement of a higher level of government. The collective action problem is a circumstance in which multiple jurisdictions would benefit from an action, but there is a perceived cost for any one individual to engage in the action alone (Olson 1965). When local governments initiate cooperation and negotiate agreements with other jurisdictions to provide alternative options for service delivery, the costs associated with the desired action declines. In some cases, it may be more rational for local governments to share in costs rather than go it alone (Feiock 2004).

In our scan of the literature and current practices, we find that there are several areas in personnel and purchasing where municipal governments pursue cooperative agreements with two or more other governments. In this chapter we highlight and describe current, innovative practices involving alternative modes of municipal shared service delivery. We first define alternative service delivery as local governments reorganizing and reengaging themselves to embark on a joint venture with one or more governments, but falling short of complete functional consolidation of services (i.e., combining a police and fire department). We are particularly interested in considering ways that jurisdictions cooperate but maintain individual departments.

PURSUING PERSONNEL AND ALTERNATIVE SERVICE DELIVERY AGREEMENTS

The following section focuses on a number of areas in which local governments can take advantage of alternative forms of service delivery, specifically related to personnel. They include cooperative activities like the use of mutual aid agreements, floater models, and cross-training of personnel. While we highlight police and fire services, public works, parks and recreation, and health services are examples of other areas where these or other similar models may be used to achieve local government collaboration.

Utilize Resources Available from Mutual Aid

Local government services are sized and staffed primarily for typical day-to-day operations, with some room for larger-scale demands that may occur. For instance, in fire suppression, the vast majority of incidents are likely routine emergency medical calls or minor fire incidents that can be handled with a minimal number of firefighters (labor). However, when an emergency occurs that is beyond the capability of those minimal resources, the day-to-day operations become overwhelmed. This section discusses how municipal-based services can be shared among jurisdictions when the demand for services exceeds the capabilities of the standing army of public servants available in the affected community, particularly through a mechanism called mutual aid.

The Federal Emergency Management Agency (FEMA) defines mutual aid agreements as "agreements between agencies, organizations, and jurisdictions that provide a mechanism to quickly obtain emergency assistance in the form of personnel, equipment, materials, and other associated services. The primary objective is to facilitate rapid, short-term deployment of emergency support prior to, during, and after an incident" (FEMA 2013). In addition to the large-scale disasters, manmade or natural, that we typically associate with FEMA intervention (such as hurricanes or terrorist attacks), these agreements can also be applied in smaller-scale incidents that are larger than the typical daily needs of a single jurisdiction.

Low-risk, high-cost events create a problem for municipal managers because services must be prepared to deal with an event if it were to occur. However, sizing a public bureaucracy based on the chance that an incident might occur would be highly wasteful on a day-to-day basis. Mutual aid agreements provide larger capacity by taking advantage of neighboring resources. For instance, a riot is fairly unlikely to occur in most jurisdictions, but the costs could be extremely high due to damage to public and private property and injuries, requiring a response from local government. A riot in a small town, though unlikely, might require the service of 50 police officers in a community that would typically only need a handful of patrol officers at one time. Mutual aid agreements provide the option to take advantage of the resources of other communities, providing a high level of service to the public during times of need without having to size the agency for those needs all of the time. Essentially, the study of the need for mutual aid is analogous to the study of peak load pricing.

Instead of focusing heavily on end-user pricing structures during times of peak demand, as economists may do, public administrators can instead focus on the structural arrangements of service delivery during times of excessive demand in order to develop appropriate mutual aid agreements. Therefore, it is important for municipal managers and policymakers to develop an understanding of the capabilities not only of their own jurisdiction, but also of other geographically proximate jurisdictions, whether they be municipalities, counties, or other governmental units. Additionally, those involved with the development of mutual aid agreements must consider all possibilities when planning for emergencies that might occur within their own jurisdiction. Once municipal managers and policymakers develop that understanding, they can craft the size of their own agencies, as well as the provisions found within agreements, to ensure that each jurisdiction can minimize costs while maximizing the capabilities of public service delivery.

An excellent example of an innovative mutual aid agreement comes from the City of Harrisonburg and the County of Rockingham, Virginia. Virginia has independent cities, which means that while many cities are located geographically inside counties, service delivery responsibilities do not cross jurisdictional lines. Cities are islands within counties. This is unlike cities in other states, where city boundaries are superimposed on the existing county boundaries. As a result, there are geographic challenges to service delivery. Harrisonburg and Rockingham County have developed a model for mutual aid in which a county fire station is located within the jurisdictional bounds of Harrisonburg and has primary response responsibility for the unincorporated areas within Rockingham County just outside of the city. As a result, county-employed firefighters are sometimes closer to an emergency than some city-paid firefighters and vice versa. Since it is rational to dispatch the closest fire engine to an emergency, there are times when the county firefighters are dispatched to city fires, even though county taxpayers are providing the service. The reverse is also true.

When there is a large emergency within the city, county firefighters are dispatched and serve as a fifth engine company for city firefighting operations. Conversely, since there is just one county engine company covering the areas just outside of the city limits, when there is a large emergency in the county, one or more city fire companies are dispatched along with county firefighters. This arrangement allows both the city and county to invest in minimal labor while enjoying the capabilities that would be associated with a much more robust firefighting bureaucracy.

Without this mutual aid agreement in place, taxpayers would need to place into service at least two additional engine companies to achieve the same level of service that they now enjoy, at a potential cost of well over one million dollars annually in labor alone. This figure does not include the capital, operational, and maintenance costs associated with additional fire suppression vehicles, equipment, and fire stations, which could amount to tens of millions of dollars. This agreement circumvents the political fracturing associated with independent cities and takes advantage of geography. When the peak of service demand occurs (for instance, a large structure fire), the typical institutional arrangements flex to solve the problem at hand. This dynamic structure allows for the maximization of utility derived from taxpayer investment, regardless of the jurisdiction to which taxes are being paid.

The application of municipal mutual aid agreements is not limited, though, to single-discipline services. Emergencies may often require the coordination of several different agencies within and across each jurisdiction. One example of this type of arrangement in found in Michigan's 5th District Medical Response Coalition. This organization brings together personnel from "hospitals, public health departments, medical control authorities, emergency management services, medical examiners, law enforcement, hazmat," and others to help to deal with "natural and manmade disasters of diverse causes, including those that are nuclear, biological, chemical, electromagnetic, weather-related, traffic related or violent" that might occur within southwest Michigan (5th District Medical Response Coalition n.d.). The organization and associated agreements provide "surge capacity" that might be necessary to deal with any emergency that occurs. Again, by collaborating across jurisdictional lines, local governments are able to take advantage of a much larger public bureaucracy without having to actually invest in it.

Finally, personnel in some jurisdictions might be able to specialize in certain functions that tend to be needed relatively infrequently but are immediately important when the need arises. For instance, one town in a region might develop a highly skilled team of public utility workers who have extensive experience quickly identifying and solving utility infrastructure problems. By specializing in this work, that team might be able to reduce the amount of time it takes to solve the problem as compared to others, who might need time to think through the problem. This team could be used across jurisdictional lines, improving the quality of service and eliminating the need for several municipalities in the region to develop a highly skilled team. This spreads the costs of the service across more taxpayers and reduces the marginal cost of each utility breakdown.

Though we have outlined two successful mutual aid agreements in action, it is clear that such agreements can be expanded beyond the programs that have been defined in this section thus far. While these agreements may not be appropriate in all circumstances, there is likely room for additional coordination between the personnel of each jurisdiction during peak demand situations. However, it is unlikely that a single mutual aid agreement structure will fit all situations. In addition to the well-developed mutual aid programs found within typical public safety services systems, a general guideline for the development of mutual aid agreements suggests that they should allow for expanded capacity of service delivery without the expansion of public bureaucracies for many other local

Figure 10.1 **Key Characteristics of Successful Mutual Aid Partnerships**

- Local managers have knowledge of available resources
- Local managers are willing to share
- Organizational cultures value cooperation

government typical services. Simply put, inefficiencies and a lack of peak capacity of street-level bureaucrats due to the fragmentation of local jurisdictions can be moderated by mutual aid and interjurisdictional cooperation.

There are some key characteristics of successful mutual aid agreements (see Figure 10.1). First, local government managers (and, of course, their subordinates) must have a strong awareness of the resources that are available in other local governments in the region. Second, local government managers must be willing to share resources with other jurisdictions when there is a need. Third, because these agreements must take shape quickly, organizational culture must encourage cooperation with other localities during emergencies. If those conditions are not met, the mutual aid agreement will only be worth the paper it is written upon.

Within the context of the lessons learned from the above examples of interjurisdictional agreements, the expansion of mutual aid agreements has the potential for improving the ability of local governments to provide continual services, even in times of peak demand. The possibilities are only limited by the creativity of municipal managers and policymakers.

Shift Your Resources: Using Floating Personnel

While the mutual aid model allows for jurisdictions to take advantage of the capacity of other local governments when they reach peak demand for service delivery, this does not take into account staffing issues associated with day-to-day operations. The floating personnel model allows for the sharing of resources on a day-to-day basis when there are comparable processes that need to be accomplished but one locality does not have enough staff available to perform basic functions. This is different from the mutual aid model because the implementation of floater models relies primarily on the supply of labor rather than the demand for services.

Some municipal services may require the minimum daily staffing that is necessary to provide a basic level of service. For instance, a public utilities department may require a minimum of three people to staff a wastewater treatment plant. This can be due to processes that require multiple actions at one time or for other reasons that the local government may deem necessary. Another example is fire departments requiring a minimum staffing of each company within the response system. In this case, Occupational Safety and Health Administration regulations and professional standards dictate that a minimum of one firefighter be standing by outside of a burning structure for every firefighter actively engaged in interior firefighting (Occupational Safety and Health Administration 2003a; National Fire Protection Association 2013). Other standards mandate that no firefighter should operate alone inside a burning structure (Occupational Safety and Health Administration 2003b). In a professionalized department, this suggests a minimum staffing of four at all times. Since employees are frequently entitled to vacation days and occasionally call in sick, these minimum staffing requirements have the unintended consequence of driving up overtime costs for local governments. This section discusses a staff-sharing model that may reduce the amount of overtime needed to cover minimum staffing—the floater model.

Local governments have used floater models within their own jurisdictions for many years. For instance, when a teacher in a public school system needs to take a day off, the school division may allow for a floating substitute teacher who can provide coverage at many different schools. In a floater model that takes into account municipal shared services, local governments share floating personnel across jurisdictional lines. In a fragmented system in which each local government has several floating personnel that are not shared between the jurisdictions, one local government may run out of floating personnel while another may not be using any at all. For example, during an outbreak of the stomach flu in a school, several teachers might have to take off work. As a result, the supply of substitute teachers for that jurisdiction may run dry. The neighboring school district might not be experiencing that demand for substitute teachers and might have extra capacity that could be used by the first jurisdiction. However, their floaters stand unused.

In a municipal shared services floater model, the administrative boundaries of the established institution would be softened, allowing for floating personnel to be used in multiple jurisdictions seamlessly. This could be accomplished by several different methods. First, the multiple municipal governments might create a regional organization that employs floating personnel. Such an agency would be responsible for staffing the location in which there is a vacancy. This would likely be a simple model to implement, but it results in the loss of local control over agency staffing choices. A second model would look similar to a mutual aid agreement in that each jurisdiction would employ a number of floating personnel, would inform the other municipalities of available floating personnel, and then each locality would request the number of floating personnel it needs for a certain time period. This is a more complicated model, but it would allow local jurisdictions to hire whomever they want for most vacancies.

This idea of floating personnel operating between jurisdictions seems like a simple way to reduce the amount of overtime that a community endures as a result of minimum staffing requirements. However, there are challenges with using this model.

First, while many of the services that local government provide are relatively similar to one another, the intricacies of how organizations, roles, and tasks are structured may differ considerably from one local government to another. If we are to believe the Tiebout (1956) model of sorting at the local level, the bundle of services provided by local governments within a region varies based on the demands of the public. For that reason, the challenges associated with each locality differ, and, as a result, so do the challenges to those employed there. Therefore, a person coming in from another jurisdiction to perform a public function for a short period of time may have difficulty adapting to the challenges at work that day. For instance, suburban school districts likely have different challenges from urban school districts and, as a result, a substitute teacher from the outer-ring suburbs might not be prepared to deal with a classroom in the inner city. Similarly, fire departments in a region may operate with vastly different standard operating procedures. If the floating firefighter is not as well versed in the procedures in the department he or she is floating to, his or her actions could place the rest of company in danger or, at a minimum, could be counterproductive to the operation.

A second challenge to the floater model is that assignment to the floater position may be less prestigious than a permanent location at one workplace. As a result, employees with less experience, or even poor skills, might be assigned to this floater position. Therefore, the quality of service they provide may be limited compared with full-time employees. Adding these two components together, cross-jurisdictional floating personnel might have a very large negative impact on effective provision of public services. However, if the system is managed correctly, each of these conditions can be managed appropriately.

For instance, fire departments could require that all employees takes a turn serving in the floating position and spend time learning about the operating procedures of other departments. Substitute teachers could be monitored closely by building administrators.

Though the model presents challenges to the affected jurisdiction, the benefits to taxpayers may be great. Local government managers and policymakers should consider the costs and benefits of a model like this to determine if the costs, both direct and indirect, associated with the challenges are outweighed by the savings to taxpayers. If so, it might be a reasonable shared serviced model that could be used by local governments.

Hire the Multitasker for Fire and Police: The Public Safety Officer Model

Despite the evolution of public administration theory over the last 100 or so years, public bureaucracies have largely maintained the strict institutional structures that were developed in spirit of classical organizational theory. Relying on Max Weber's description of bureaucracy, one key characteristic is the division of specialized labor, where individuals within public bureaucracies have tended to focus on a small number of tasks, becoming an expert on those particular functions rather than on the process of public service delivery as a whole (Hall 1963). This division of labor can be seen in the disciplinary departments found within municipal governments. For instance, those who work in the public works department paving streets are unlikely to be utilized by the public library system reshelving books; their specialized skills are simply not translatable between the two functions.

While specialization of labor theory suggests that those who are specialized in their smaller function within the entire production process will be more efficient than someone who has to be skilled at all of the tasks, this division of labor likely leads to organizational inefficiencies due to the inability of public personnel to provide a dynamic set of services. Anyone who has ever dealt with a large public bureaucracy has a story of having to talk with six different people to accomplish one small task. Strict definitions of job responsibilities that create silos of public service delivery lead to the inflexibility of public employees and, as a result, a frustrating experience for end users. While specialization likely increases the capability of an individual to perform his/her particular function, which increases the efficiency in that role, the overall process is likely made more inefficient by creating difficulties with coordination, one of Luther Gulick's seven major functions of management (Gulick 1937). This section documents how some municipal governments have attempted to break down the silos of bureaucratic operations by de-specializing public employees and utilizing the public safety officer model. This model will be discussed and the concept will be applied to other functions of local government, as well.

The public safety officer (PSO) model in this context is defined as the complete consolidation of municipal police and fire departments that had previously been separate in their administration and operations. Kenneth Chelst (1988) explains that this merger would require the cross training of all existing police officers and firefighters. In his study in Michigan, Chelst notes that many employees were also to be trained as emergency medical technicians. Additionally, any future employees would be trained as both firefighters and police officers.

The consolidation of function does not stop with field personnel. Since the two departments are merged, there is no longer a need for two sets of administrative services functions, such as department-specific human resources, finance, planning, and so forth. Additionally, instead of two command structures (presumably a chief and one or several deputy/assistant chiefs in each department), those functions could be consolidated into one command group. Theoretically, this consolidation could result in a substantial decrease in the number of personnel that are required to perform the functions of the previously split departments. It is important to note that emergency medical services are kept separate under the PSO model.

Why Might a Community Consider the PSO Model?

In addition to political advocacy that has called for the reduction of public sector expenditures, local governments have been required by limited local revenue to reduce the cost of doing business. While some fire and police departments have been immune to the same reductions in public sector expenditures experienced by programs and services that are less palatable to conservative policymakers, those departments remain among some of the most expensive in municipal government. In an attempt to reduce the cost of providing police and fire services within a community without reducing the level of services, local governments may consider the idea of consolidation of police and fire department functions.

The theoretical financial gain made by consolidation of police and fire personnel comes from cross training personnel. This could potentially lead to more dynamic public sector employees who could perform a broader array of functions on a day-to-day basis. For instance, a police officer trained as a firefighter could theoretically serve as an arson investigator. Given the proper training, the person who is already a police officer already understands criminal procedure and investigative techniques. Adding knowledge of fire behavior seems like a natural progression toward skills otherwise left to another public official, the fire marshal. On the opposite side of the arrangement, in municipalities that already have full-time fire departments, firefighters trained as police officers could enhance police patrols when they would otherwise be waiting for another alarm.

Inherently, the primary benefit of the PSO model is that the same functions of local government service delivery can likely be achieved with fewer personnel on duty. This relies on the notion that departments are staffed on a day-to-day basis with a complement of personnel that is greater than the number needed at any one time. If we think of bureaucrats as producers of public services, the public safety officer model attempts to take advantage of economies of scope by producing multiple public services within the same agency. By taking advantage of economies of scope, the municipality can reduce the number of inputs, in this case labor, and still achieve the same outcome—public service delivery. The incentive to engage in the PSO model is, thus, financial. However, this requires that we think of personnel as inputs that can be manipulated without negative effects on the organization's environment and service users.

Challenges of the PSO Model

Some organizations are not convinced that the PSO model is the panacea that advocates conclude it is. Primarily, arguments against the model focus on the complex personnel issues that are, some claim, avoided by separating the two organizations. The International Association of Fire Fighters (IAFF), the labor union of firefighters, points to several issues that may not be accounted for in the model presented by PSO advocates. Admittedly, the IAFF is not a disinterested organization, but their arguments merit consideration.

In a 2009 document titled "Fire and Police Consolidation: An Ineffective Use of Resources," the IAFF points to nine major problems with the PSO model, ranging from declining morale of employees to the decline in quality and quantity of services available. For each of the problems associated with the model, the document provides written arguments and, in some cases, empirical evidence to back the claims. The most meaningful arguments, though, are those citing the inability of firefighters and police officers to be specialists in both areas. They argue that fire and police consolidation will result in inadequate job training and inadequate on-the-job experience. These are the two major problems that are associated with the actual provision of public services. It is reasonable to say that most citizens, when calling for either police or fire services, expect those who respond to be highly competent.

It is also reasonable to suggest that when tasked with two jobs as different from each other as policing and fire protection, any single individual might have a difficult time achieving a high level of competency at both. Thus, while the PSO model might reduce costs over time, it could also result in employees who are less competent in either discipline. According to notions of specialization in public services derived from Adam Smith's ideas about industrial production, using multitaskers might actually reduce the efficiency with which public services are provided. Of course, the choice to use the PSO model requires a calculation of costs and benefits associated with the program.

Challenging the Assumptions

While the assumptions of both arguments are consistent with economic and organizational theory, in practice those assumptions have not always held true. First, the assumption that the quality of service will decline is refuted by Chelst (1988) in his analysis of a merger of police and fire services in Gross Point Park, Michigan. He found that post-merger, on fire and rescue incidents, the first trained person arrived on scene an average of 85 percent faster than pre-merger. While the time frame of arrival of major firefighting equipment was unchanged, presumably the arrival of that first officer can be thought of as increased service delivery, potentially having the opportunity to start emergency medical care sooner, making a quick rescue of trapped person, or knocking down a fire when it is still in the incipient stage. This should of course be qualified with the fact that the use of response time is an output-based performance measurement (Melkers and Willoughby 2005). While internal performance measures can be important for managerial decision making, from the perspective of service delivery, external measures can also be used (Kelly and Swindell 2002). Outcomes-based performance measurement has become pervasive in the literature because of recent findings that the reliance on administrative output data fails to adequately predict a program's true impact (Halachmi 2002; Heinrich 2002) and that many times, what is being measured has very little to do with what the agency's services or programs are intended to provide (Behn 2003).

On the other side of the equation, the IAFF makes reference to two cities that have tried the PSO model and have decided to revert to two separate departments. Of particular interest is the story of Daytona Beach, Florida. In the 1970s, Daytona tried the PSO model in an attempt to enjoy financial savings (IAFF 2009). However, nine years after implementing the model, the city found that it had spent nearly one million dollars more on this model than it would have with the two departments as separate entities. The departments remain separate today. This should be qualified with the statement that it is also possible that abandoning the model was a result of endogenous characteristics of the affected cities and their politics rather than a complete failure of the model.

When considering a potential merger of police and fire departments through the PSO model or even a partial merger, local government policymakers and managers should seek the advice of competent policy analysts to determine the merger's likely impact.

Every municipality is different, so the outcomes of the consolidation of police and fire into a PSO model system will vary. The analysis of this question should take into account both the potential financial and operational gains that could be realized by consolidation and the potential negatives associated with the action. Clearly, problems of decreased service delivery and lower morale might have costs that are difficult to quantify up front but should be considered in the equation nonetheless. Once those impacts are assessed, policymakers should be able to find a proper solution to the question given what they believe to be in the best interest of the community as a whole.

This discussion of the public safety officer model is offered as an example of how bureaucratic silos can be broken down to allow public personnel to be more flexible in their job functions, potentially resulting in cost savings for the community. Of course, this model could be applied to other municipal services. For instance, in 2010, Elkton, Virginia, a small community in the Shenandoah Valley, was able to use existing Department of Public Works personnel when they brought garbage collection back in-house after decades of contracting out. By expanding the responsibilities of existing employees, the town administration was able save nearly $100,000 per year doing the work in-house. Though the existing personnel had been trained to perform basic maintenance and other operations around town, it was a simple task to train them on garbage collection operations.

An implementation strategy that requires a more dynamic use of personnel is innovative for municipal governments because public organizations have traditionally been quite hierarchical. In order to see the potential cost savings and service improvements associated with more dynamic personnel, managers must be willing to alter their service delivery paradigms away from time-tested arrangements and public personnel must be willing to try new things.

ENGAGE IN JOINT PURCHASING AND COOPERATIVE CONTRACTING

Besides contracting out individually to private companies for services, local governments can often save money by entering into joint purchasing consortiums, where buying in bulk leads to a larger discount. These consortiums can also reduce administrative costs and ease workloads. As more and more services are contracted out and purchasing requirements have become more complex, workload administration has increased. In the recession, local government officials strain to continue to meet their objectives and seek new and innovative tools to cope. Joint purchasing and cooperative contracting practices can help ease this strain.

Administrators form cooperative contracts or joint purchasing agreements when one or more parties identify a common requirement suitable for cooperative purchase and sign a written agreement. Such agreements can be facilitated by a state law/state organization or a council of governments; in some cases, a local government reaches out to another local government. They are typically based on common requirements of two or more local governments, which can be cities, towns, villages, counties, school districts, or other special districts (typically taxing entities). Initially, such agreements were typically utilized for gasoline and fuel. Now they are used for things like information technology services, software, furniture, copiers, printing, carpeting, wireless radios, paper, and fleet vehicles.

CONSIDER OPTIONS FOR STATE FINANCIAL ASSISTANCE ENCOURAGING COOPERATION

In fiscal year 2005–2006, the State of New York enacted the Shared Municipal Services Incentive (SMSI) program. It is a $2.75 million grant program that was created to help local governments work to consolidate services, reduce spending, and lower taxes. It allows municipal governments to apply for state-level grants to cover the start-up costs associated with shared services plans, cooperative agreements, mergers, consolidations, and dissolutions (NYSAC 2006).

The State of Illinois provides an excellent example of how leadership in this area can come from the state level and how a council of governments can be used to facilitate joint purchasing among local governments. The Illinois Department of Central Management Services (CMS) offers local governments the opportunity to save time and money when purchasing commodities, services, and equipment. CMS offers this for commodities such as automobile repair parts, bulk electricity, computer hardware and software, defibrillators, mowers and tractors, rock salt, and vehicles. CMS allows any unit of local government to join this voluntary program. The state then develops the specifications, conducts the bid process, makes the awards, and creates the contracts. The entire process is transparent via the Illinois Procurement Bulletin (IDCMS 2013). Another organization also developed in Illinois is a Joint Purchasing Program for Local Government Agencies that serves four councils of governments: the DuPage Mayors and Managers Conference, Northwest Municipal Conference, South Suburban Mayors and Managers Association, and the Will County Governmental League.

EXAMPLES OF REGIONAL COUNCILS AND COOPERATIVE ACTIVITY

When local governments seek to innovate in response to service demand, regional councils—a smaller unit of government than states—are often used as the network to facilitate cooperation among two or more governments (Wolf and Bryan 2009). Not only do they serve the information dissemination function of best practices, they can also oversee joint purchasing programs and provide technical assistance. One Alliance of Innovation Award–winning program is the Municipal Partnering Initiative (MPI) between the Village of Glenview and City of Lake Forest, Illinois. Originally established by a regional council of governments, and motivated by the recession, the MPI encountered two major obstacles: First, there was the major undertaking of reviewing bid specifications, service-level needs, current contract costs, and the design of new bid specifications. Second, the partnership required overcoming the collective action problem of 18 different communities (ICMA 2012). By working together, the MPI towns saved from $405,500 to $545,500 for each town participating. This allows local governments to go forward with additional projects that they did not know would be financially feasible. The program works because vendors are open to negotiating to acquire additional business, but local government staffs learn best practices from each other through the network. Local governments participating can also buy in bulk and receive the same products and services for less if vendors are guaranteed an increased customer base. Services provided include crack sealing, resurfacing, concrete, sewer lining, sewer testing, leak detection, hydrant painting, water meter testing, emergency contractor assistance, and cold patch paving (ICMA 2012).

SHARE CAPITAL AND RESOURCES WITH OTHER LOCAL PARTNERS

Co-location of services, both real and virtual, constitutes another area for innovations that cities and counties may consider. This includes sharing Web sites, buildings, or information centers to create one-stop shopping for citizens. The City of Charlotte and Mecklenburg County, North Carolina, not only share a Web site but are located in the same building. Citizens can call 311 to get information on both city and county services. Not only does this save money, it helps citizens obtain access information and services more efficiently (City of Charlotte and Mecklenburg County 2013). Additionally, 311 can increase the accountability of both governments by being transparent about which unit of government is responsible for providing a specific service, thus avoiding giving citizens the run around.

Dallas County and the City of Irving, Texas, were recently honored by the Texas Municipal League (2009) for their cooperative efforts in creating and building the Irving Health Center through an interlocal government agreement. Studies dating back to the 1990s demonstrated that there were almost 100,000 residents in the area classified as indigent or on Medicare or Medicaid. Twenty-six percent of this population was at or below 200 percent of the federal poverty level. Taxpayers were footing the bill for expensive emergency room services if the uninsured did not have access to a clinic where they could be diagnosed and treated before a condition became an emergency. In 2004, the local governments entered into an interlocal government agreement that allowed the health center to open in 2007 (TML 2009).

CONCLUSION

State and local governments in the United States continue to be the laboratories of democracy, inventing new ways to share services. There are a variety of ways local governments can cooperate to deliver services without having to functionally merge two departments or governing structures. In this chapter, we highlight several examples where jurisdictions work together to improve the overall quality and efficiency of service delivery. Mutual aid provides help during emergency situations where one jurisdiction may be overwhelmed by an unusual event such as a wildfire or hurricane. Working together can provide additional relief in the form of personnel, back-up computer systems, and the lending of expensive equipment. Floater models for joint jurisdictions are often a quick-fix solution to cover local government service delivery gaps, especially when a jurisdiction experiences an uneven demand for service or needs to expand its pool of workers without incurring the expense of overtime or wearing out the current workforce. Cross-training, such as the implementation of PSOs, while more challenging to implement in the short term than other alternative service delivery arrangements, can certainly pay off for specific areas, such as police and fire in smaller communities. Joint purchasing and one-stop shopping also offer the promise of more efficient and effective local government services. All of these alternative forms of municipal shared services offer the promise of improving the efficiency and effectiveness of service delivery at the local level. But local governments should be careful to negotiate an agreement and monitor implementation, just as they would with any other contract with a private company.

KEY POINTS

- It is important to look outside of your organization for potential resources that are useful to local governments, not just in times of crisis.
- Alternative models can be applied to physical, human, and financial resources.
- Sharing services can improve service delivery and save money, but only if services are performed carefully and consider the context of the local government.
- Using experiences from other communities can help to build models that fit your own community.

REFERENCES

Behn, Robert. 2003. Why measure performance? Different purposes require different measures. *Public Administration Review* 63(5): 586–606.

Chelst, Kenneth. 1988. A public safety merger in Grosse Point Park, Michigan—A short and sweet study. *Interfaces* 18(4): 1–11.

City of Charlotte and Mecklenburg County. 2013. Web site. http://charmeck.org/Pages/default.aspx.

Federal Emergency Management Agency (FEMA). 2013. Preparedness overview. www.fema.gov/preparedness-0.

Feiock, Richard C., ed. 2004. *Metropolitan Governance: Conflict, Competition, and Cooperation.* Washington, DC: Georgetown University Press.

5th District Medical Response Coalition. N.d. About us. www.5dmrc.org/about-us/.

Gulick, Luther. 1937. Notes on the theory of organization. In *Papers on the Science of Administration*, ed. Luther Gulick and L. Urwick, 3–45. Concord, NH: The Rumford Press.

Halachmi, Ari. 2002. Performance measurement, accountability, and improved performance. *Public Productivity and Management Review* 25(4): 370–374.

Hall, Richard H. 1963. The concept of bureaucracy: An empirical assessment. *American Journal of Sociology* 69: 32–40.

Heinrich, Carolyn. 2002. Outcomes-based performance management in the public sector: Implications for government accountability and effectiveness. *Public Administration Review* 62(6): 712–725.

Illinois Department of Central Management Services (IDCMS) 2013. About CMS. www2.illinois.gov/cms/About/Pages/default.aspx.

International Association of Firefighters (IAFF). 2009. *Police and Fire Consolidation: An Inefficient Use of Resources.* Washington, DC. www.iaff.org/09News/PDFs/PSOSystems.pdf.

International City/County Management Association (ICMA). 2012. Municipal Partnering Initiative: Glenview, IL; Lake Forest, IL. 2012 ICMA Program Excellence Award Winner: Community Partnership. http://icma.org/en/icma/knowledge_network/documents/kn/Document/304199/Municipal_Partnering_Initiative__Glenview_IL_Lake_Forest_IL.

Kelly, Janet, and David Swindell. 2002. A multiple-indicator approach to municipal service evaluation. *Public Administration Review* 62(5): 610–621.

Leland, Suzanne, and Holly Whisman. 2011. *The Promise of Collaborative Governance*. A white paper produced for the Scripps Howard Center for Civic Engagement at Northern Kentucky University.

Melkers, Julia, and Katherine Willoughby. 2005. Models of performance-measurement use in local governments: Understanding budgeting, communication, and lasting effects. *Public Administration Review* 65(2): 180–190.

National Fire Protection Association (NFPA). 2013. *NFPA 1500: Standard on Fire Department Occupational Safety and Health Program.* Quincy, MA.

New York State Association of Counties (NYSAC). 2006. *The Shared Service Incentive Program: A Policy Primer.* Albany, NY, July. http://nysac.org/policy-research/documents/sharedservicesbriefing.pdf.

Olson, Mancur. 1965. *The Logic of Collective Action: Public Goods and the Theory of Groups.* Vol. 124, Harvard Economic Studies. Cambridge, MA: Harvard University Press.

Occupational Health and Safety Adminstration. 2003a. "Procedures for IDLH Atmosphere." Title 29, *Code of Federal Regulations*, Pt. 1910.134(g)(3)(iii).

———. 2003b. "Procedures for Interior Structural Firefighting." Title 29, *Code of Federal Regulations*, Pt. 1910.134(g)(3)(4).

Smith, Adam. 1776. *Wealth of Nations: An Inquiry into the Nature and Causes of the Wealth of Nations*. London: Methuen.

Texas Municipal League. 2009. Municipal Excellence Awards. www.tml.org/municipal_award.asp.

Tiebout, Charles. 1956. A pure theory of local expenditures. *Journal of Political Economy* 64(5): 416–424.

Wolf, James F., and Tara K. Bryan. 2009. Identifying the capacities of regional councils of government. *State and Local Government Review* 41(1): 61–68.

About the Editor and Contributors

Charles R. Abernathy has served as county manager in McDowell County, North Carolina, since 1987. He has also served in the dual capacity of county manager and economic development director since 2000. He received his PhD from the University of Tennessee, Knoxville, in 2009. Abernathy teaches a graduate course in public administration at Appalachian State University. He has published articles in *Public Administration Quarterly and Public Management* on the consolidation of services and economic development.

Daniel E. Bromberg is an assistant professor of public administration at the University of New Hampshire. His research focus is on issues of public management in relation to business–government relations, technology implementation, and collaborative governance. Dr. Bromberg received his PhD from the School of Public Affairs and Administration at Rutgers–Newark in 2009.

Jered B. Carr is the Victor and Caroline Schutte/Missouri Professor of Urban Affairs and director of the L.P. Cookingham Institute of Urban Affairs at the Henry W. Bloch School of Management at the University of Missouri–Kansas City. His current research and teaching interests focus on public service cooperation, metropolitan governance, and civic engagement. His research has been published in a wide range of journals in public administration, political science, and urban affairs. He serves as a co-editor and the managing editor of the *Urban Affairs Review*.

Anthony Cresswell's teaching and research career spans over four decades, focusing on public policy, management, and technology innovation. Prior to retiring in 2012, he had been at the University at Albany since 1979, with faculty appointments in Educational Administration and Information Science, and in the Center for Technology in Government (CTG). From 1999 to 2012, Dr. Creswell served as deputy director and interim director of CTG, working with a variety of government, corporate, and university partners to conduct applied research on the policy, management, and technology issues surrounding information use in the public sector. Prior to arriving at the University at Albany, Dr. Cresswell served on the faculties of Northwestern University and Carnegie Mellon University, and as a faculty adviser in the U.S. Office of Management and Budget. In addition to research and teaching in the United States, he has worked in information system and policy analysis projects in local, state, and federal governments in the United States and in Africa, Asia, the Middle East, and Caribbean. He has published widely in scientific and professional literature. Dr. Cresswell holds a doctorate from Columbia University.

Sydney Cresswell serves as the local government policy adviser to Governor Andrew Cuomo, and was recently appointed to the New York State Financial Restructuring Board for Local Governments. She focuses on issues related to municipal stress, and has been part of the governor's mandate relief efforts. She is also in the early stages of a team effort that will create the state's first local government data resource. Prior to her appointment as a policy adviser, Ms. Cresswell directed the Program on Local and Intergovernmental Studies (POLIS) for the Rockefeller College of Public Affairs and Policy at the University at Albany, where she was also the assistant dean. POLIS examines intergovernmental systems and practices in partnership with state and local governments in New York State. She did her doctoral work in policy studies at the University at Albany and is currently ABD/PhD.

Richard C. Elling is professor emeritus of political science at Wayne State University in Detroit. During his more than four-decade career, his research and teaching has focused on public management, intergovernmental relations, and state politics and governance. His publications include the book *Public Management in the States: A Comparative Analysis of Administrative Performance and Politics* (1992) and co-authorship of *The Political and Institutional Effects of Term Limits* (2004). He also authored the chapter on "state bureaucracies" in six editions of *Politics in the American States*. He is most recently the co-author (with Kelly Krawczyk and Jered Carr) of "What Should We Do? Public Attitudes About How Local Government Officials Should Confront Fiscal Stress" (in *Local Government Studies,* forthcoming).

William D. Hatley is an adjunct faculty member in the Department of Political Science at Wayne State University in Detroit, Michigan, teaching classes in political science, public administration, and public policy. He also regularly teaches graduate-level classes in MPA and MPP programs for the University of Michigan at Dearborn, Oakland University, and Eastern Michigan University. Before earning his PhD and starting a teaching career, he worked for 25 years at the local government level as a city attorney, director of planning and development, and as an economic development director. He is also a licensed attorney and has maintained a private practice since 1986. He has worked on several projects to facilitate collaboration between communities, nonprofits, and resident organizations. He is a regular attendee and panel presenter at the annual meetings of the American Society for Public Administration.

Michael R. Hattery is a senior fellow and director of local government studies at Rockefeller Institute of Government, University at Albany–SUNY. He has a range of experience as a student of state and local government. He has conducted applied research as well as community-based technical assistance and adult education for state and local officials. His work and interests are centered in the areas of public finance, organization, and service delivery. He has done significant work in the areas of management capacity building, budgeting, and analysis of intergovernmental service delivery options, particularly among local governments in non-metropolitan regions.

Christopher V. Hawkins is an assistant professor in the School of Public Administration at the University of Central Florida. His research focuses on metropolitan governance, urban sustainability, urban politics, and the application of network analysis to understanding planning and policy decisions. His research has been published in *Public Administration Review, The American Review of Public Administration*, and *State and Local Government Review*, among others.

Alexander C. Henderson is an assistant professor in the Department of Health Care and Public Administration at Long Island University, Post Campus. He holds a BA and MPA from Villanova University, and a PhD in public administration from Rutgers University–Newark. He previously served as a chief administrative officer, operational officer, director, and volunteer with several emergency services organizations in suburban Philadelphia.

Suzanne Leland is a professor of political science and public administration at University of North Carolina at Charlotte. She directs the Gerald G. Fox MPA Program, and teaches and researches urban politics, state and local government, and intergovernmental relations. She is the co-editor of *Case Studies of City-County Consolidation* and *City-County Consolidation: Promises Made, Promises Kept?* with Kurt Thurmaier. Her publications also have appeared in *Public Administration Review, Public Budgeting and Finance, The American Review of Public Administration, Administration and Society, Journal of Urban Affairs,* and other journals.

Lauren Miltenberger is an assistant professor of public administration at Villanova University. Dr. Miltenberger teaches courses in public and nonprofit human resources, decision making, public policy, and public administration. Her current research interests are human services system partnerships between nonprofits and the government and human capital management strategies within the nonprofit sector. Dr. Miltenberger has a PhD in urban affairs and public policy from the University of Delaware. Prior to joining the faculty at Villanova University, Dr. Miltenberger held executive leadership positions in the nonprofit sector.

Ricardo S. Morse is an associate professor of public administration and government at the UNC School of Government in Chapel Hill, North Carolina. He teaches and advises state and local public officials in the areas of collaborative governance, strategic visioning, and leadership. He also teaches in the school's Master of Public Administration (MPA) Program. He has published more than two dozen articles and book chapters and is lead editor of two books on public leadership, *Transforming Public Leadership for the 21st Century* (2007) and *Innovations in Public Leadership Development* (2008), both published by M.E. Sharpe. Morse holds BA and MA degrees in public policy from Brigham Young University and a PhD in public administration/public affairs from Virginia Tech.

Mildred E. Warner is a professor in the Department of City and Regional Planning at Cornell University, where her work focuses primarily on local government service delivery, economic development, and planning across generations. Dr. Warner's research explores the impact of privatization and devolution on local government and the role of human services as part of the social infrastructure for economic development. Her work shows potential for market-based solutions in public service delivery but also raises cautions about the uneven incidence of market approaches in depressed inner-city and rural areas. Prior to her professorship at Cornell, she served as a program officer with the Ford Foundation in New York City and as associate director of Cornell's Community and Rural Development Institute. Dr. Warner has a PhD in development sociology and a master's in agricultural economics, both from Cornell University, and a BA in history from Oberlin College.

Reid A. Wodicka serves as the town manager for Woodstock, located in the Shenandoah Valley of Virginia. Additionally, Wodicka is a doctoral candidate in the interdisciplinary PhD in Public Policy program at the University of North Carolina at Charlotte. He has worked in local government management in localities in Virginia and North Carolina.

Eric S. Zeemering is an associate professor in the Department of Public Administration at Northern Illinois University. His research on local government management and policy has appeared in *Public Administration Review, State and Local Government Review, Urban Affairs Review,* and other journals and edited volumes. He is currently writing a book about policy definition and governance relationships for urban sustainability in Baltimore.

Index

t denotes table; *f* denotes figure.

T

CPSIA information can be obtained
at www.ICGtesting.com
Printed in the USA
BVHW012251230420
578342BV00005B/200